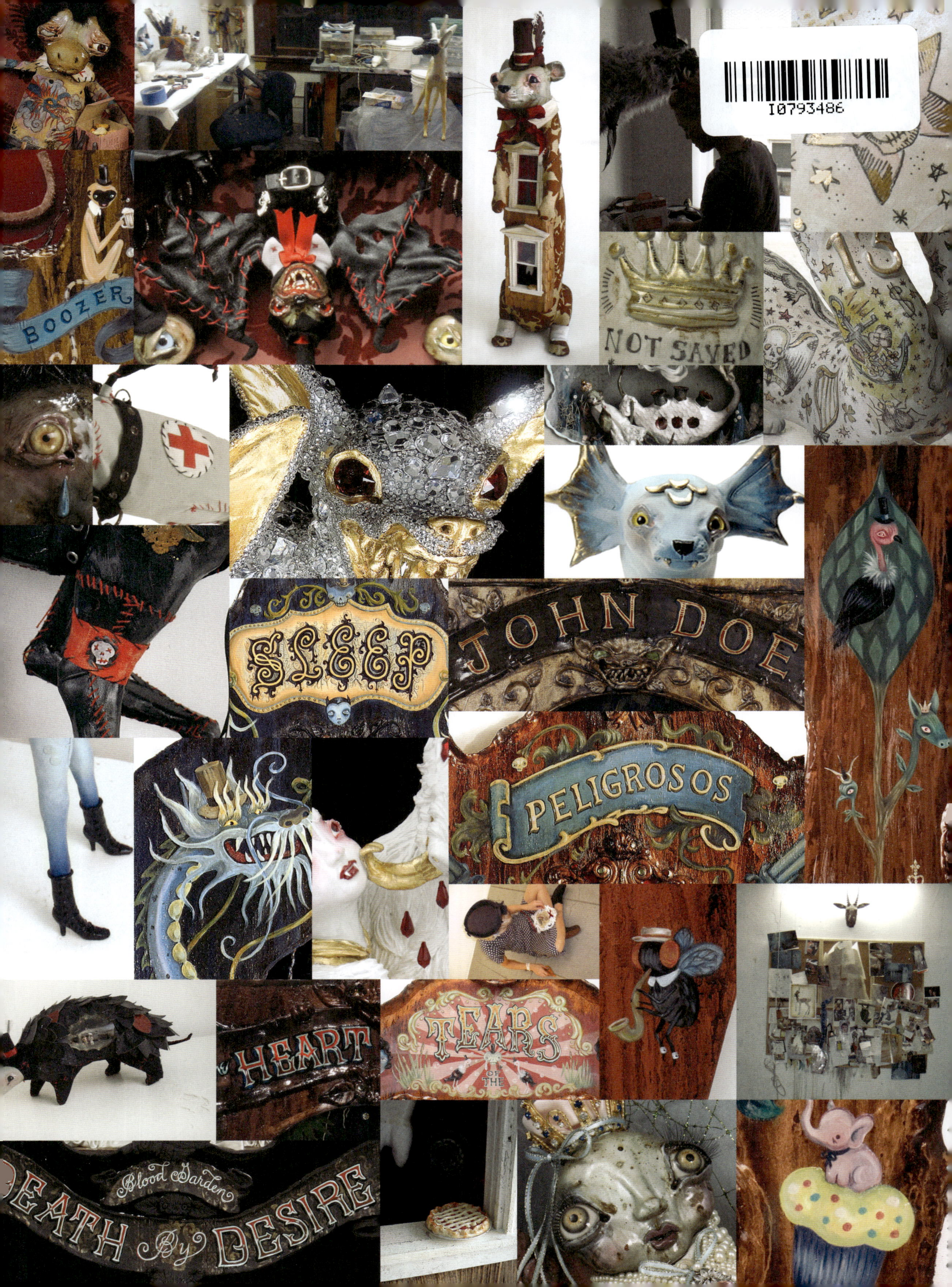
BOOZER
NOT SAVED
15
SLEEP
JOHN DOE
PELIGROSOS
HEART
TEARS OF THE
Blood Garden
EATH By DESIRE

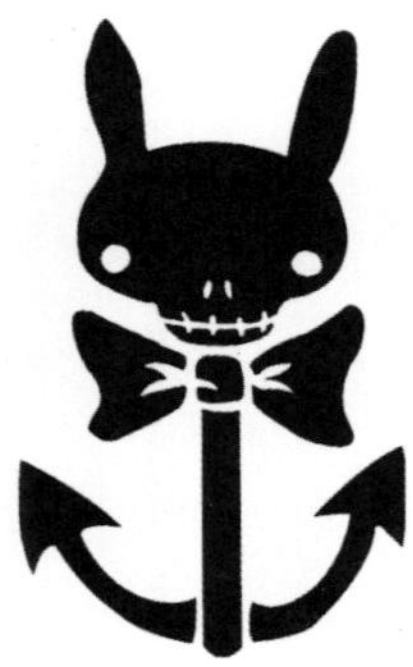

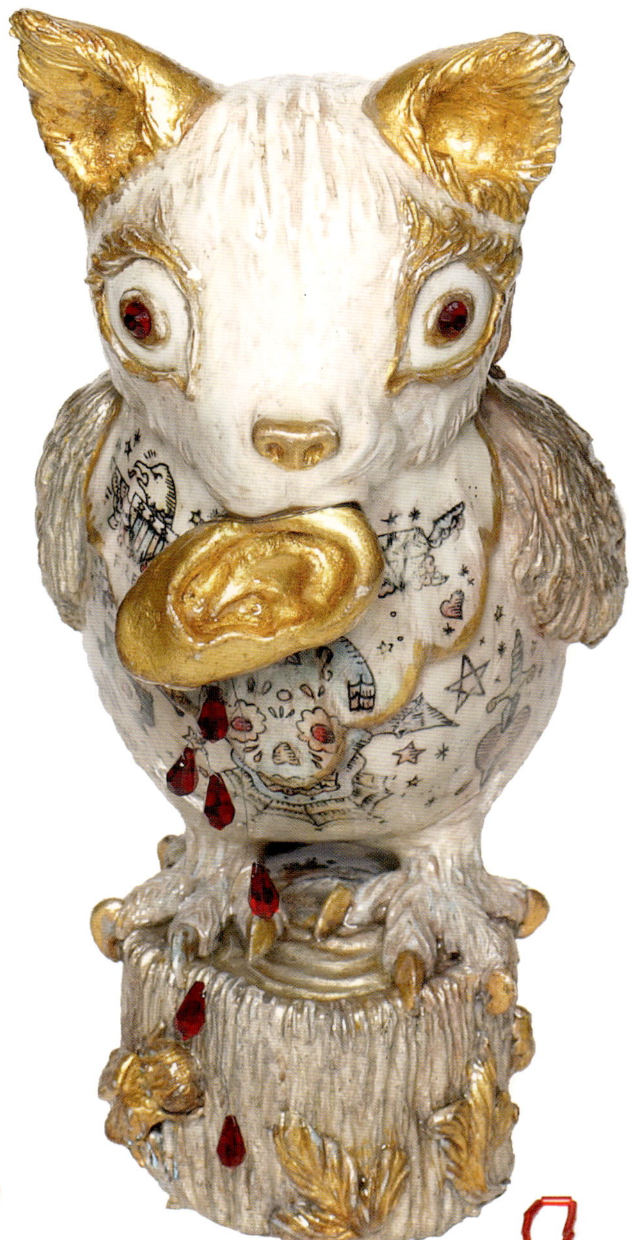

Incurable Disorder

For my darling daughter,
Sadie Valentine Slade

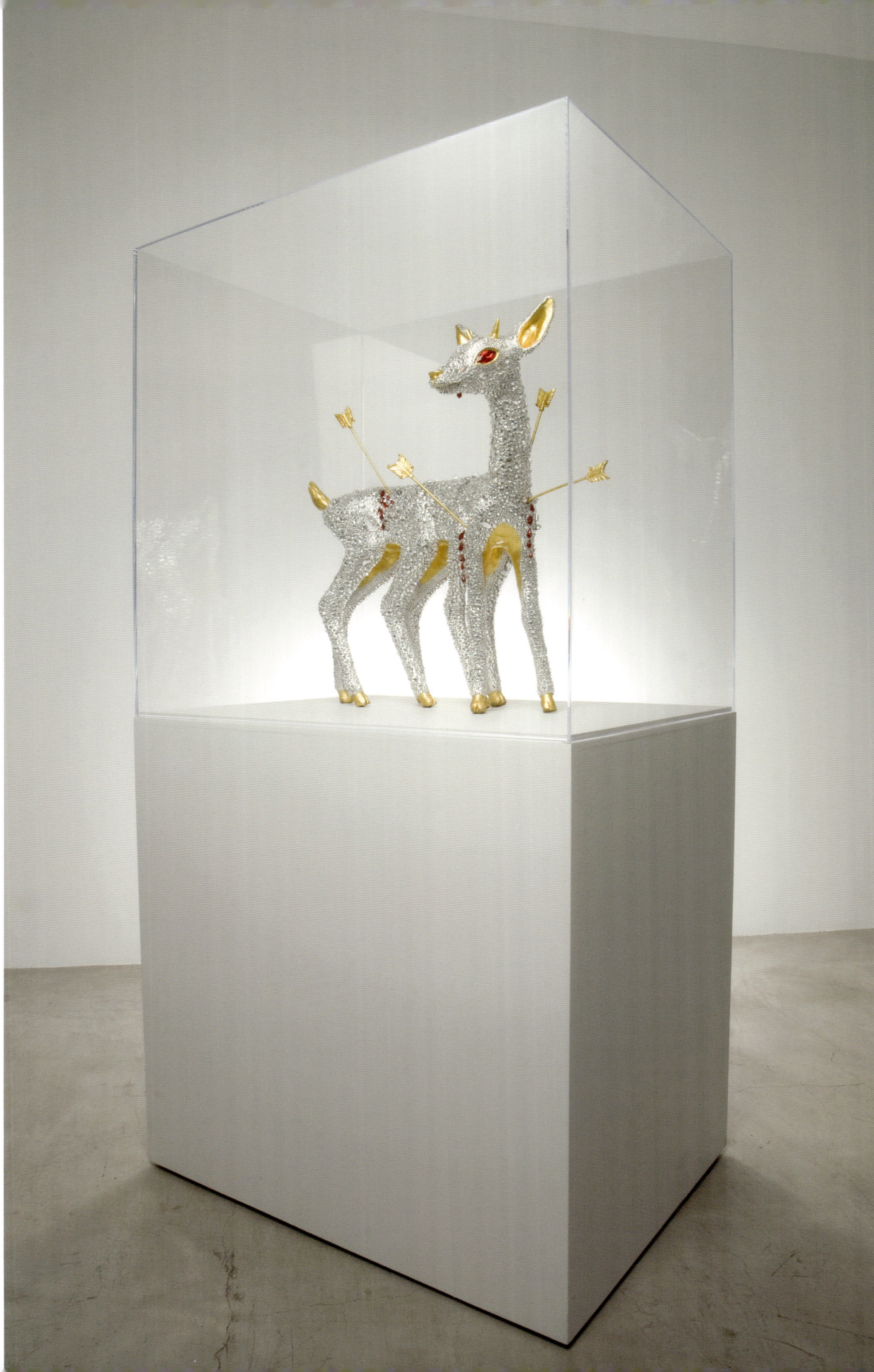

Incurable Disorder

The Art of

Elizabeth McGrath

Last Gasp of San Francisco

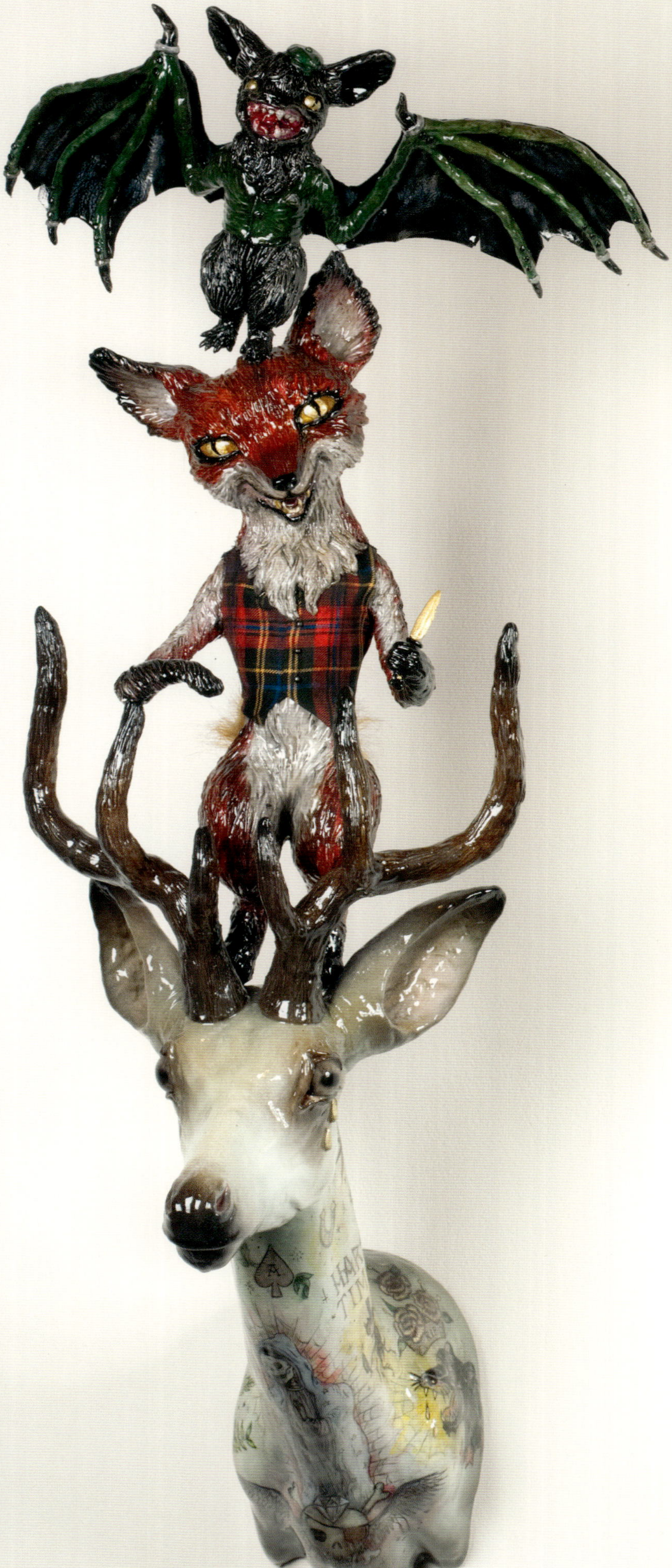

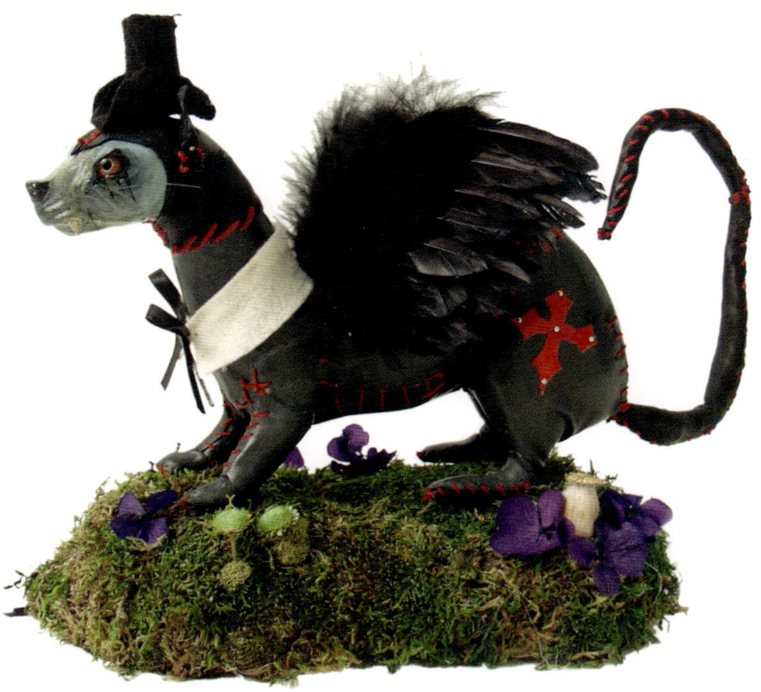

I love Liz McGrath's work. I love the oddness. I love the weirdness. I am so attracted and drawn to it, and not just because I'm also odd and weird. For me, my passion for her work is rooted in one specific moment in my life that changed the way I would look at and appreciate what she does on a much deeper and personal level.

When I was growing up in West Virginia, hunting was a big part of my family's and my community's life. Most of my relatives hunted, and most of my classmates. Hunting season was such a big deal in my state that I even remember them changing the dates for Thanksgiving vacation at my school just so it would better coincide with deer season. It was most likely this influence that caused me to have a fascination of and desire to own a collection of mounted animals.

In my childhood mind, these were the equivalent of pure grown up manhood. They lined the walls of my cousin's living room, staring down at me with those forlorn eyes. There were quail and bucks and geese and ducks. In my mind, these were the symbols of not only someone who had seen the world, but someone who had conquered it! These were the trophies of men who had been stronger and faster than the wild animal kingdom, and they brought home their spoils from the hunt to show their tribe how powerful they were.

I dreamed of going on safaris. Of tracking my own wild animals that would one day grace the walls of my own lodge-like abode. And I think that was what was running through my head when, on my 12th birthday, my grandfather gave me my first rifle. It was a .22 with a shoulder stock that he had hand crafted and sanded and stained into the smooth beautiful yellow pine rifle that I now held in my hands. I was overjoyed. It was the greatest gift I'd ever gotten. It crushed the bike I got for Christmas the year before and was leagues beyond my Atari 2600.

"You want to shoot it?" he asked, and we raced out the back door, him as excited as I was. My father used to work for the phone company, so we had a couple of those giant wooden spools that cables would come on in our back yard. We set an empty plastic milk jug in front of one of the spools and I fired my first shot. It was exhilarating. We backed up a little further, and we walked he talked about where we would be able to hunt up at their country house. I reloaded, took a deep breath, aimed, and fired. As soon as the shot rang out, there was the yelp of my dog as she went running across the back of our yard.

After my first shot, she apparently hid behind the target for safety, and my grandfather and I never saw her.

We chased her into the woods where she collapsed into the leaves at the base of a tree. I was speechless as I stood there watching her die. Watching her pant, whine and cry. Tears streamed down my face as I watched her take her last breaths, and then my grandfather buried her in the woods.

You can't help but be affected by something like this. After that day, I only went hunting a few times into my teens and I pretty much never wanted an animal's head anywhere near my house. And I think that's what attracted me most to the beautiful horrors that are the work of the amazing Liz McGrath.

They are the carnival and the spectacle, the hunter and the hunted, the loss and the prize. Each piece of brilliance makes us look at what we fear and what we consider to be beautiful. They hold a mirror up to our own scruples and force us to rationalize or justify our own choices and inadequacies. They bring into question any sense of superiority and make you realize that you yourself could soon be the tattooed and mounted trophy of another mighty hunter.

In this world, we are all game. And while we have yet to become the dissected subjects of another's collection, Ms. McGrath's art shows us that it's only a matter of time. Her creatures and characters take on all our traits and personalities, our good and bad, and she's put them all on the wall for the world to see. Sinners and saints are both welcome here, and its our faults and foibles that then become the showpieces.

I have witnessed her work make people visibly uncomfortable. I have seen people close their eyes and walk away from her sculptures. And I have seen others stare in awe, speechless at what they are consuming. It's both heart attack & resuscitation. For me, it's a celebration. It's an acceptance of the miracle that is both life and death. In all of her work, I find the laughter and joy that make life worth living as well as the irony that in the end we may just end up being stuffed and stuck on the wall for someone else's enjoyment.

Are we art or artist? Victor or prize? Only time will tell.

Morgan Spurlock

WHAT IS GREAT ART? WELL, IT'S SUBJECTIVE. WE ALL RESPOND TO A WORK OF ART DIFFERENTLY AND FOR DIFFERENT REASONS. EACH OF OUR EXPERIENCES, ISSUES, SIMPLE LIKES AND DISLIKES COME TOGETHER TO FORM OUR PERSONAL TASTE, OUR OPINION OF WHAT MAKES A PIECE FANTASTIC. EVEN AFTER ALMOST TWENTY YEARS IN THE ARTS—AS A CURATOR, GALLERIST, CONSULTANT AND WRITER—I CAN'T ALWAYS PREDICT WHAT SOMEONE ELSE WILL CONSIDER GREAT WORK. BUT I'M VERY CLEAR ABOUT WHAT WORKS FOR ME.

I want to be made, not just to think, but also to feel. I want to respect the artist's process. I don't care if your piece is a stick in the ground—think it through, craft it beautifully, make me feel something, help me see differently. Then you have me! My fantasy outcome for any work in progress is that the artist really sweats creating it and that his or her passion pays off in the end with a meaningful connection to an audience well beyond the studio.

For all of these reasons and more, I find Elizabeth McGrath's work so profoundly delicious, so elegant, powerful and moving, that at times it breaks my heart. It did the first time I saw one of her dioramas in the 1990s and continues to do so today. So much so, that when I was planning to open my own gallery, I knew McGrath would be among the artists I would invite to show. The vulnerability, honesty and craftsmanship of her work represented everything I wanted my gallery, and my life, to be—open, brave, well executed and thoughtful.

On the surface McGrath's lovingly made sculptures and paintings can be downright adorable, pulling at our heartstrings with sweet faces and whimsical colors. Upon closer inspection, an unsettling discomfort sets in. Is that sparkly deer actually bleeding crystal blood drops? Why is the grim reaper rowing a boat through that dik dik's belly? Is that seal girl's iceberg home really melting away below her flippers?

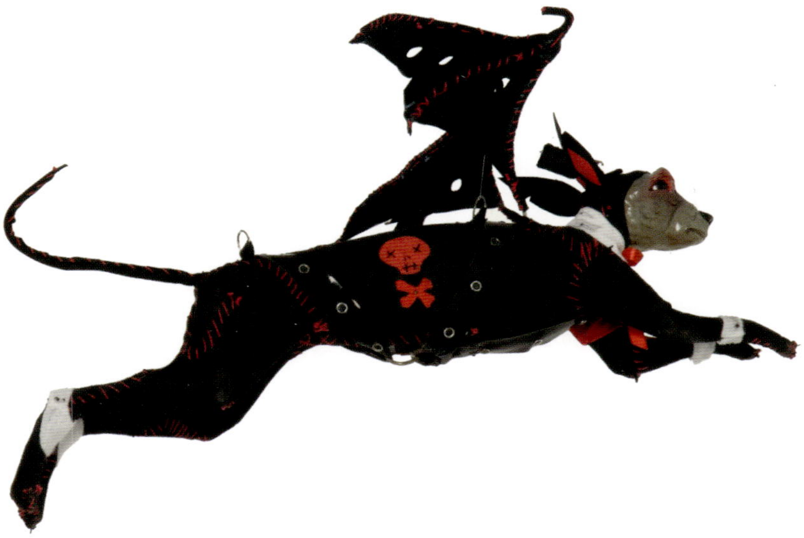

The answer is almost always yes because McGrath's magical creatures are almost always in peril. And the cause of that peril, the blame for their circumstances, undoubtedly falls squarely on the shoulders of humanity. But what can I do? Oh yes, that's right. I'm part of the problem. There's plenty I can do.

McGrath created "White Castle," a 23" x 9" x 23" sculpture of an armadillo carrying a tree house, for the first exhibition at Sloan Fine Art. I remember unpacking it and setting it on the counter to study. The complexity of the sculpture was awe-inspiring. The texture of the branches and the expression on the animal's face were delicately sculpted, then painted an eerie, unnatural blue. Each leather leaf on the tree and scale on the armadillo's back was carefully cut out and strategically placed. The rustic little tree house could have stood alone as a single beautiful work of art. It was a gorgeous piece. I was dazzled by it. But once I got past how pretty it was, I noticed that the poor little armadillo was crying black tears and struggling under the weight of its burden. I was moved to sadness. I couldn't help but wonder; what struggles do armadillos face in 2008? I can honestly say, I had never before considered the plight of the armadillo.

You see Elizabeth McGrath tricks her audience. She lulls us with the beauty of her work. Like magpies we're drawn to their sparkle and charm. Then she hits us, sometimes brutally, with a deeper message. And it's not just limited to our relationships with animals. McGrath also reminds us of our responsibility to Mother Nature. From the most subtle comments like the skull and crossbones on an animal we eat, to houses built on the backs of creatures—such as the giant armadillo—whose homes are being destroyed by deforestation, to magnificent beasts dripping glossy and black from the residue of an oil spill; McGrath gives us beautiful work, lovingly made, with passion and heart. But she also makes us think.

I'm less likely today to toss a recyclable bottle in the trashcan and more likely to send donations to appropriate environmental charities, in part due to my relationship with McGrath and my respect for her work. It has filled my gallery with beautiful objects, my heart with joy and sadness, my mind with food for thought and ultimately made me a better person. If that's not great art, as far as I'm concerned, nothing is.

Alix Sloan

SOME PEOPLE'S IMAGINATIONS LEAD TO SPACE TRAVEL, BROADBAND INTERNET AND ELECTRICITY. MINE LEADS TO DAMAGED ANTHROPOMORPHISED ANIMALS WHO WOULD RATHER BITE THAN BE HEALED. AS A SCULPTOR I TRY TO SOLIDIFY AS MUCH OF THE FANTASTICAL DETAILS OF MY IMAGINED CREATURES AS MY TALENTS WILL ALLOW.

The conception of these brainchildren is hard to pinpoint. They stem from the emotional encounters I have with humans, landscapes, and objects, and are further shaped by the constant stream of words and images that survive my mind's filter. Once I have the skeleton of an idea the rest comes automatically, but staying on task through the many hours it takes to complete one of these works requires a heavy dose of news radio, stories, and audio books. For instance the chapter titled "Altarwise by Owl Light" started with a Dylan Thomas poem but grew during "The Mists of Avalon" by Marion Zimmer Bradley. The chapter titled "With Tomorrow's Scream" also started in the lines of a Dylan Thomas poem but took form through "The Stand" and "The Shining" by Stephen King. "American Animals" came to life through many sources including radio podcasts like "This American Life" and short stories by David Sedaris.

If the words have left a physical mark upon the works, I haven't noticed, but when I see the finished pieces it takes me back to the story or vice versa, like memories from a vacation. It is when I am in the middle of a story, in the middle of a show, late at night with no one around that I feel at peace. Throughout this book I added some of the lines that have been my fuel.

Most of the works you will see are created with Magic Sculpt (a two part resin epoxy similar to clay), foam, fiberglass, resins, gold leafs, various paints, wood, fabrics and limited found objects. I like experimenting with new materials but feel most comfortable with Magic Sculpt built over wire armatures, airbrushed and varnished. If it is a very large piece I will carve it from a block of foam or make a wood armature. Sometimes I use objects that are similar to the size and shape I am looking for, such as five gallon water bottles or foam taxidermy forms.

Because Magic sculpt is a tool-destroyer, my weapons of choice are my hands, toothpicks, the backs of paint brushes and wet Q-tips. It is hard for me to achieve fine details on smaller pieces with these tools so many of the works are quite large.

If I use a found object it is because the object has somehow inspired the piece. For "Deer House" I came across a family-run doll house store and felt compelled to purchase their old stock of intricately detailed doors and windows. While spending time in traffic at a freeway underpass I noticed that a barely

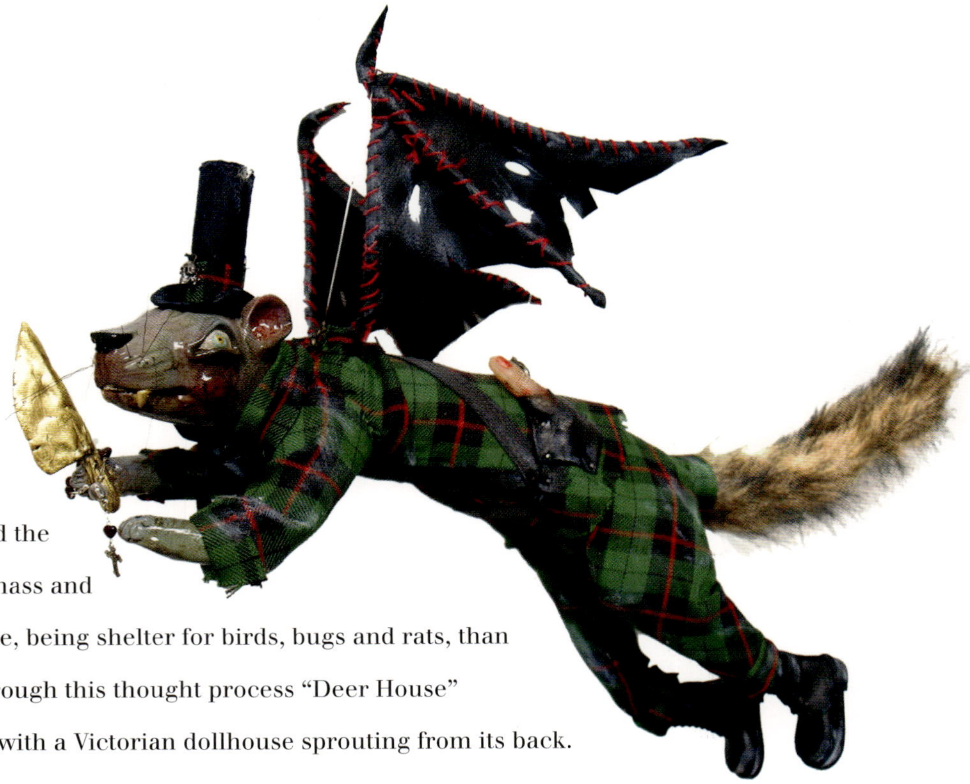

recognizable couch was fighting with the landscape, and the landscape was winning! Vines covered its rotting fabric and filth-covered plastic bags hung like moss to bare coils. I imagined the wildlife that must inhabit this sinking mass and wondered if the couch was happier here, being shelter for birds, bugs and rats, than having to support the butts of man. Through this thought process "Deer House" was born. An upholstery covered fawn with a Victorian dollhouse sprouting from its back.

While touring through the Southwest with my band, Miss Derringer, I became infatuated with the quartz crystals we encountered at the gas stations and roadside attractions. I was told you can feel them humming if you listen closely. I gathered as many of the humming crystals as I could which went on to become the feathers for "Lord Crane." A character whom I imagine could adorn the labels of snake oil liniments.

These beasts are always with me. They are projects I can never let go of, lurking, waiting to be recognized, demanding to be born. Once dislodged they are a constant intrusion till they are realized. It is sometimes hard to accommodate the chores of daily existence. I am relentlessly reminded that their being is unfulfilled. These are my obsessions.

Elizabeth McGrath

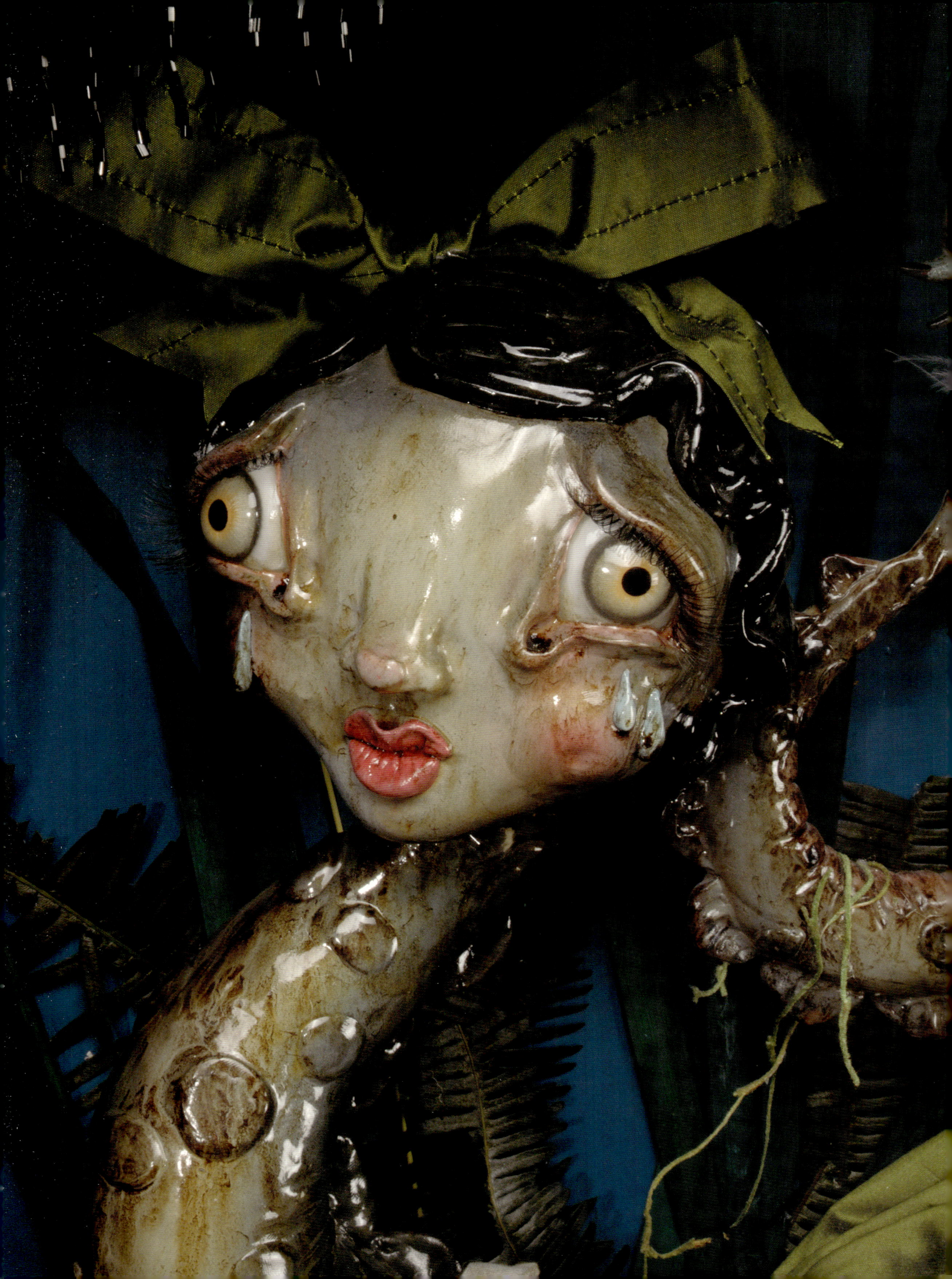

Tears of the Crocodile

What are young men made of, made of?
What are young men made of?
Sighs and leers and crocodile tears;
That's what young men are made of.

Excerpt from
"What all the world is made of"
ROBERT SOUTHEY
(1774-1843)

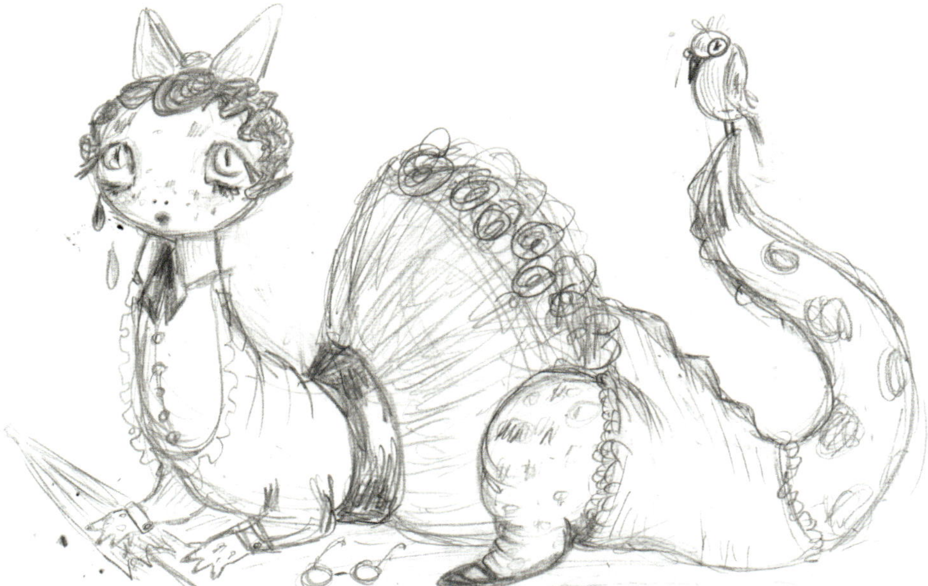

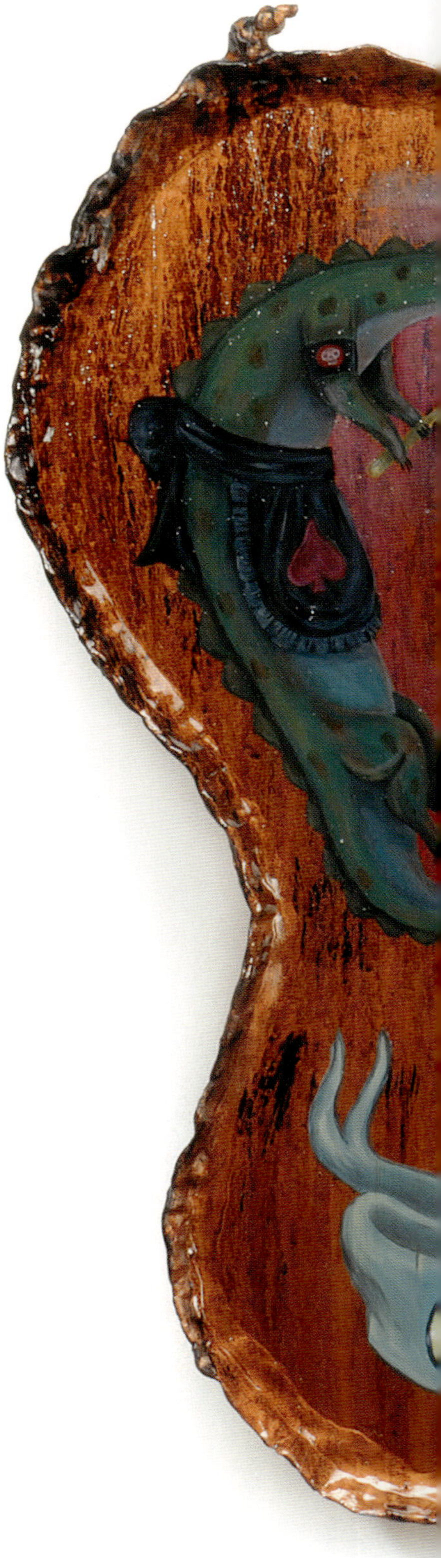

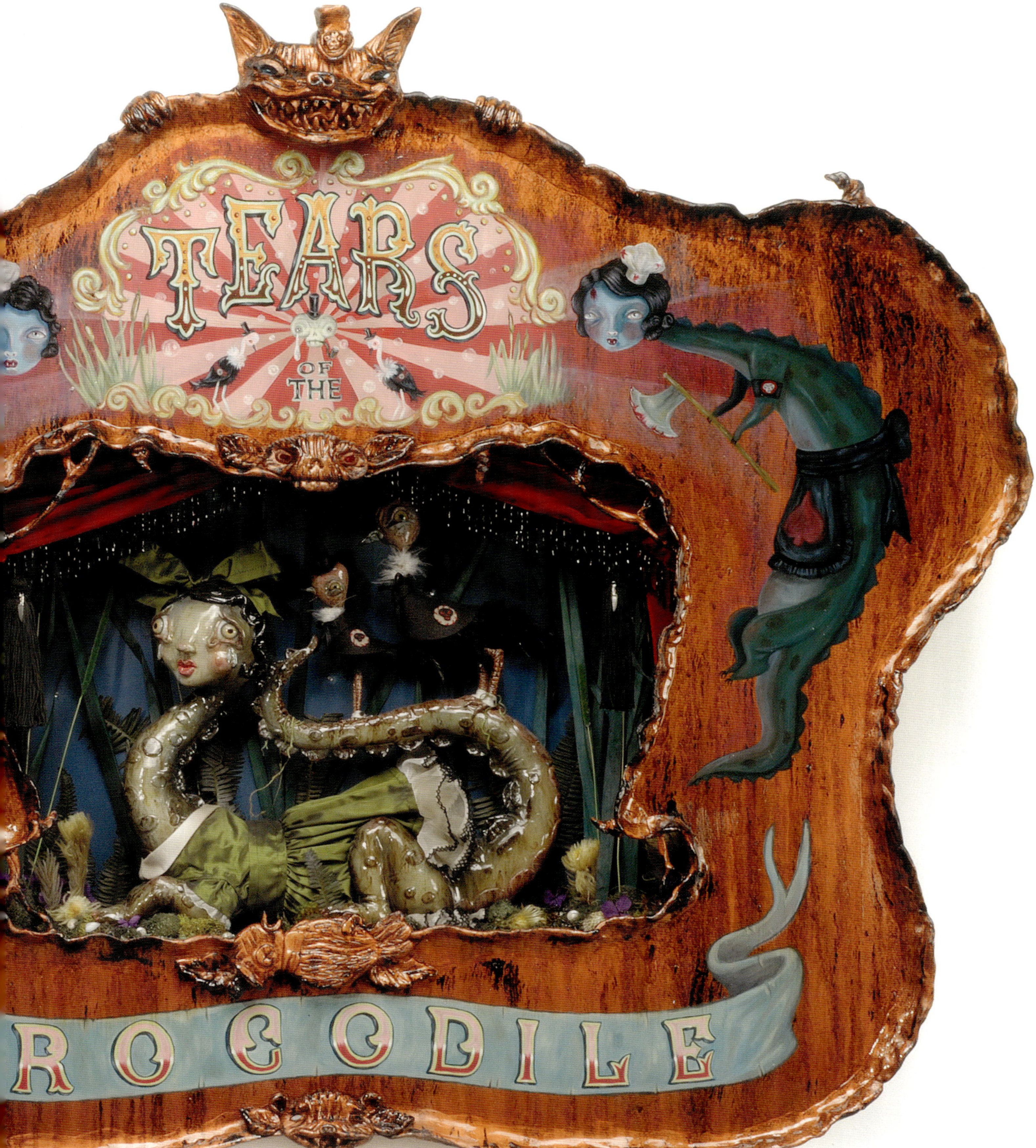
TEARS
OF THE
ROCODILE

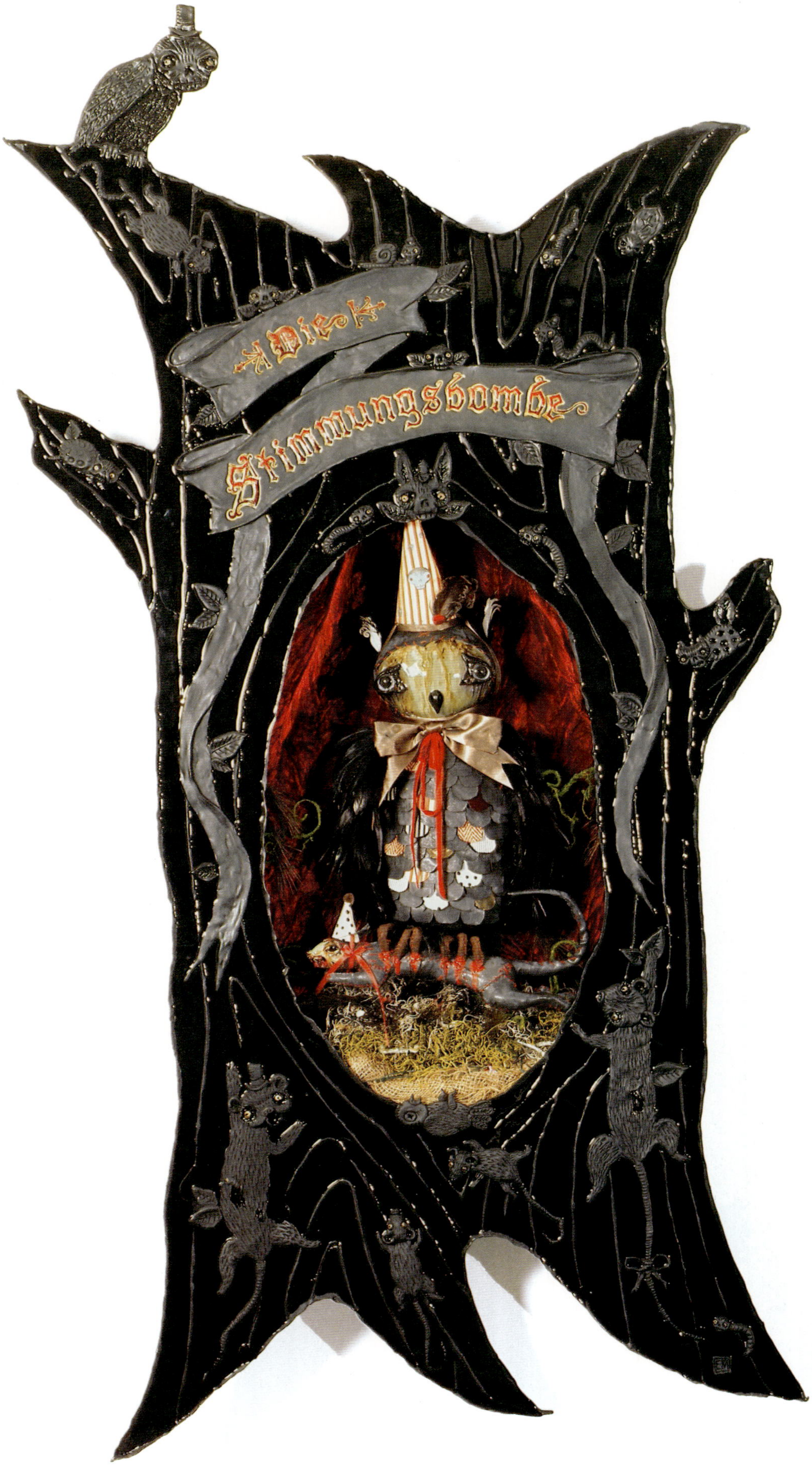
Die
Stimmungsbombe

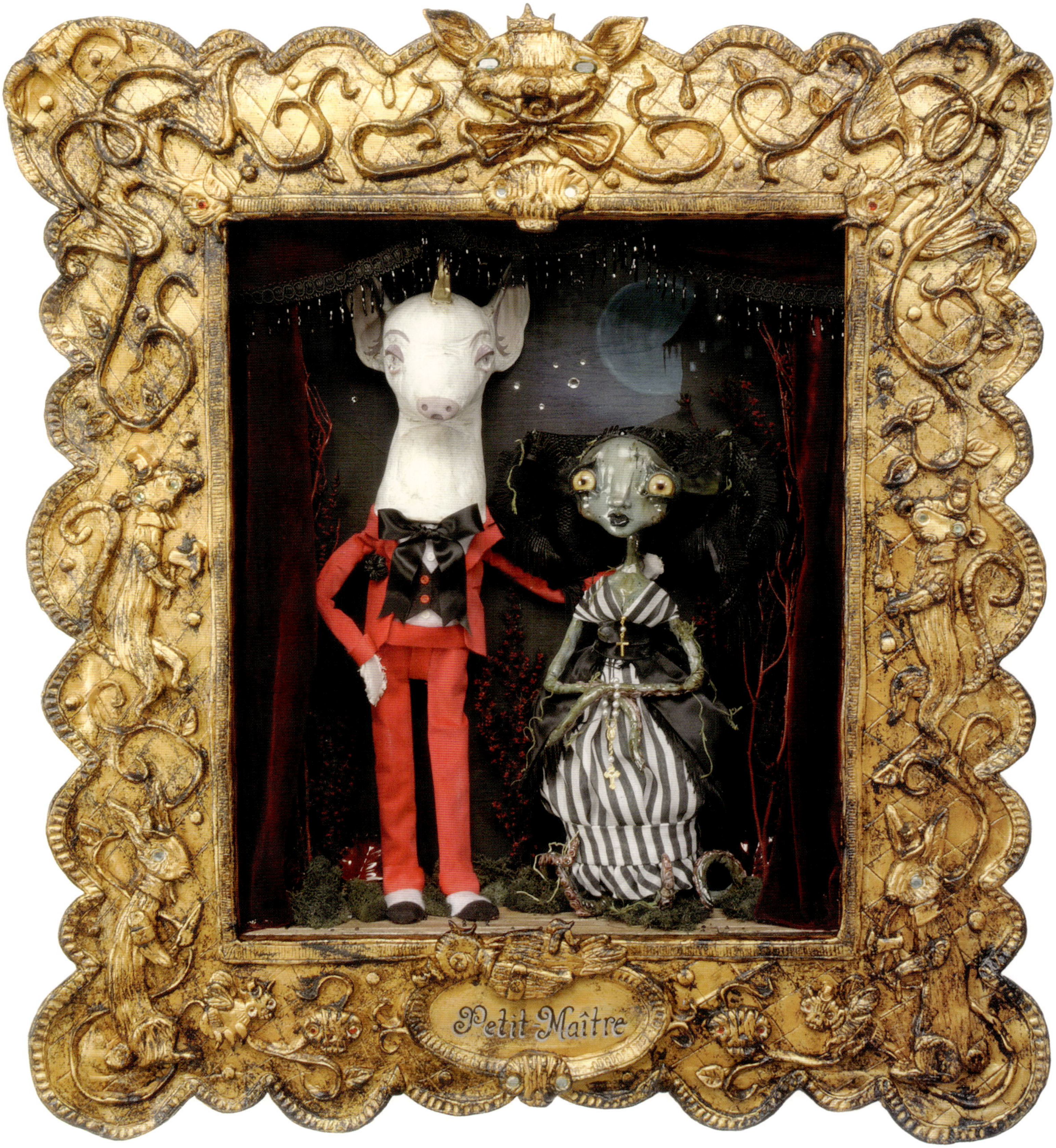
Petit-Maître

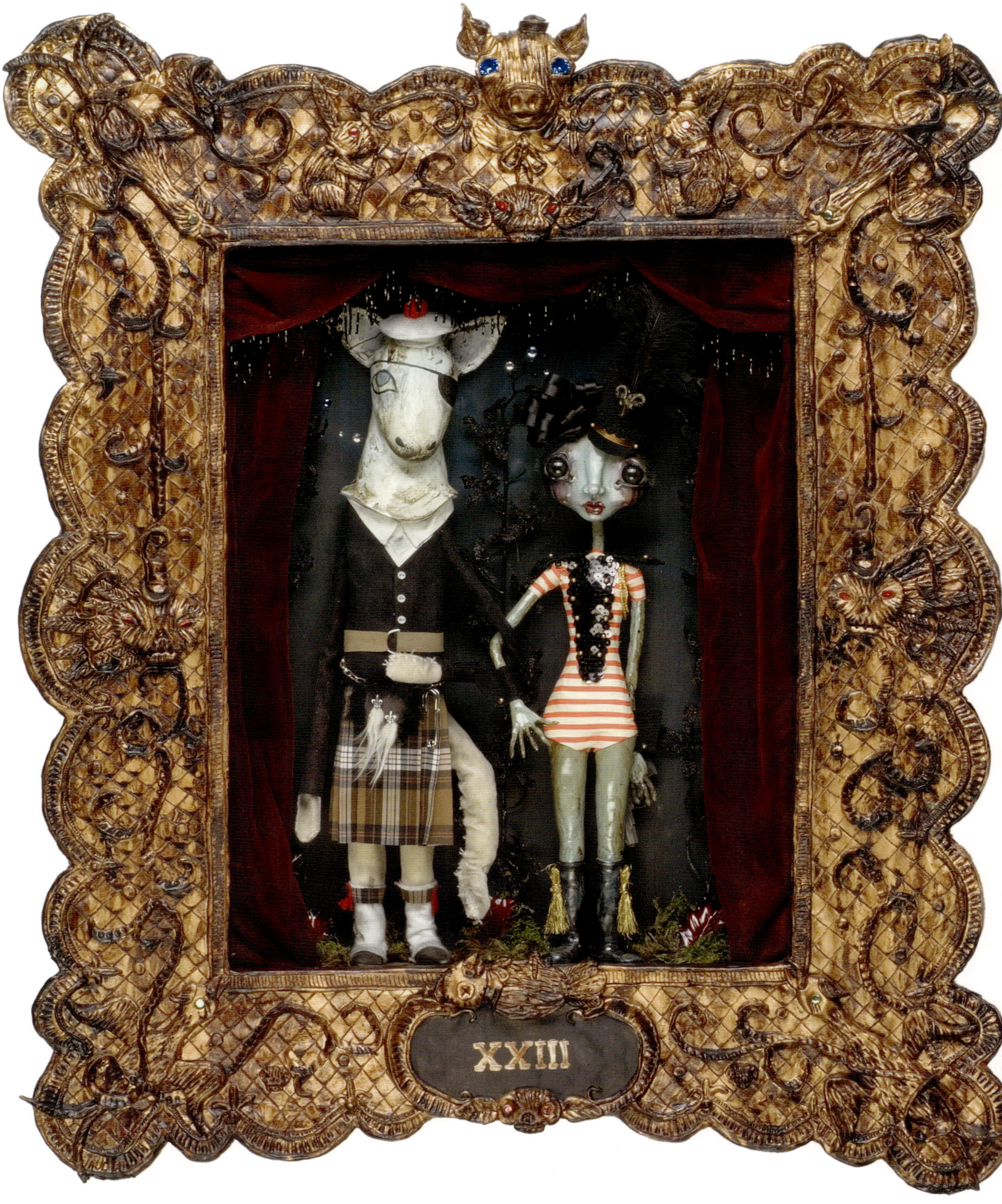
XXIII

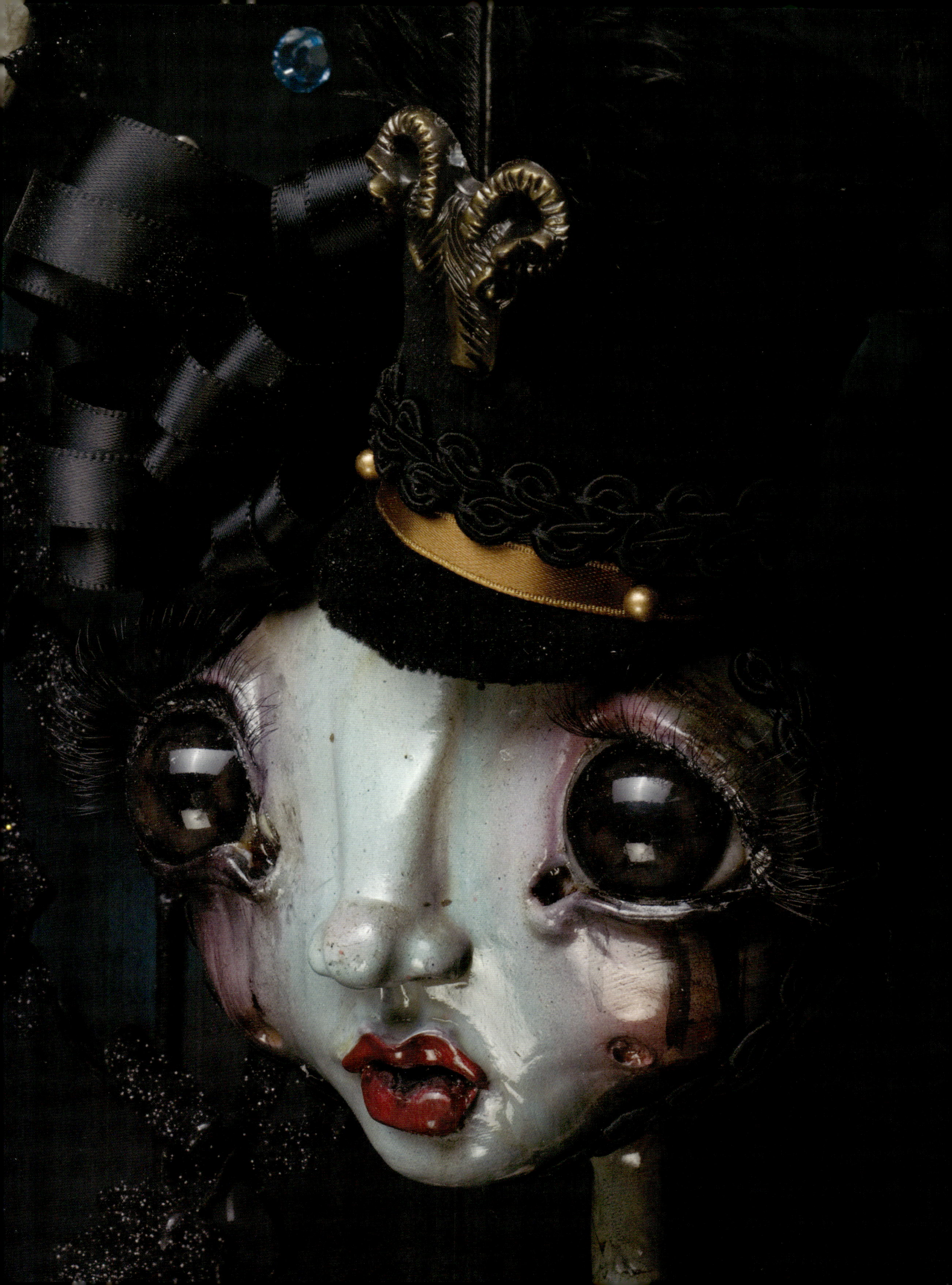

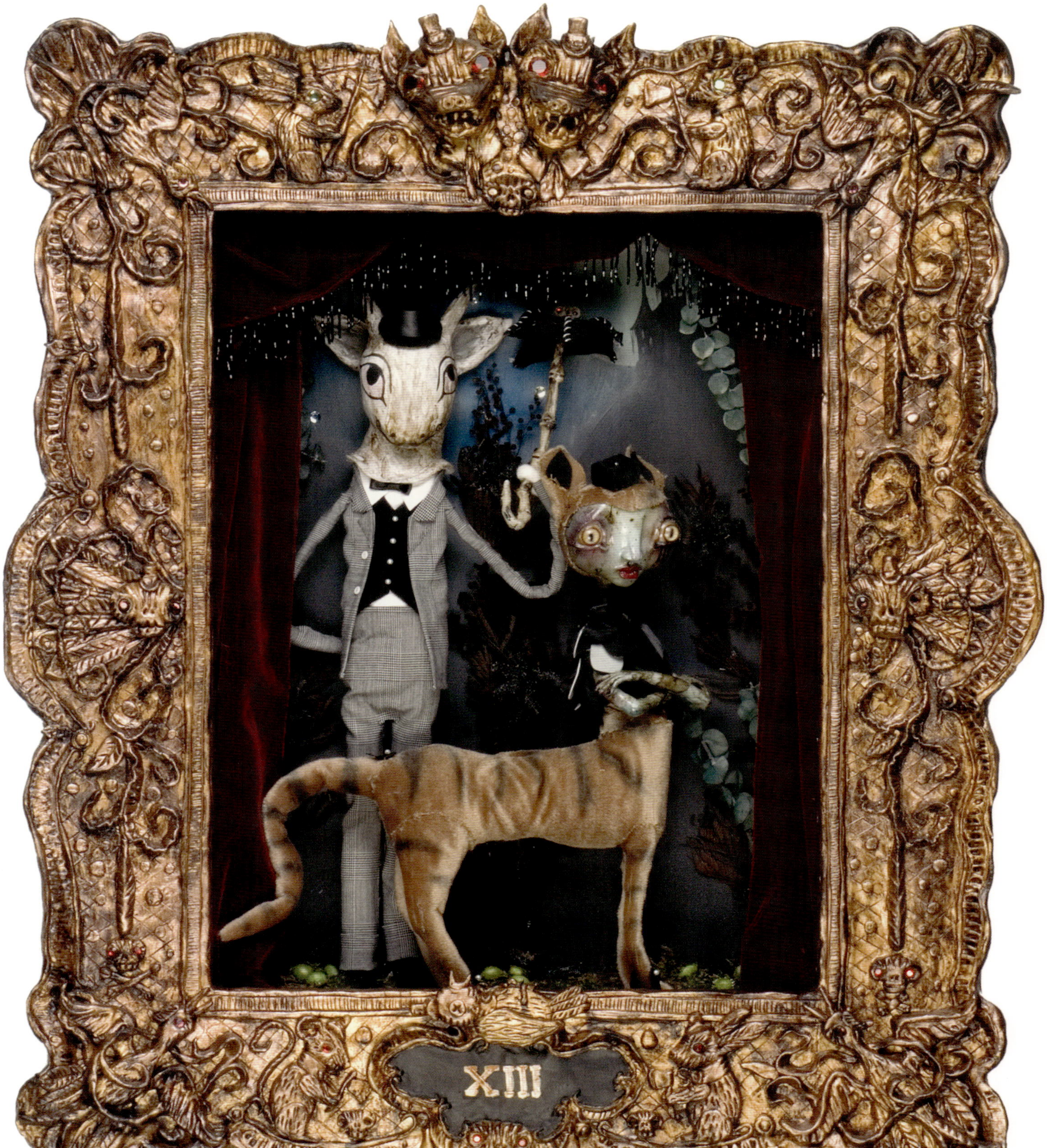
XIII

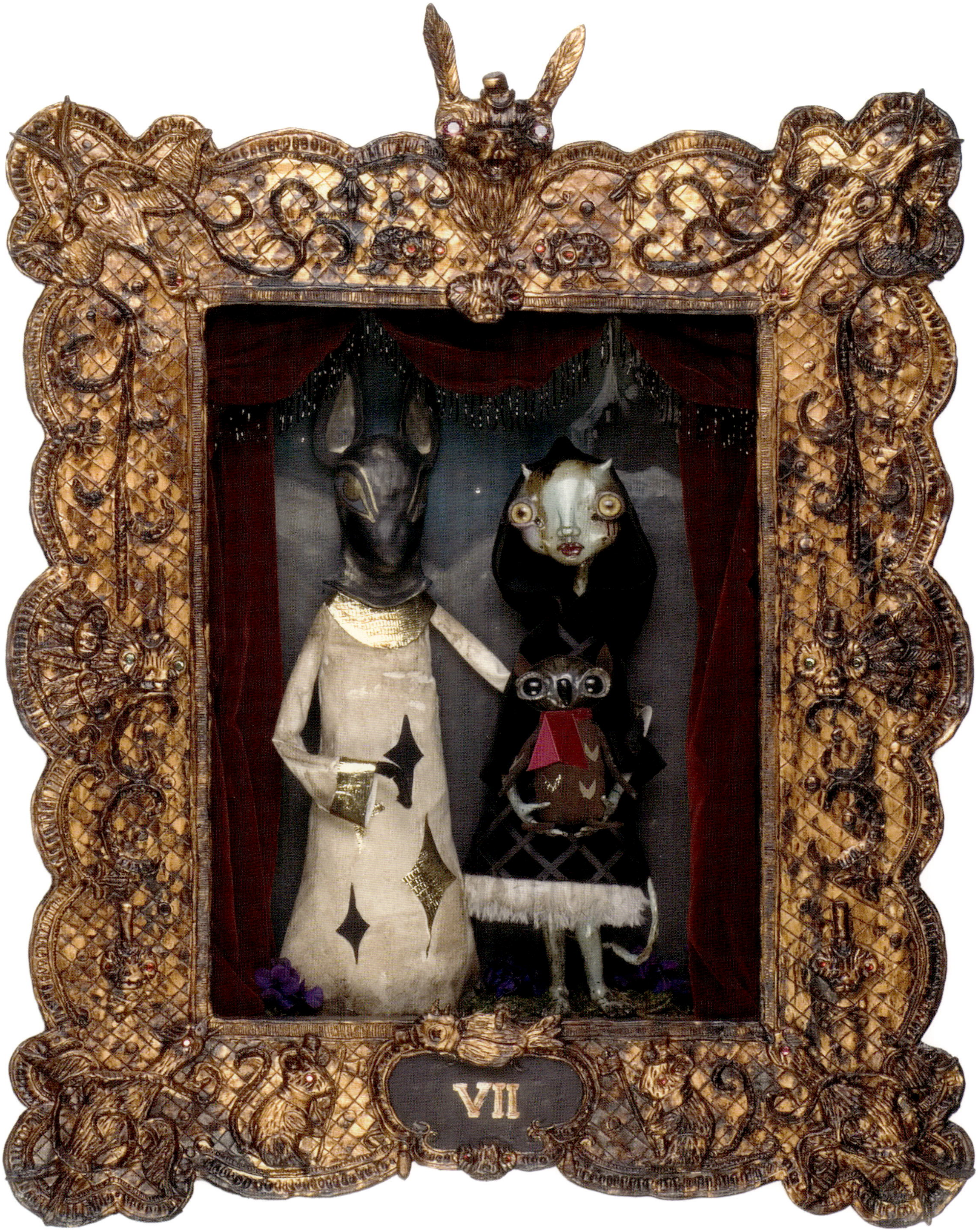
VII

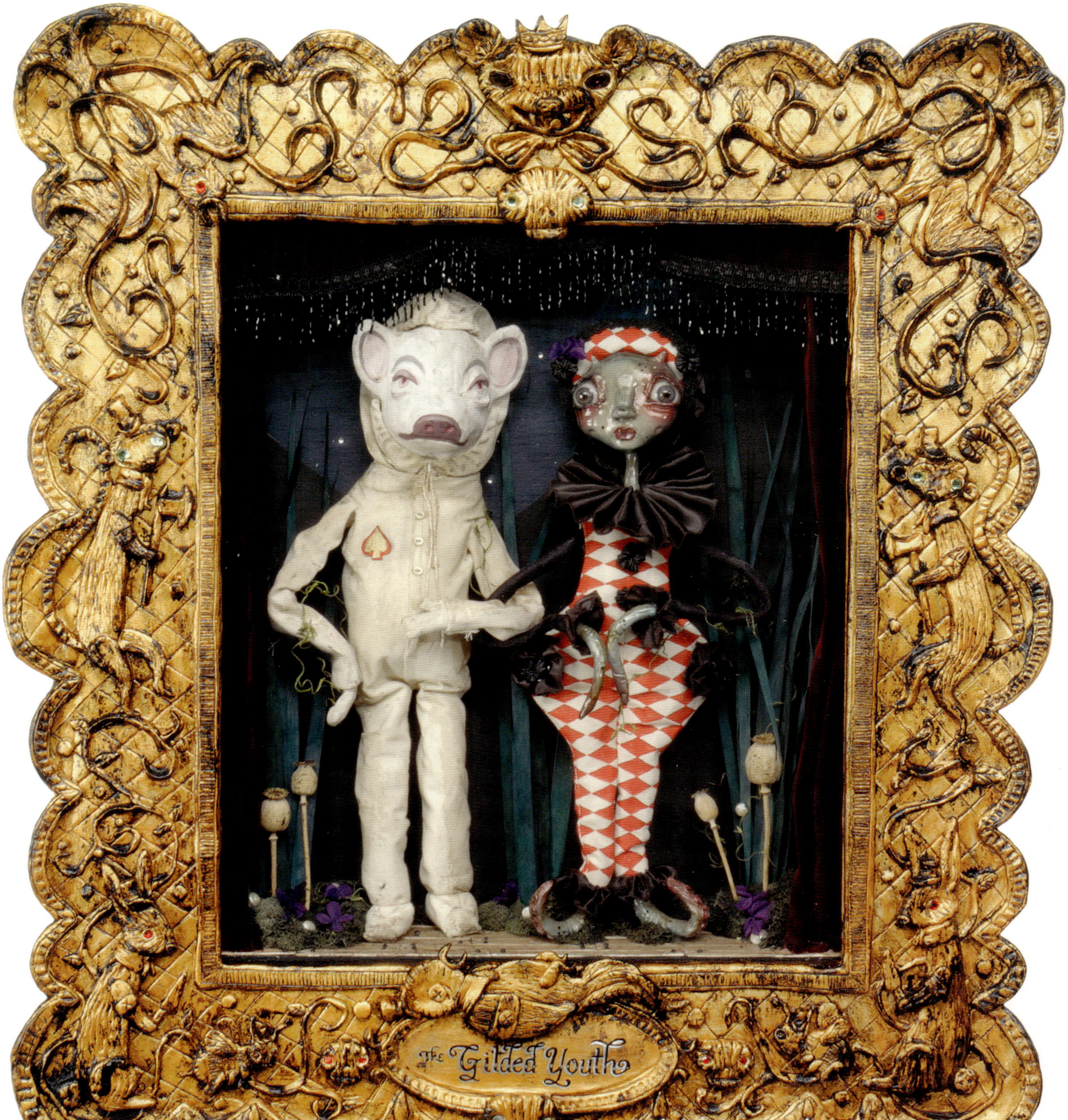
The Gilded Youth

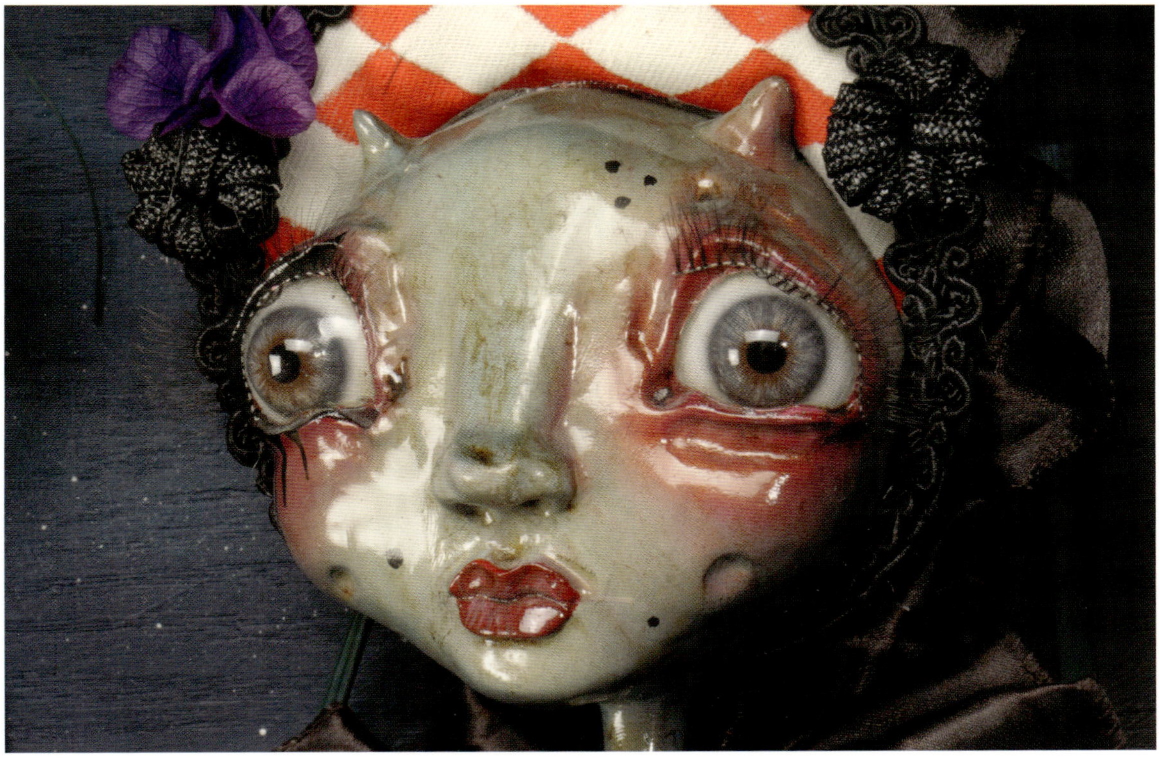

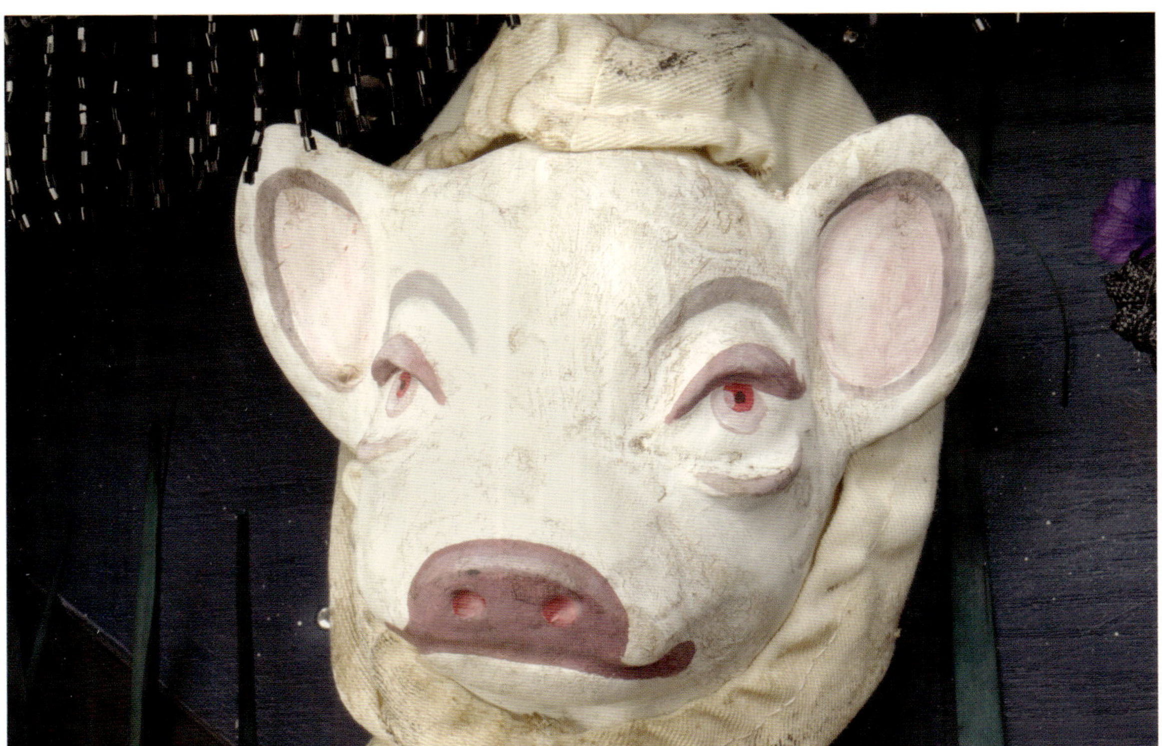

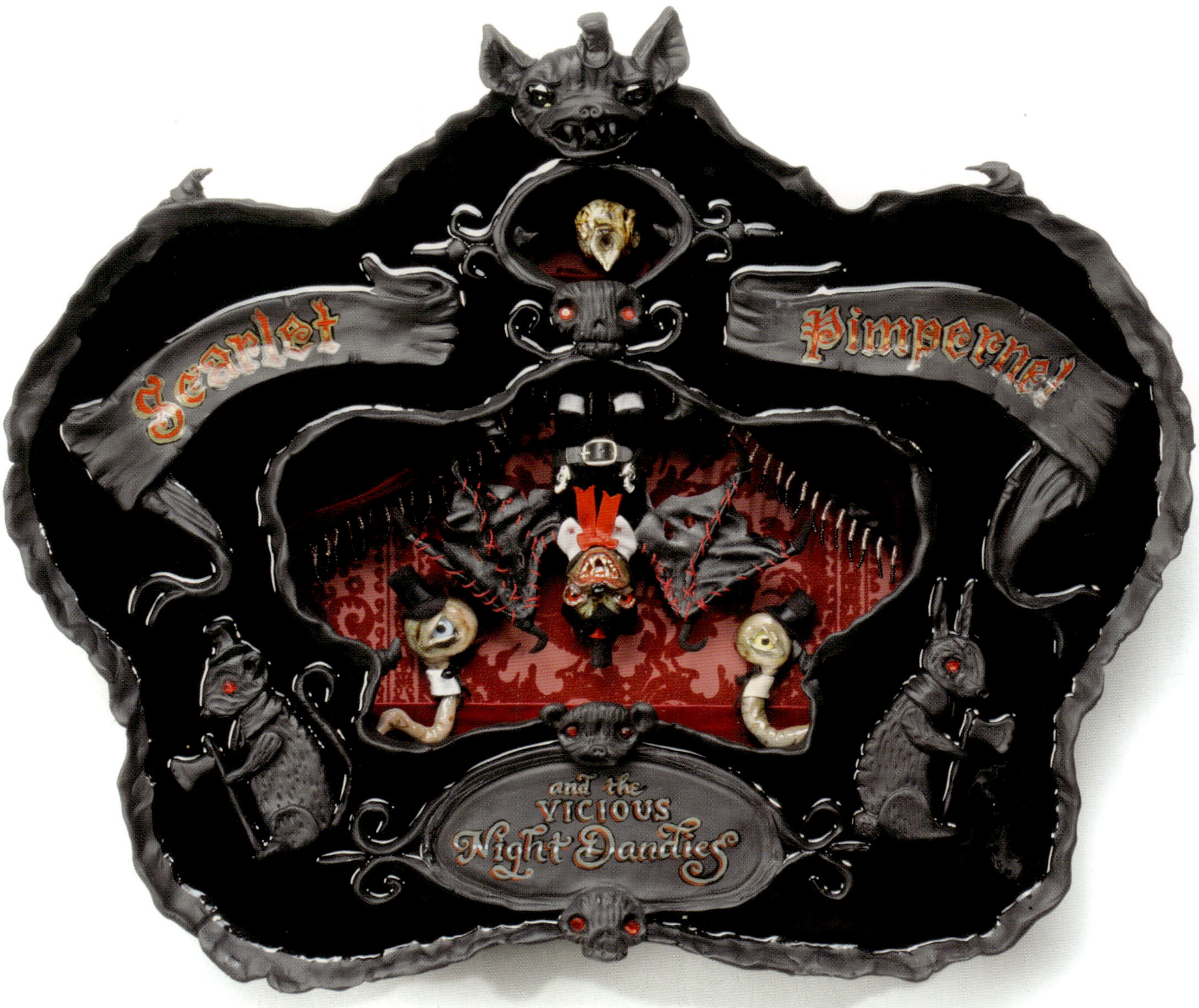
Scarlet
Pimpernel
and the
VICIOUS
Night Dandies

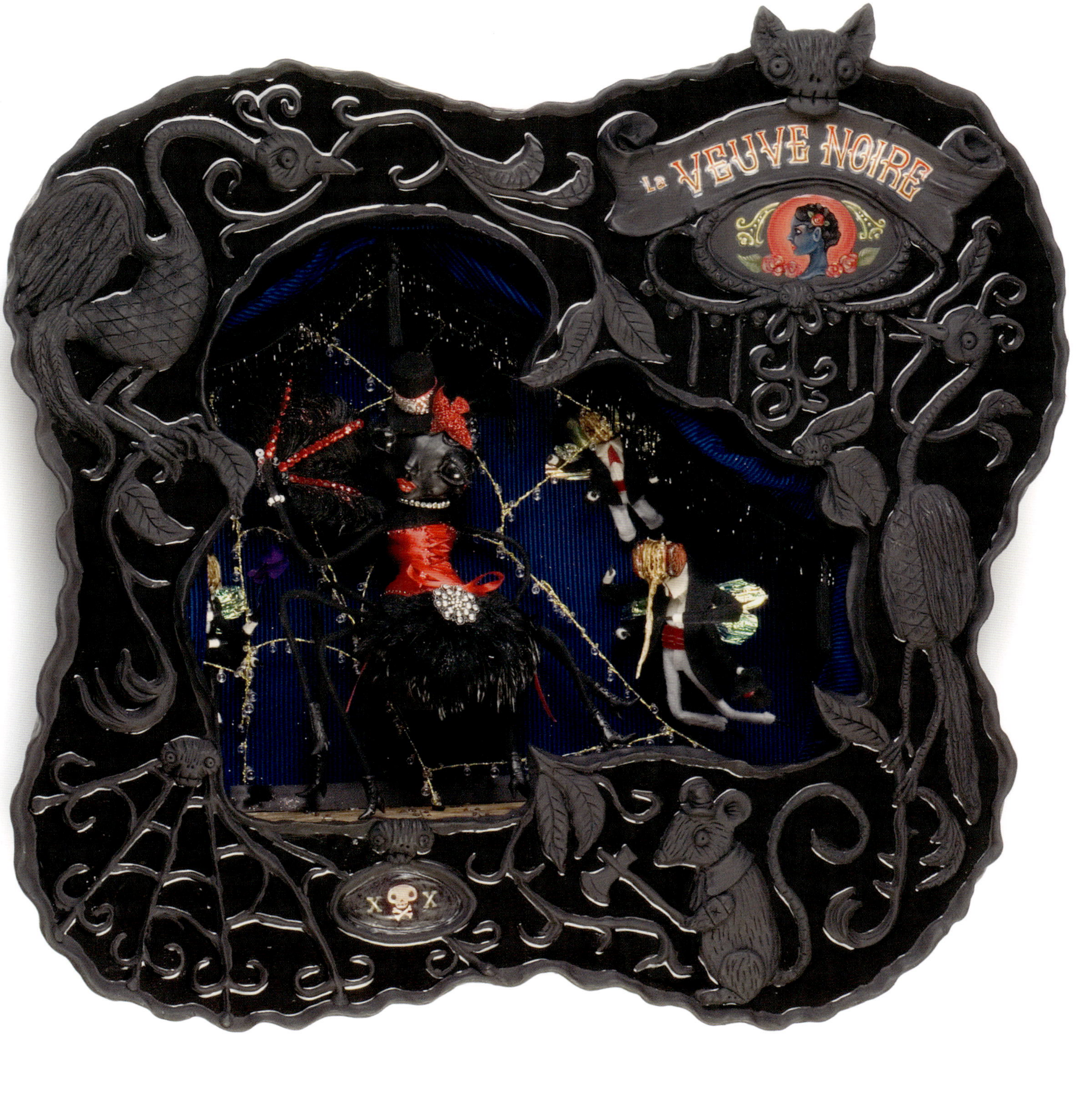
La VEUVE NOIRE

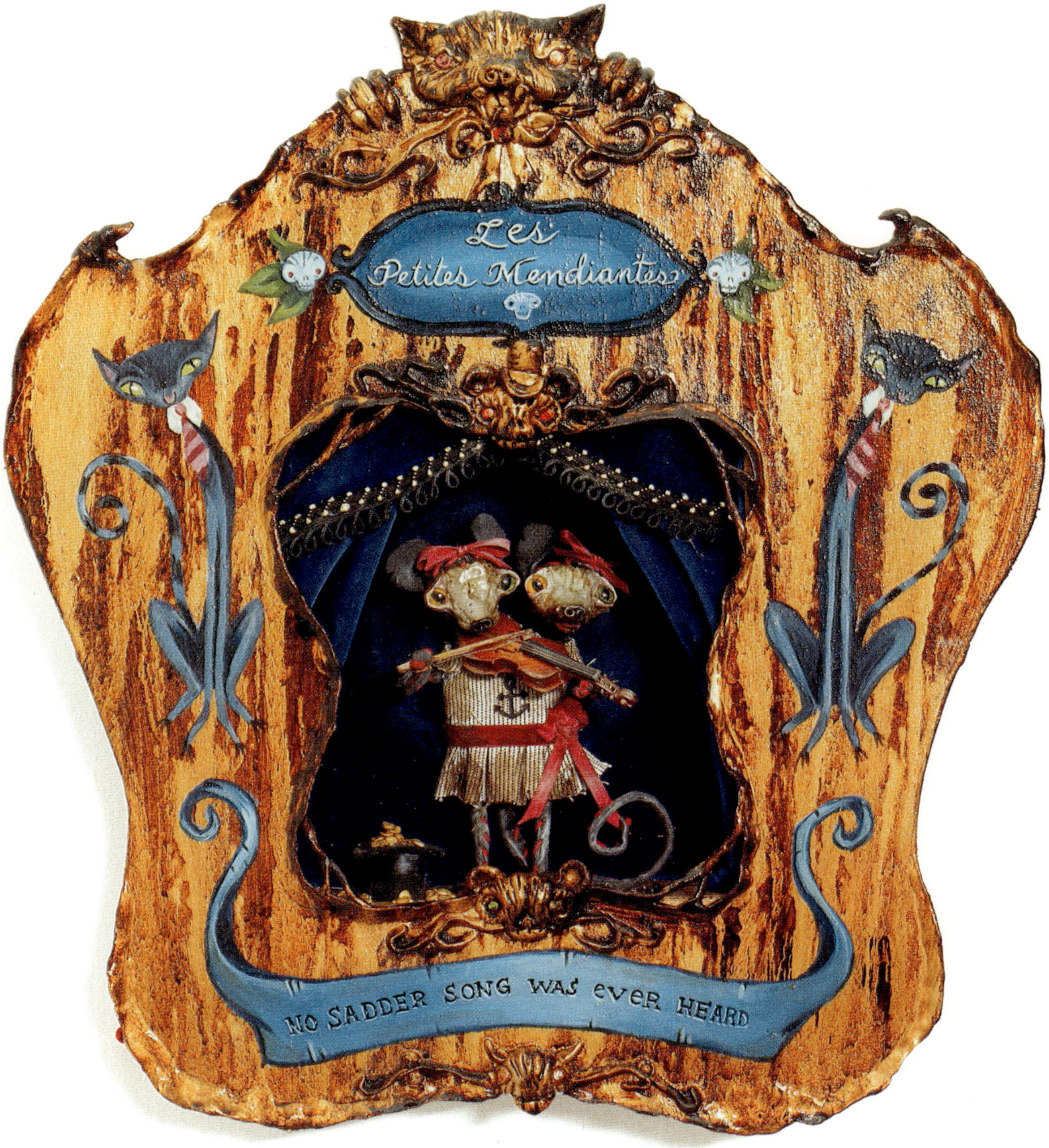
Les
Petites Mendiantes
NO SADDER SONG WAS EVER HEARD

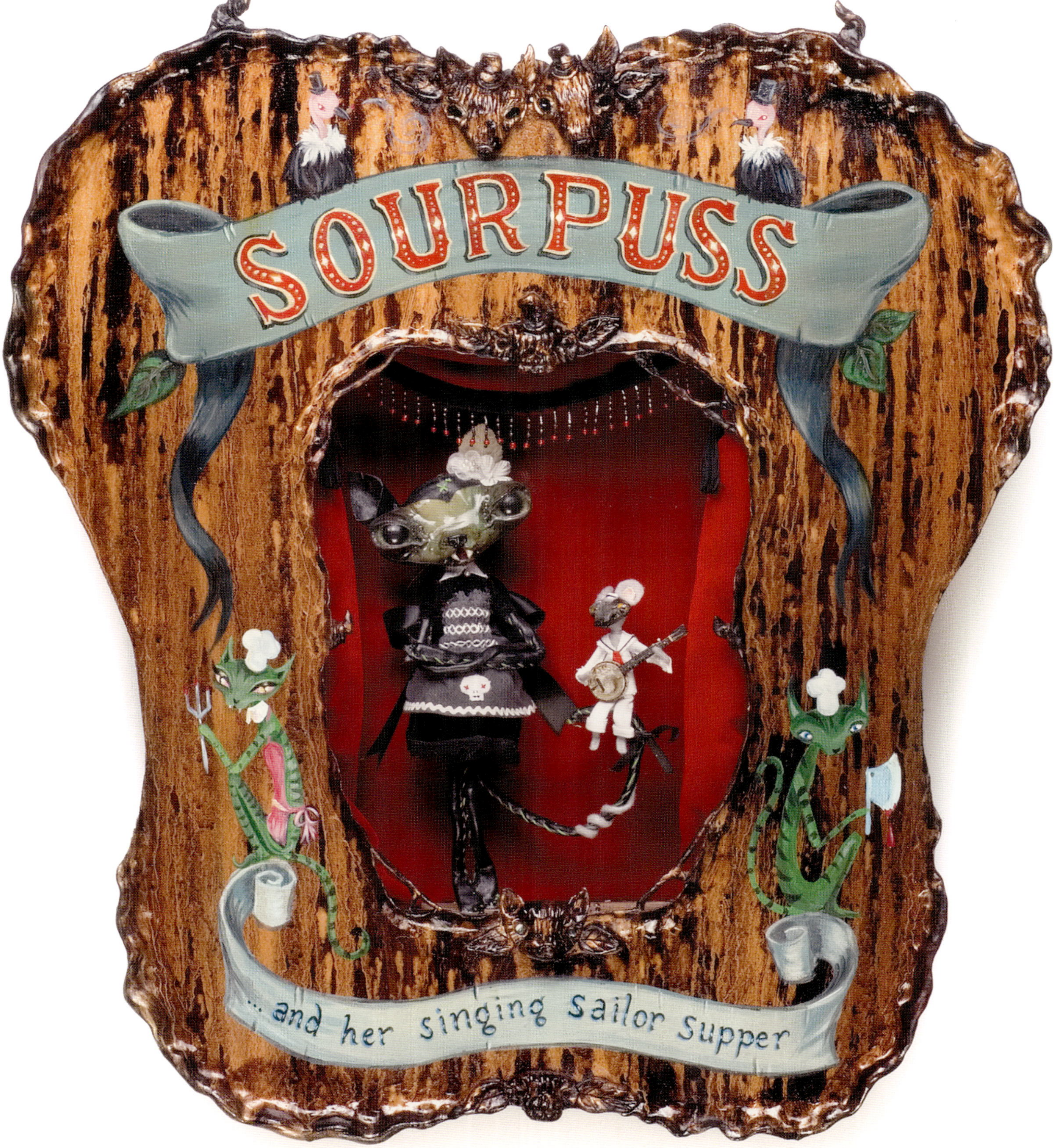
SOURPUSS
...and her singing sailor supper

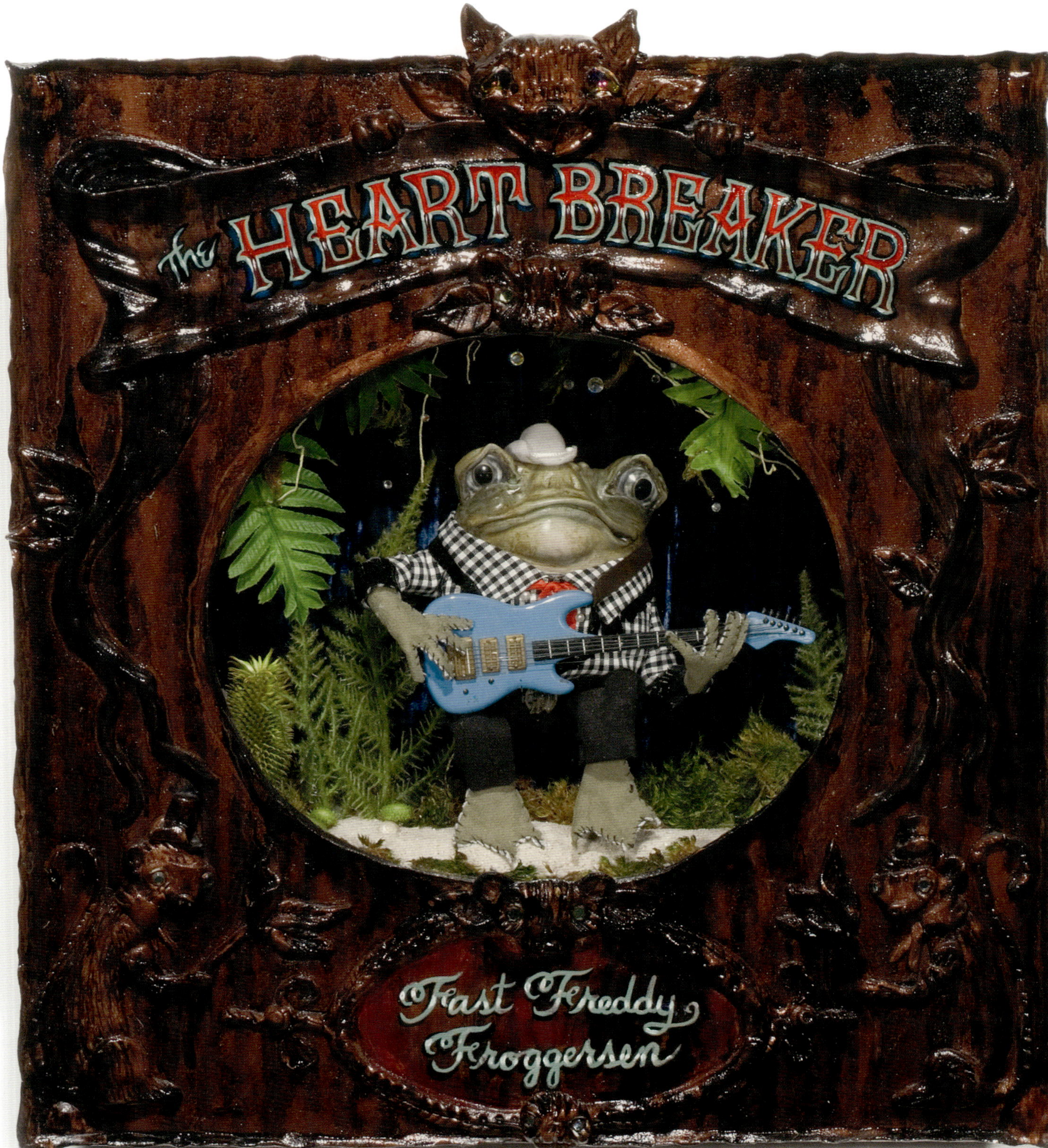
the HEART BREAKER
Fast Freddy
Froggersen

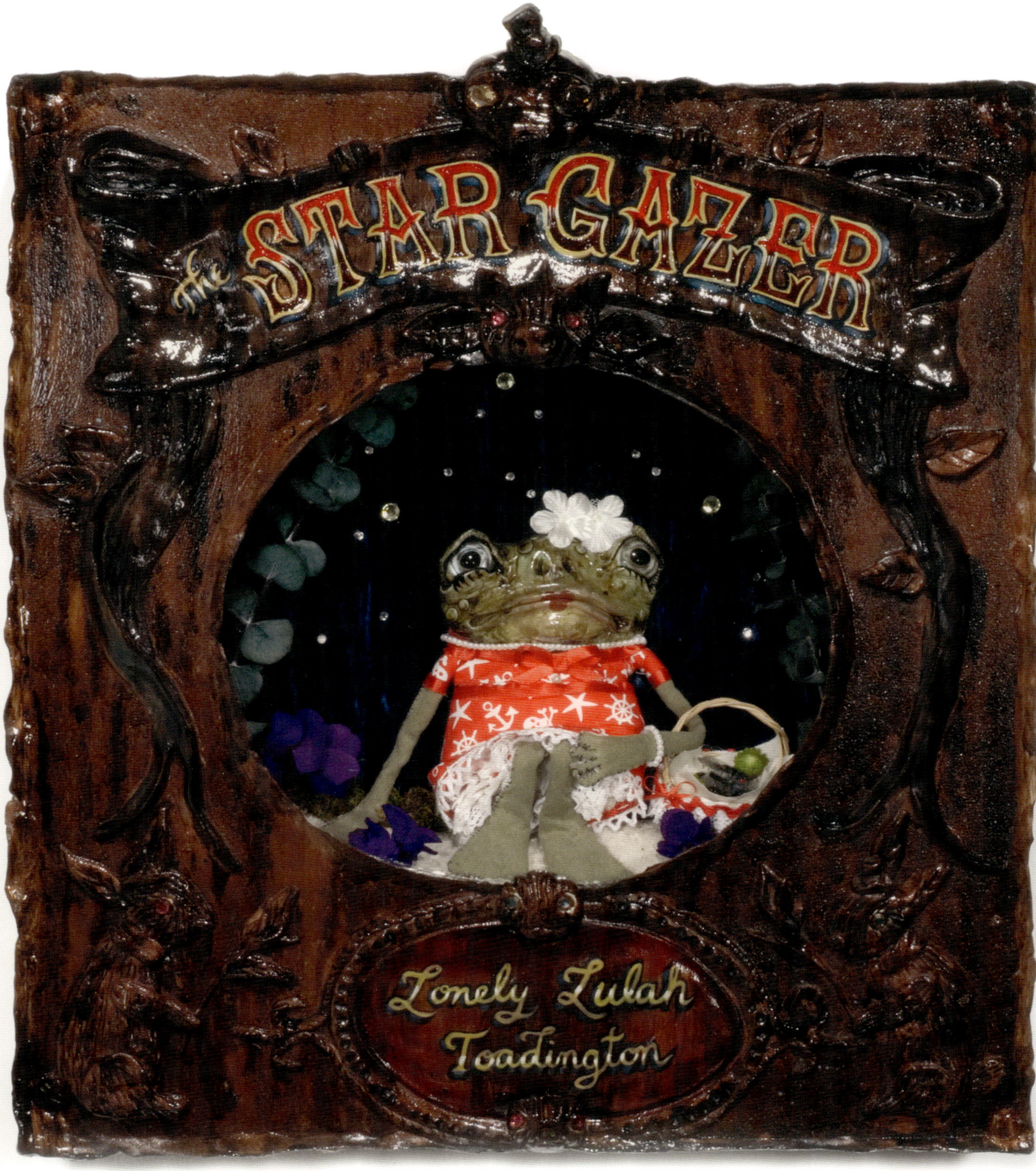
the STAR GAZER
Lonely Lulah
Toadington

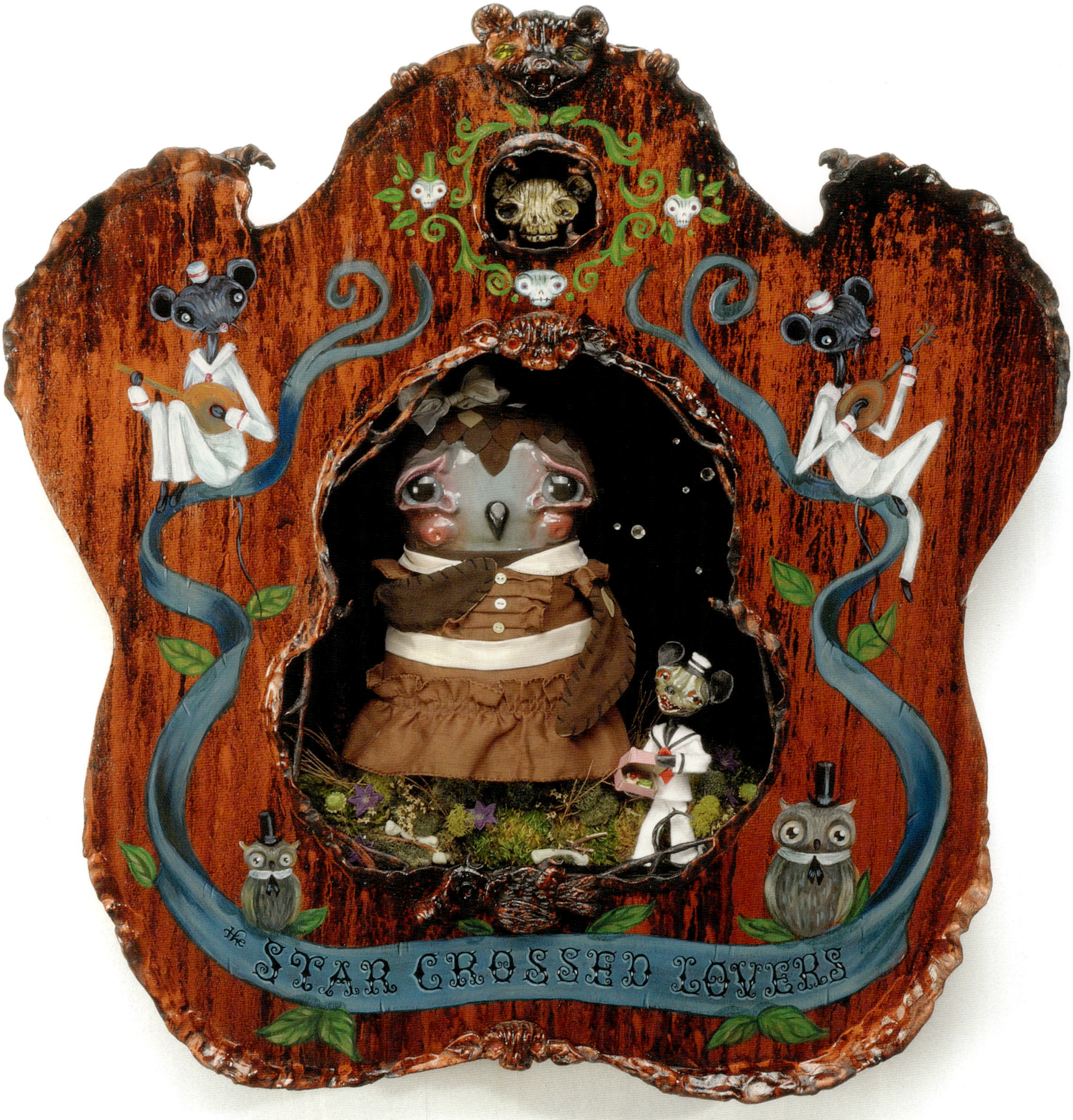
the STAR CROSSED LOVERS

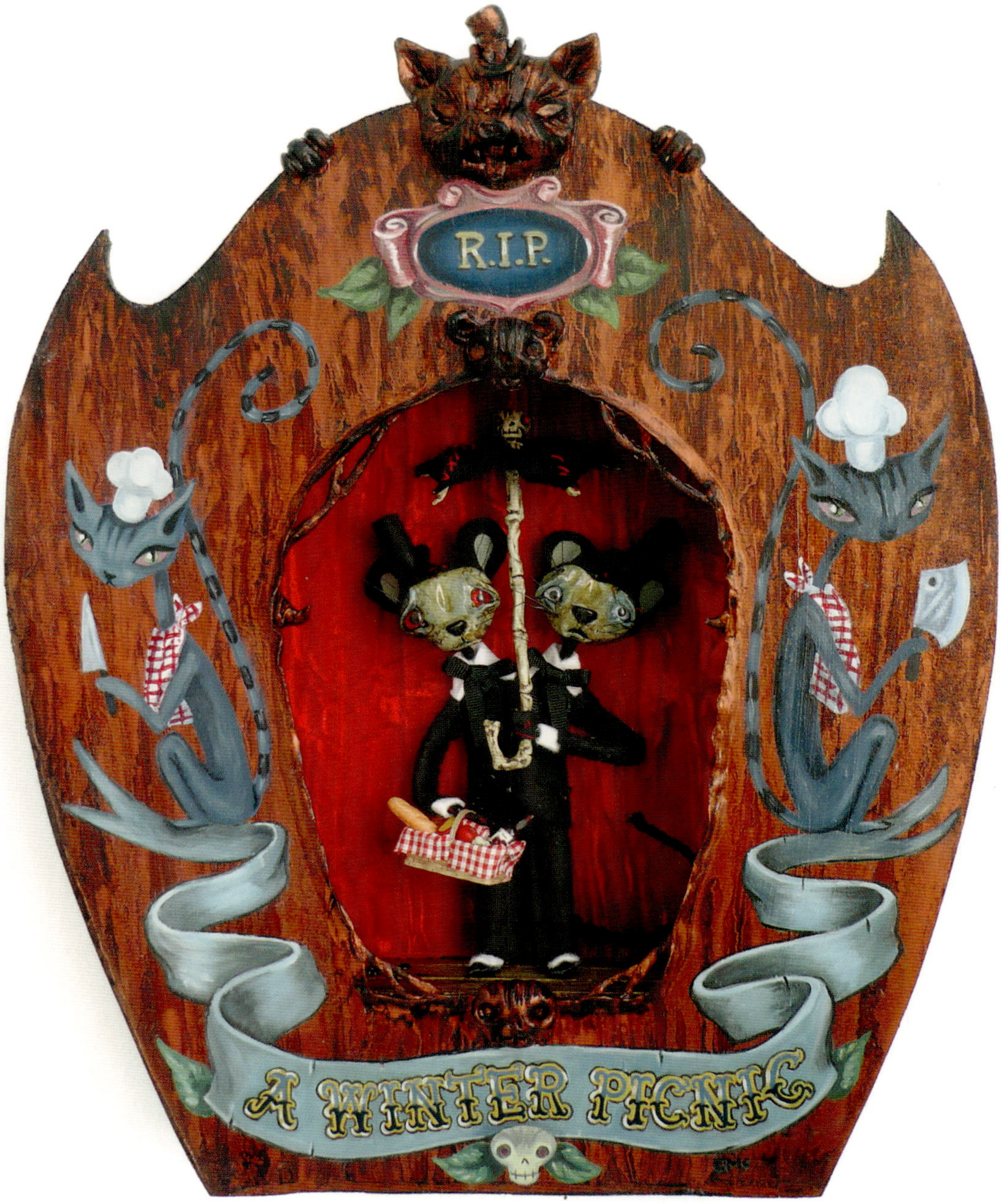
R.I.P.
A WINTER PICNIC

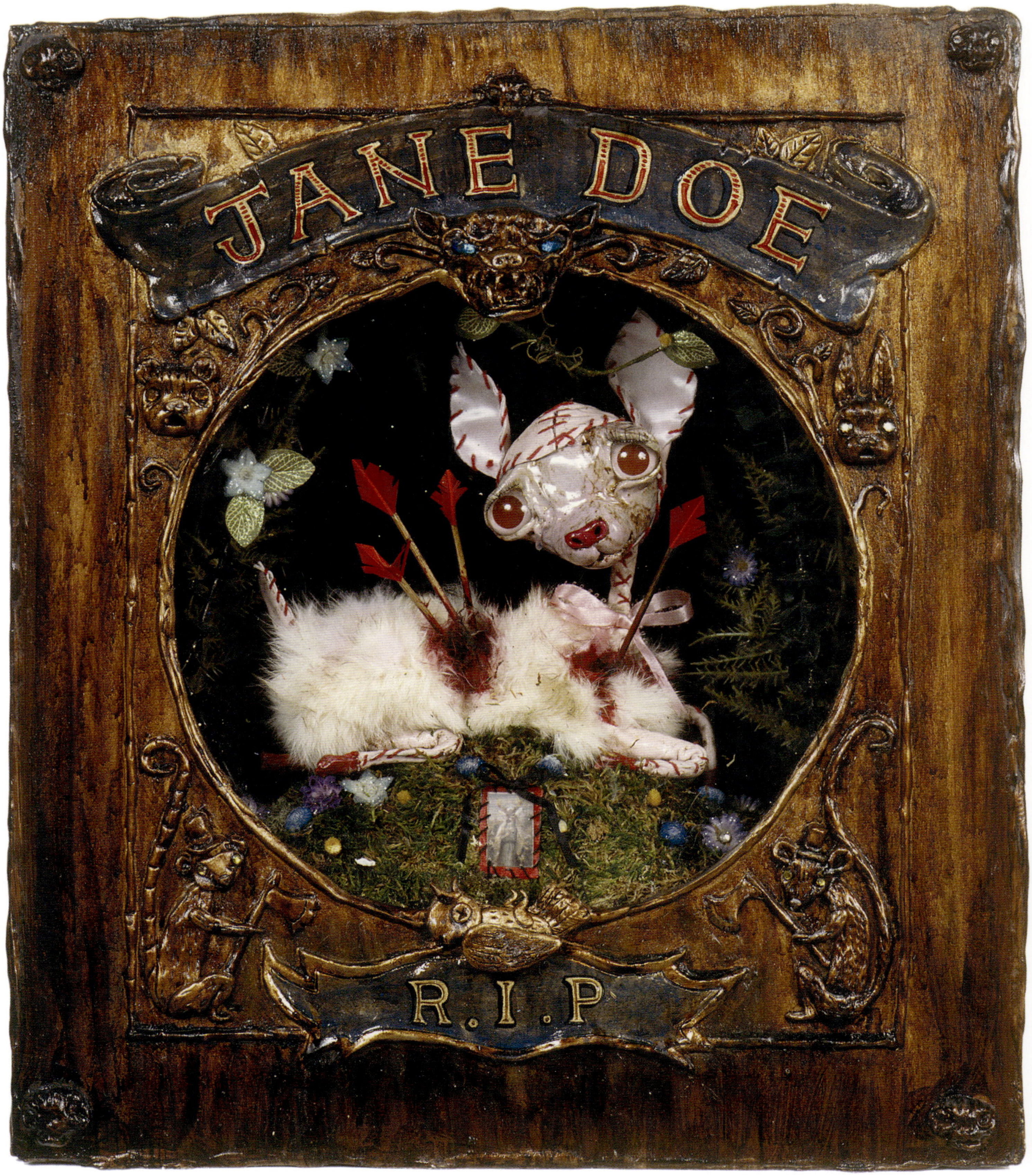
JANE DOE
R.I.P

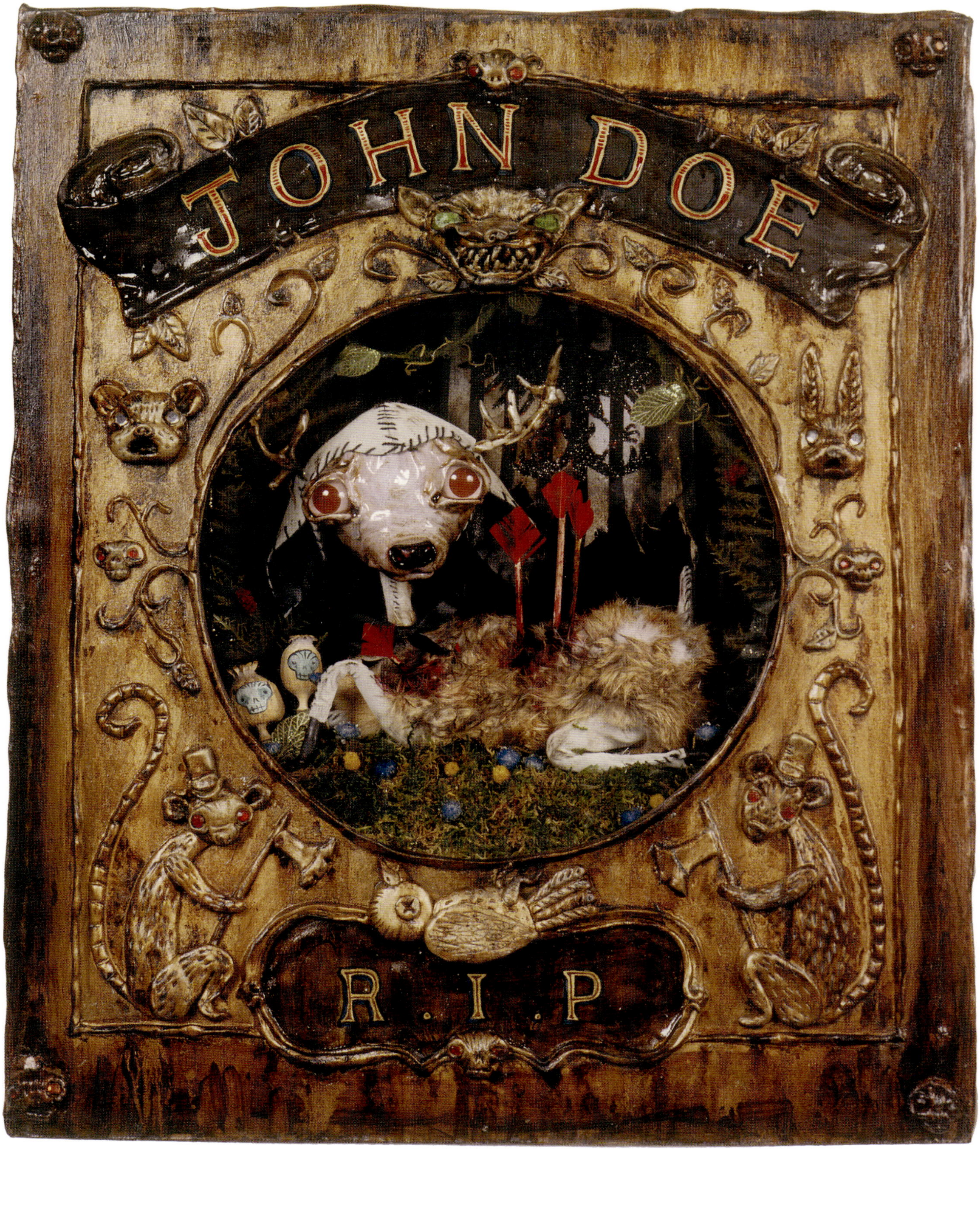
JOHN DOE
R.I.P

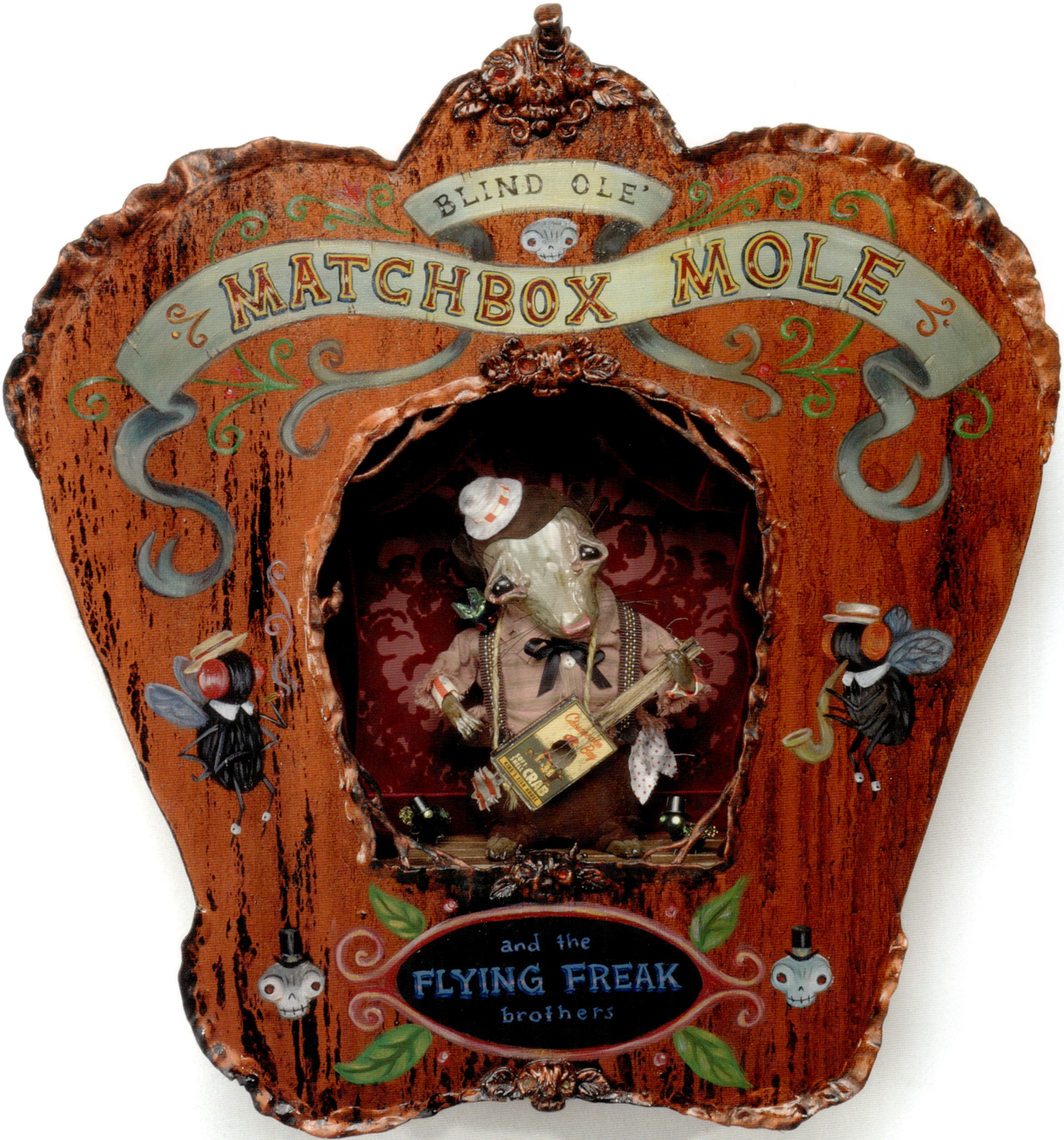
BLIND OLE'
MATCHBOX MOLE
and the
FLYING FREAK
brothers

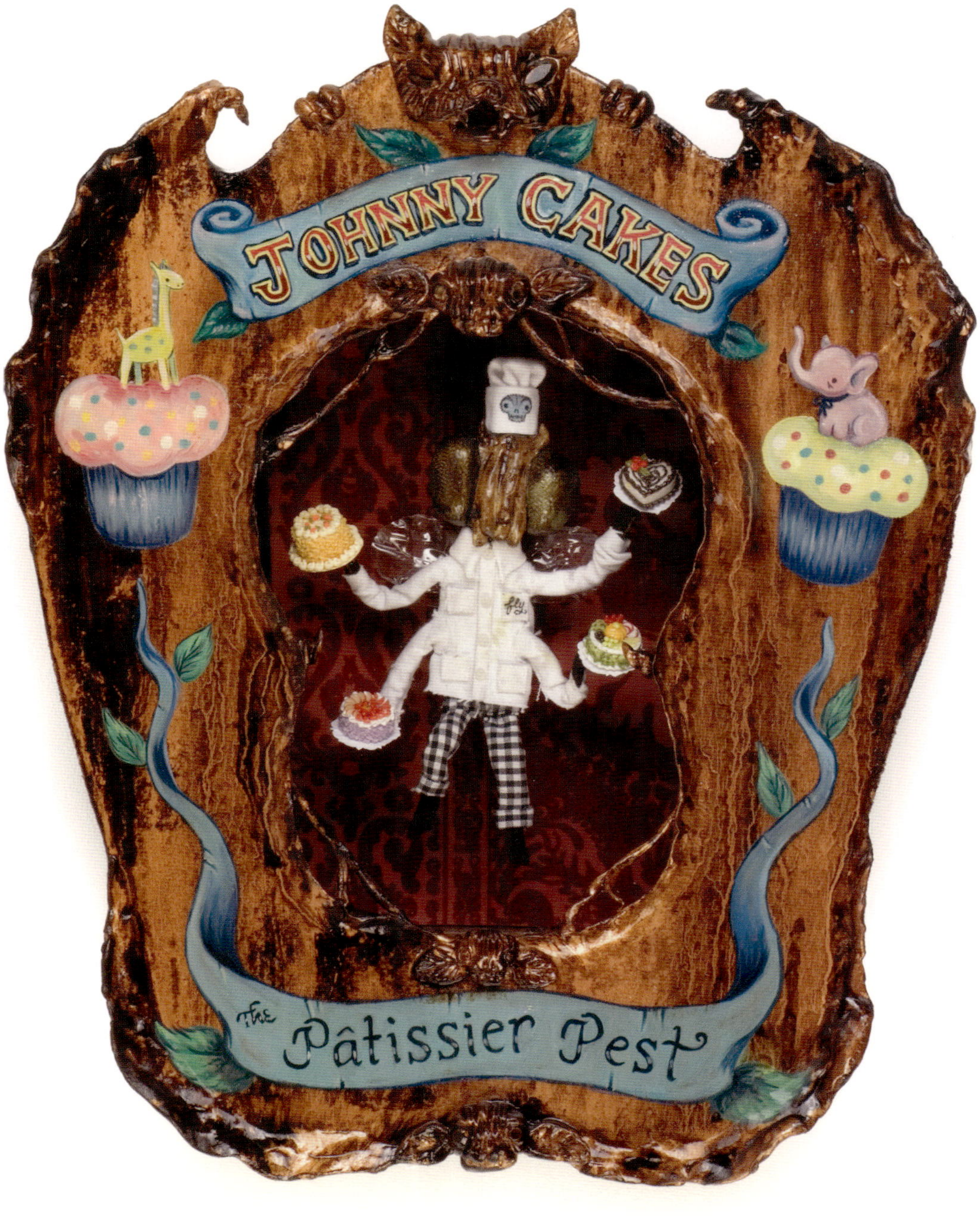
JOHNNY CAKES
The Patissier Pest

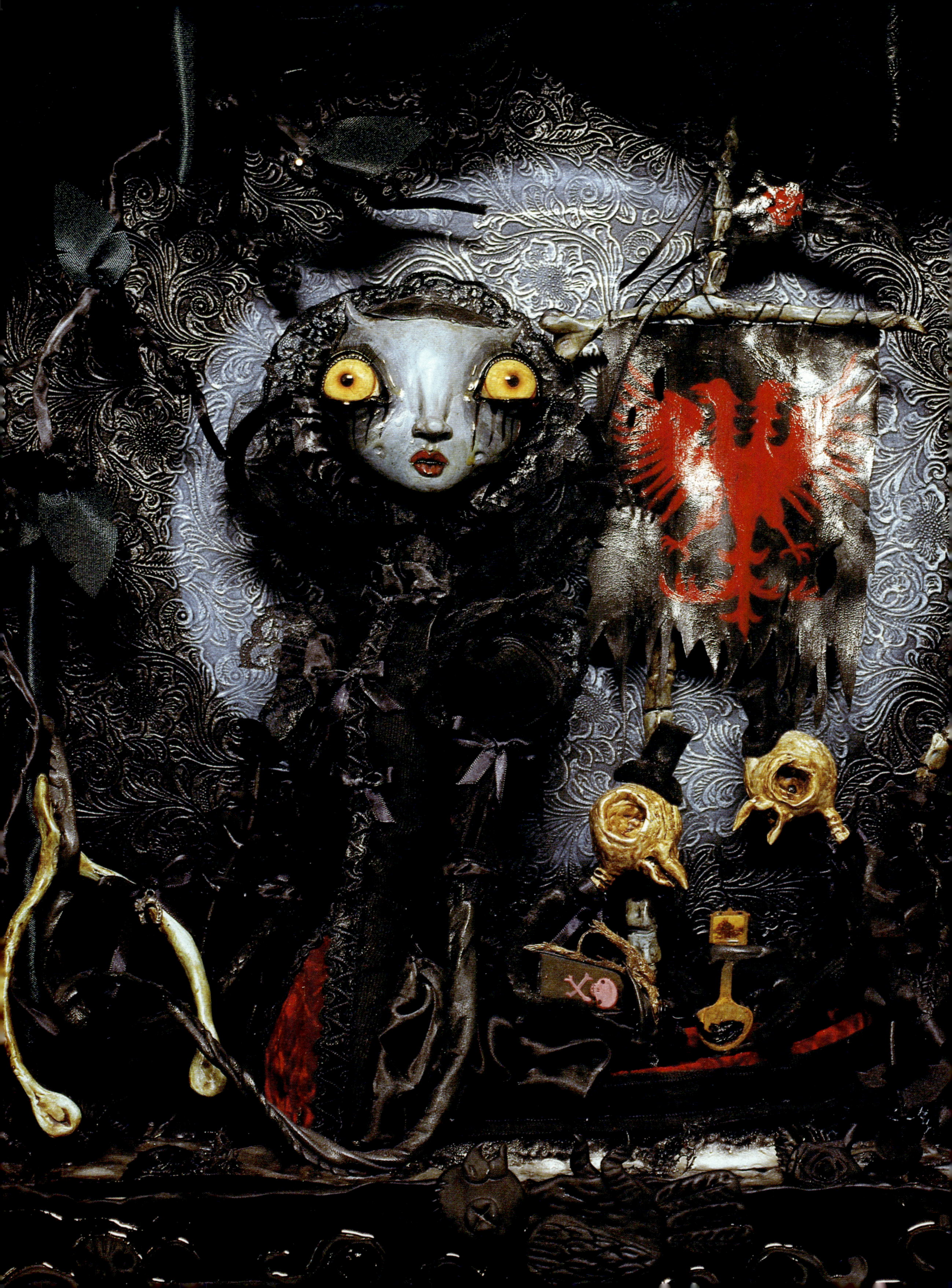

Altarwise by Owl-Light

Altarwise by owl-light in the half-way house
The gentleman lay graveward with his furies;
Abaddon in the hangnail cracked from Adam,
And, from his fork, a dog among the fairies,
The atlas-eater with a jaw for news,
Bit out the mandrake with to-morrows scream.
Then, penny-eyed, that gentlemen of wounds,
Old cock from nowheres and the heaven's egg,
With bones unbuttoned to the half-way winds,
Hatched from the windy salvage on one leg,
Scraped at my cradle in a walking word
That night of time under the Christward shelter:
I am the long world's gentlemen, he said,
And share my bed with Capricorn and Cancer.

Excerpt from
"Altarwise by Owl Light"
Dylan Thomas
1936

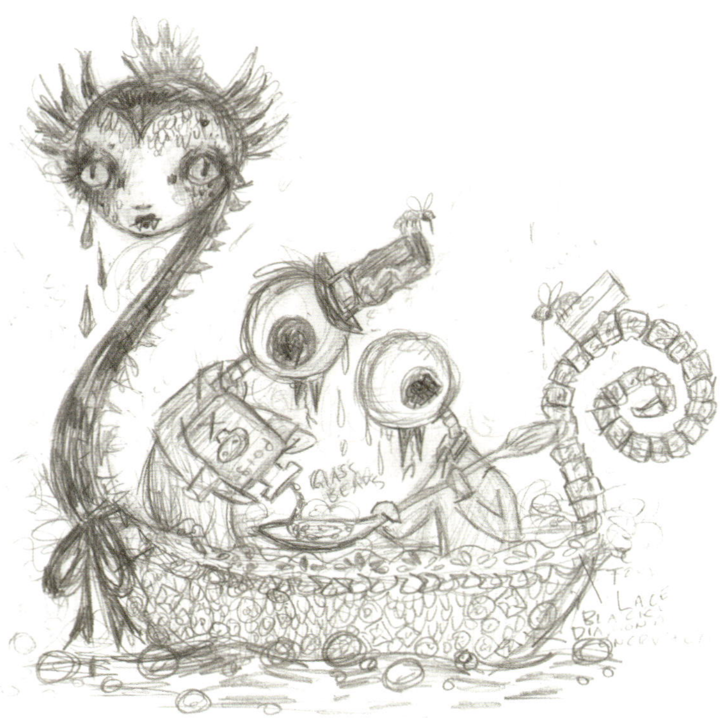

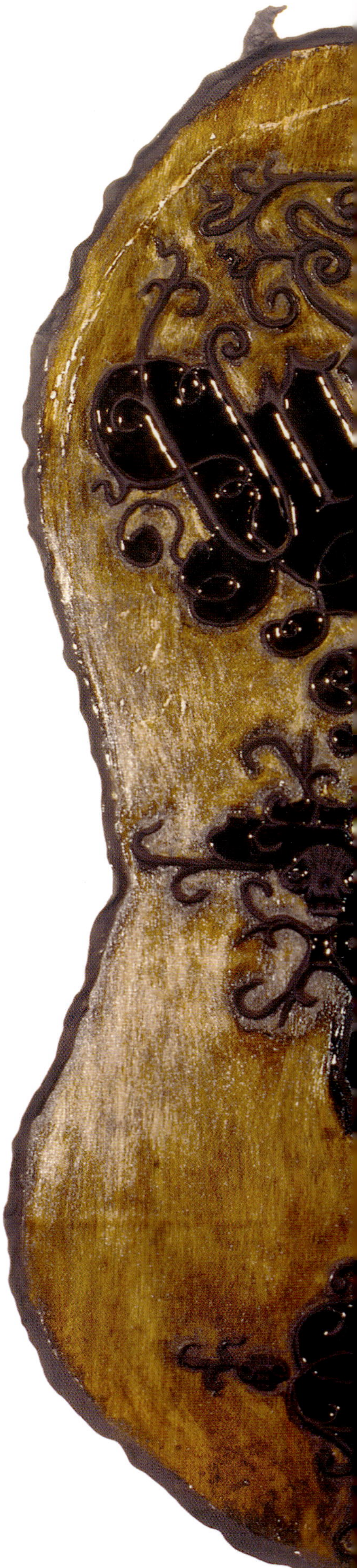

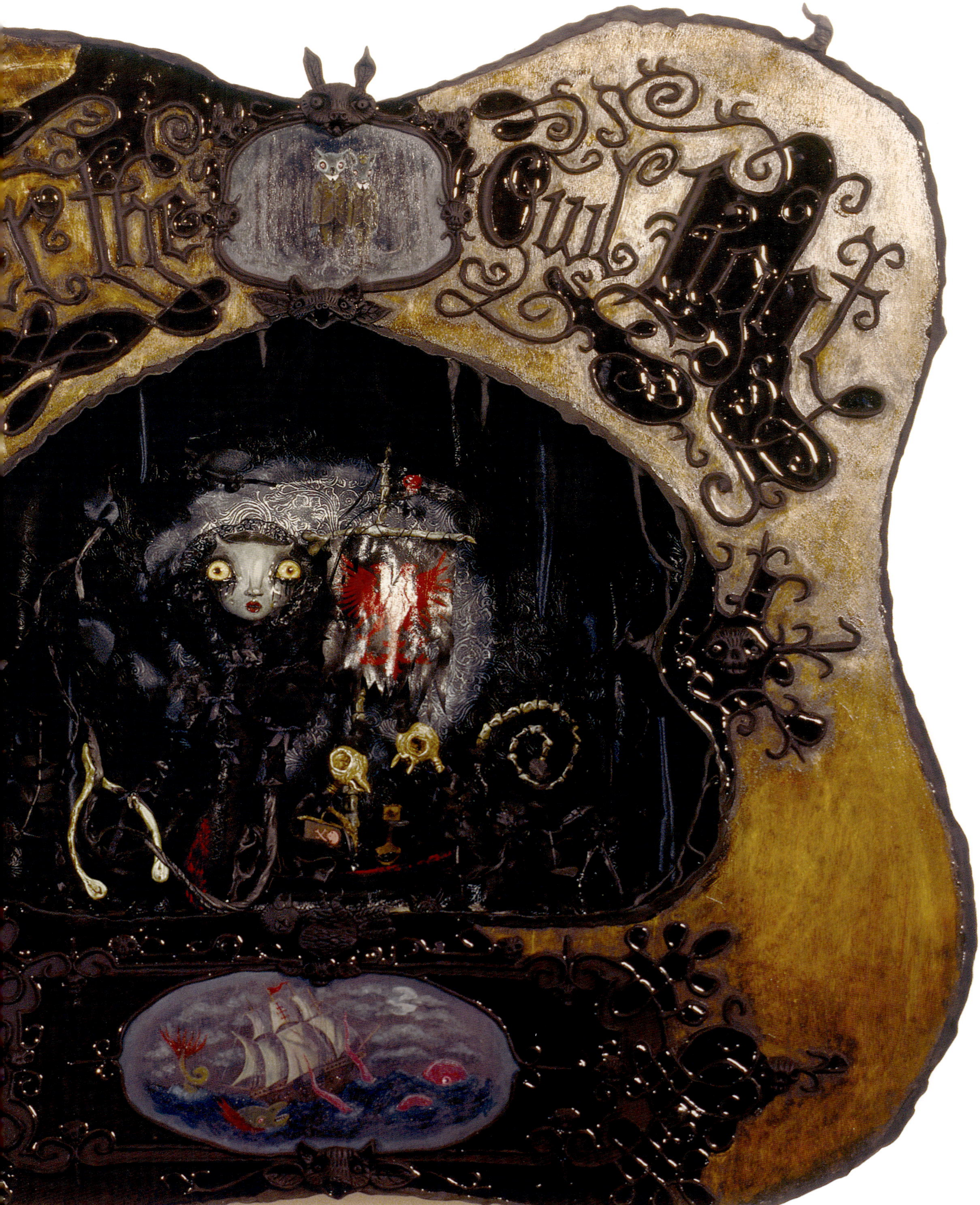
the Owl Light

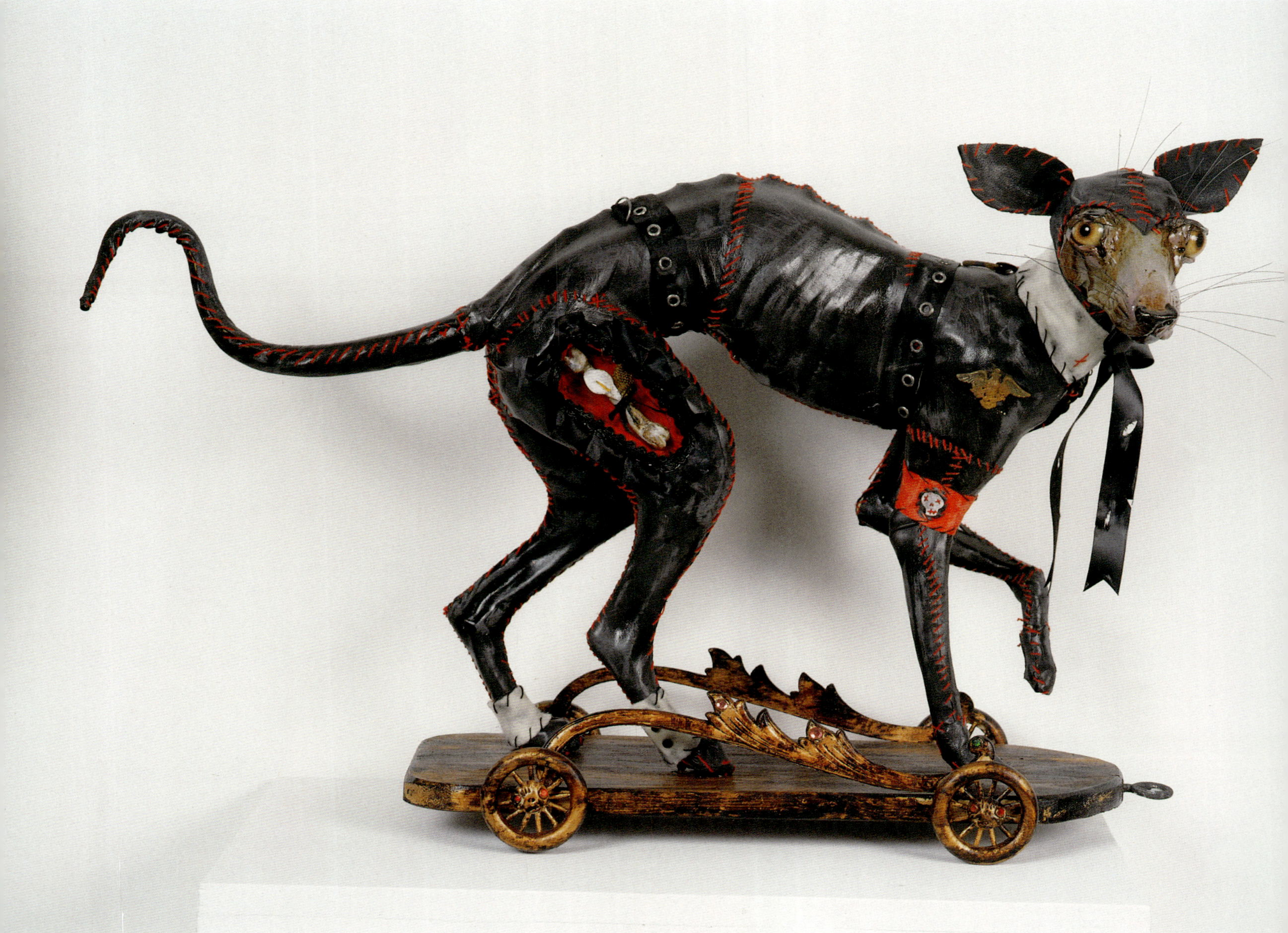

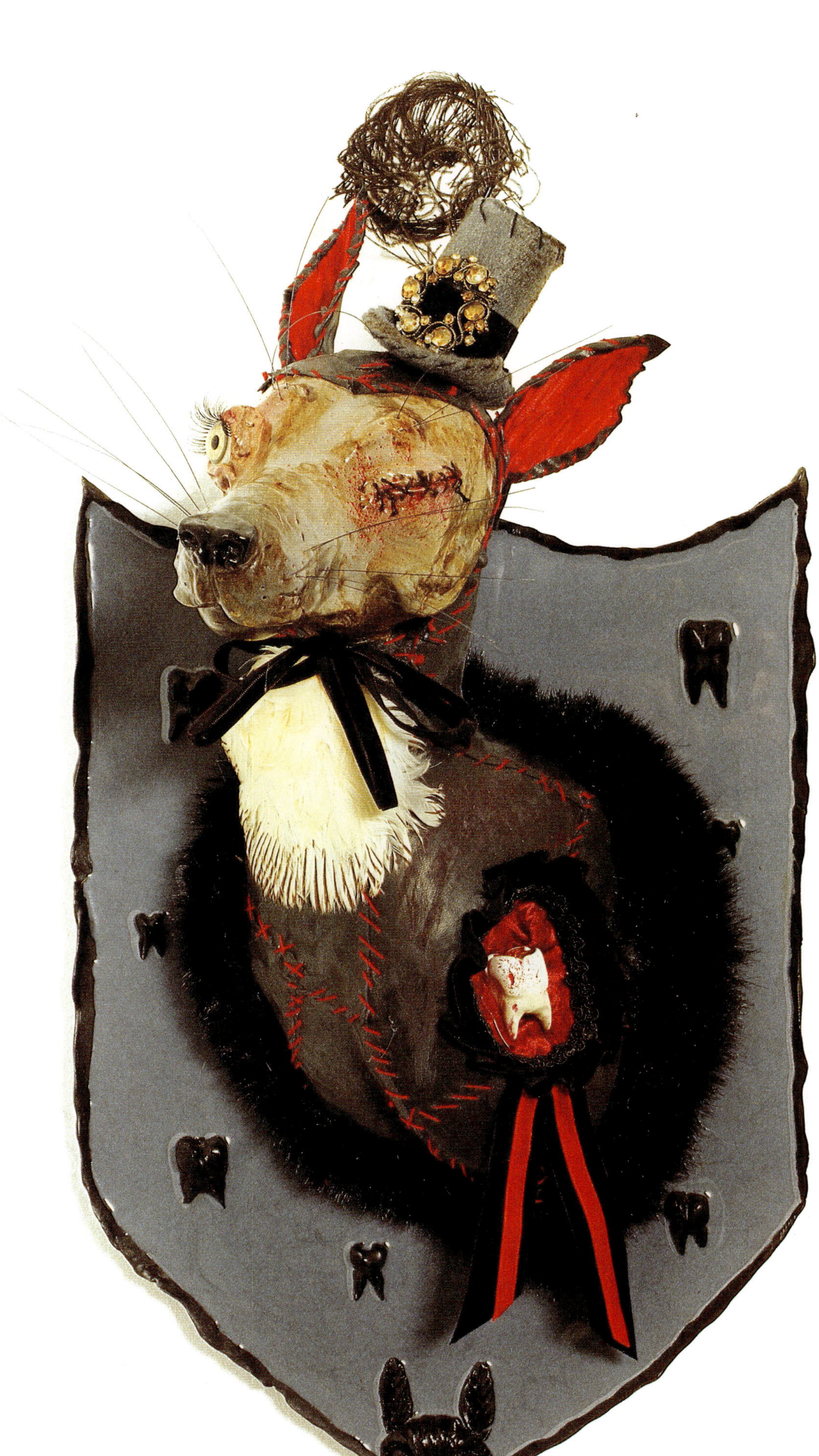

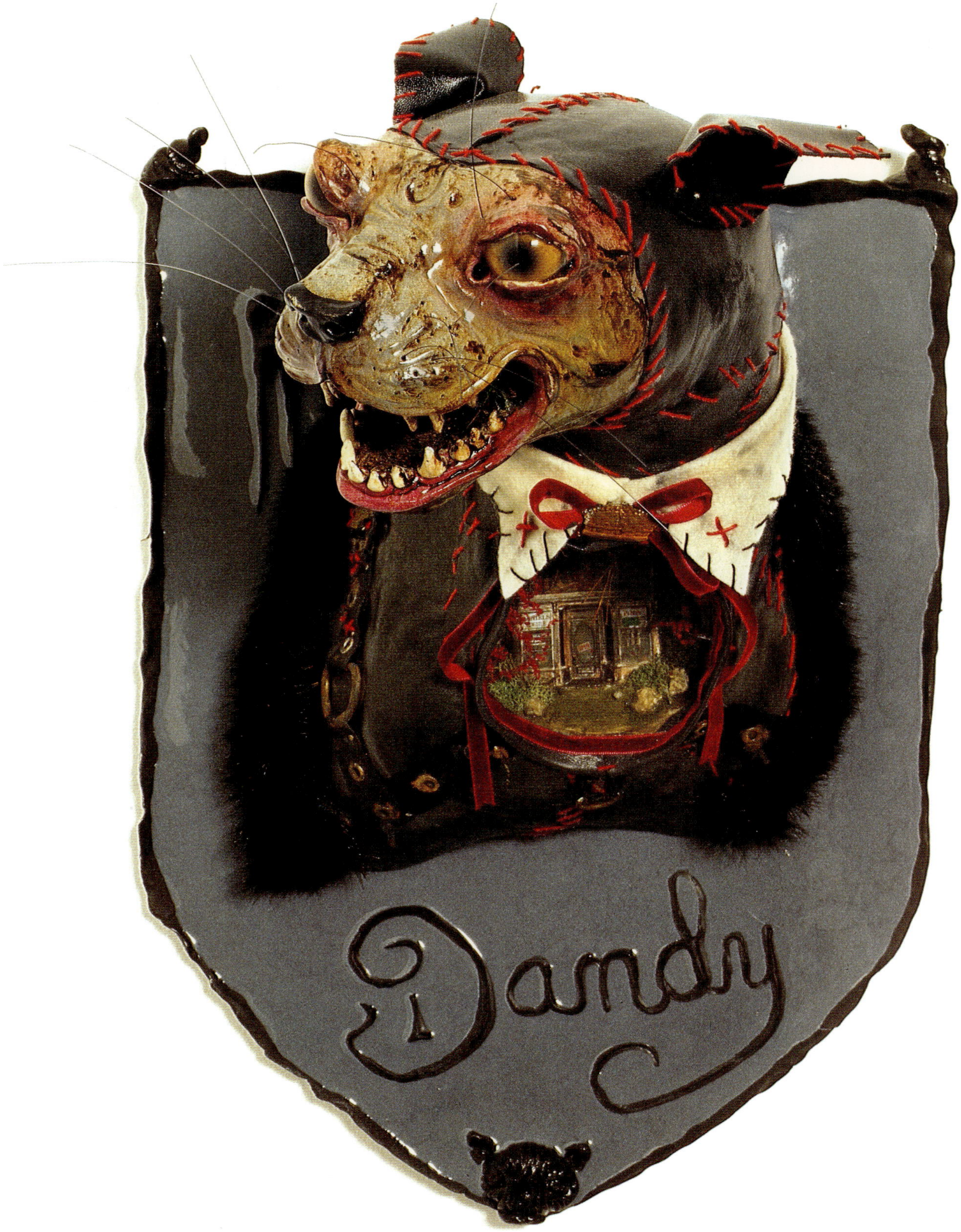
Dandy

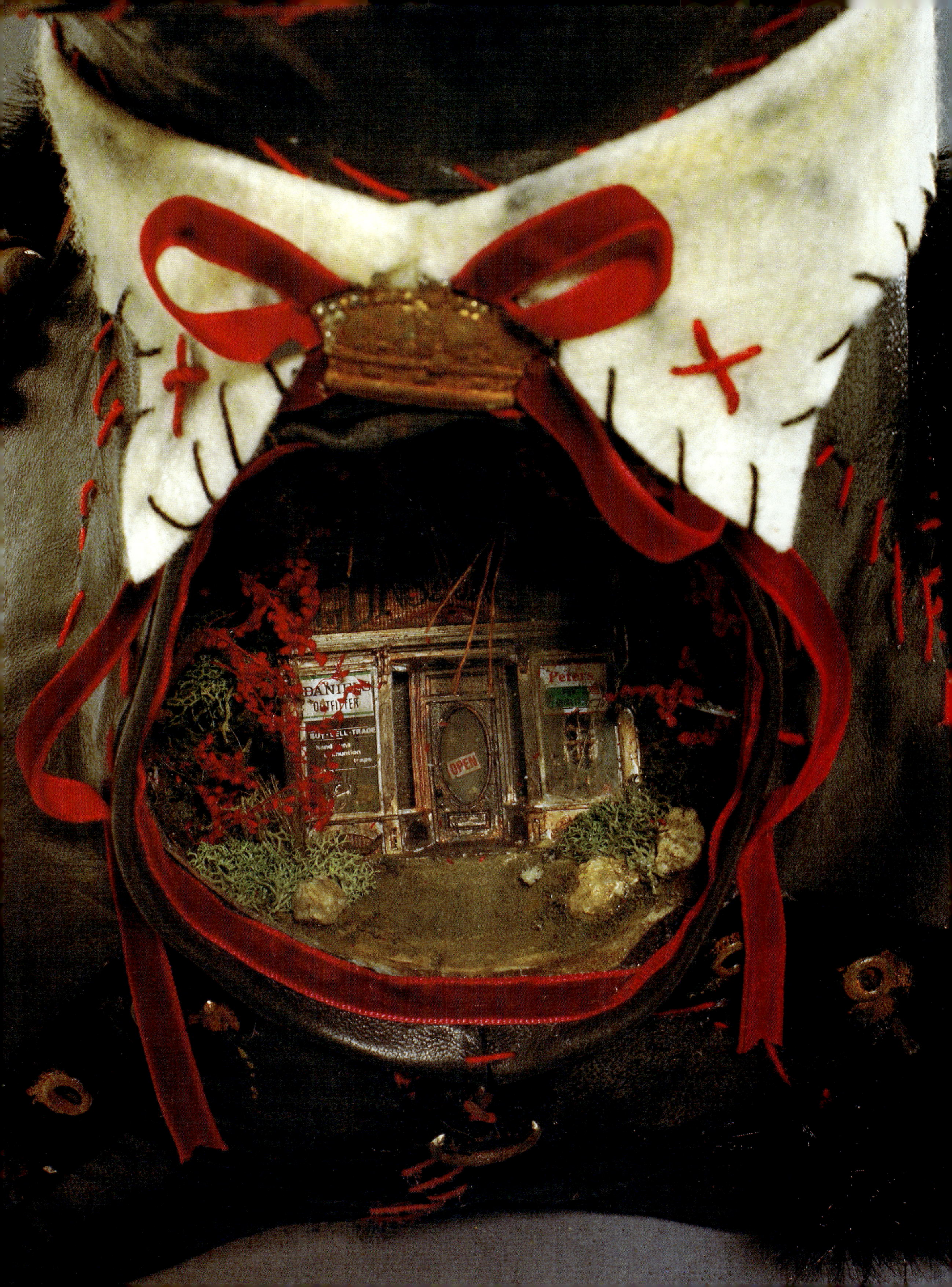
OUTFITTER
OPEN
Peters

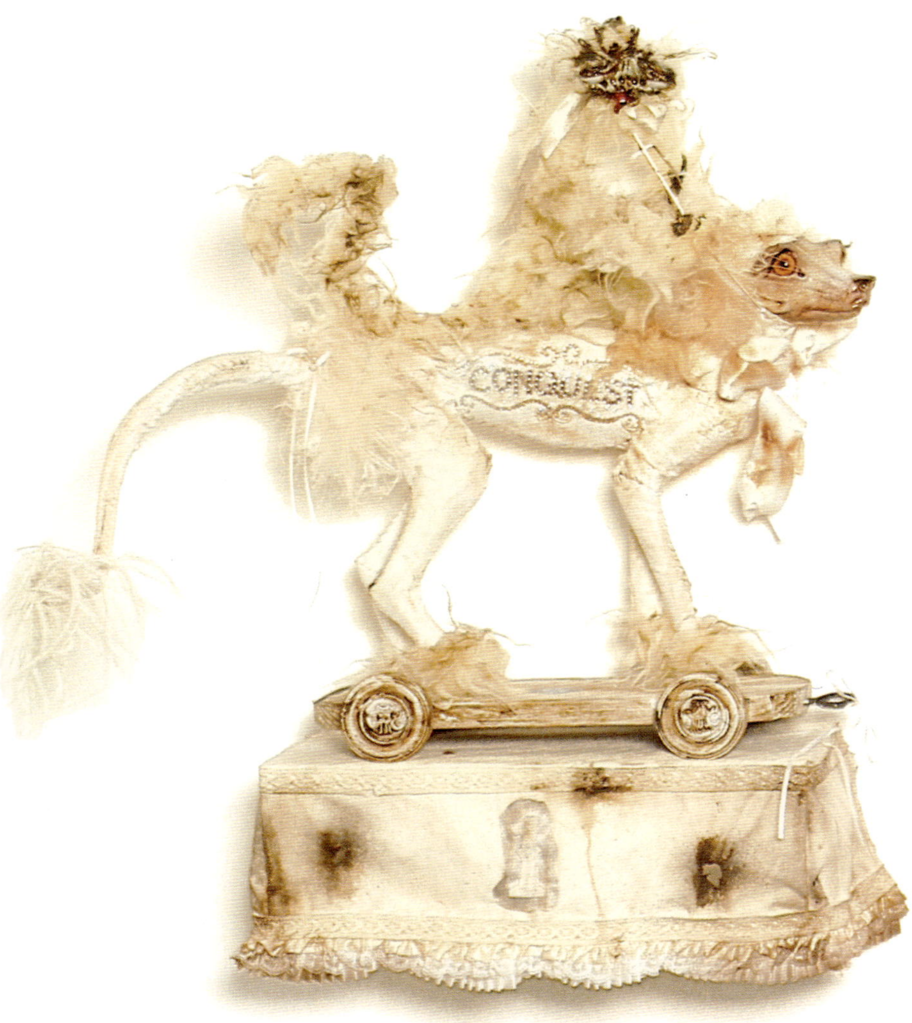

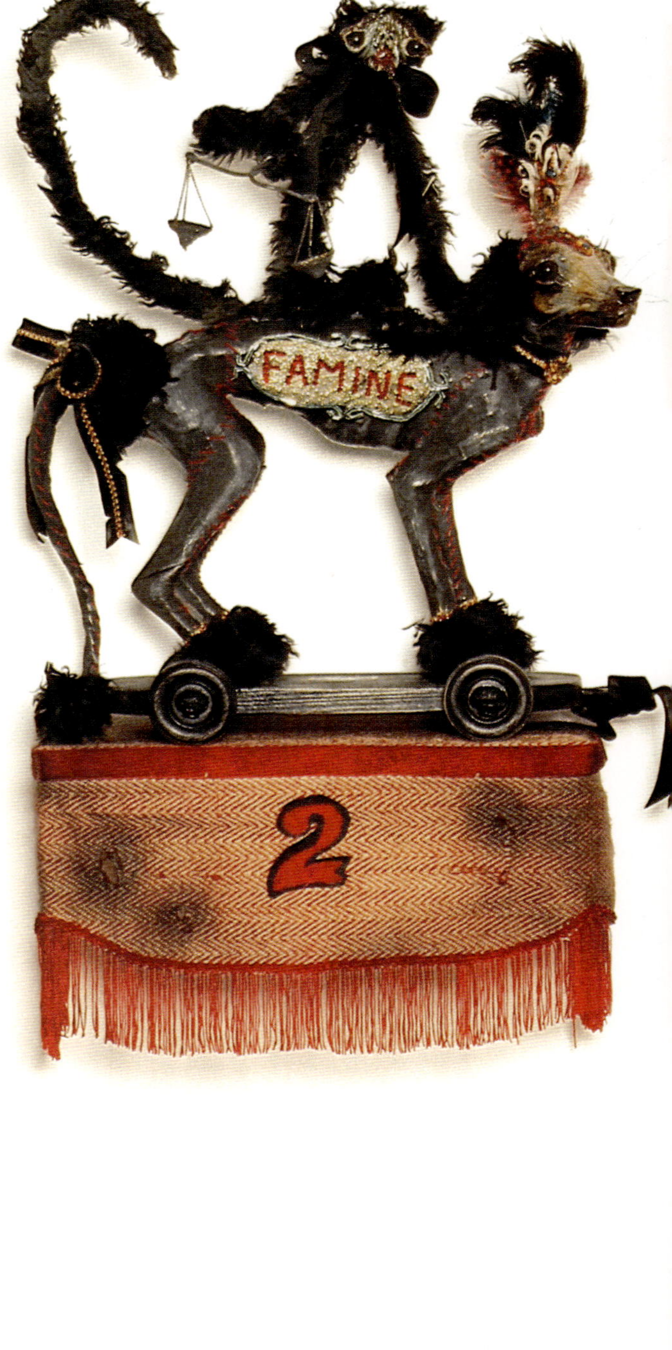
FAMINE
2

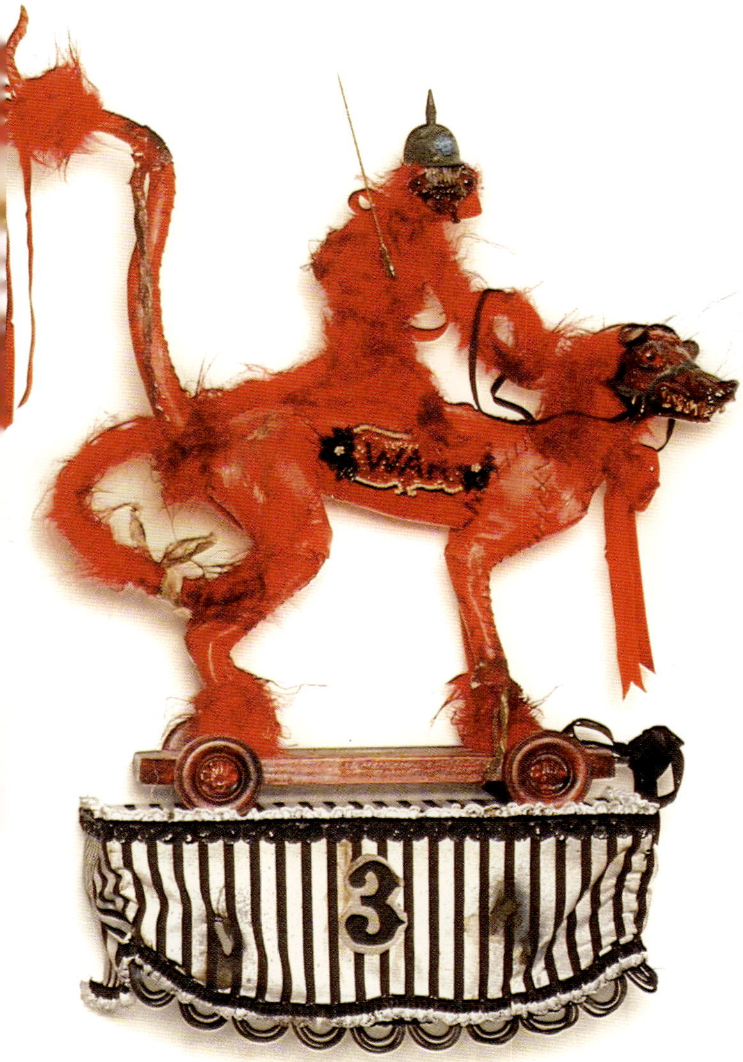
WAR
3

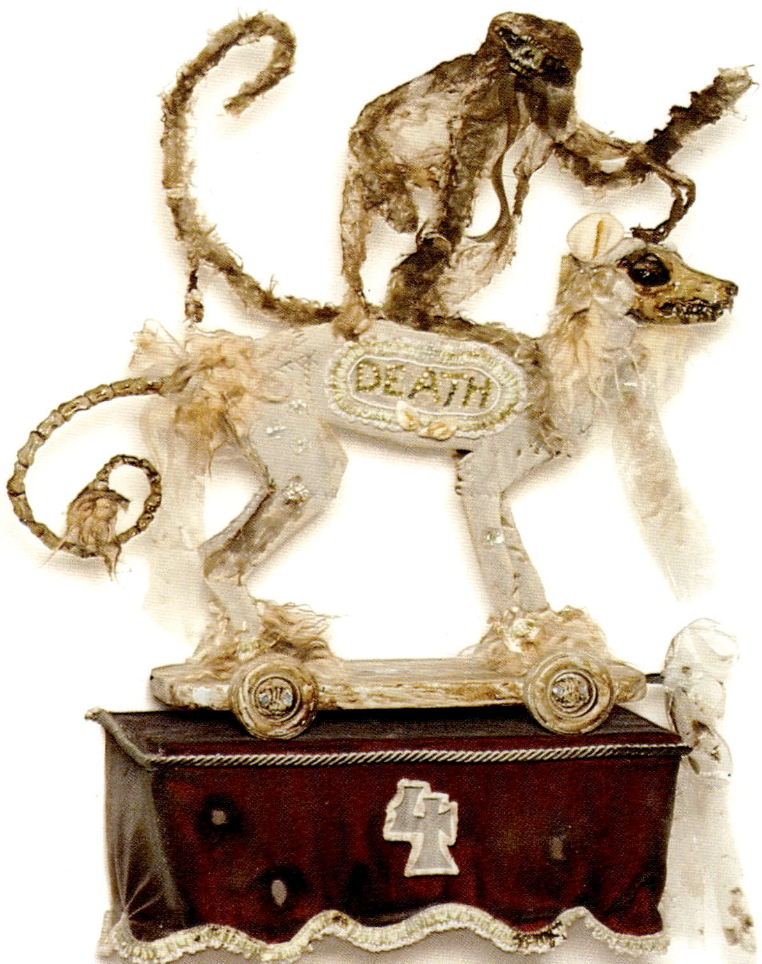
DEATH
4

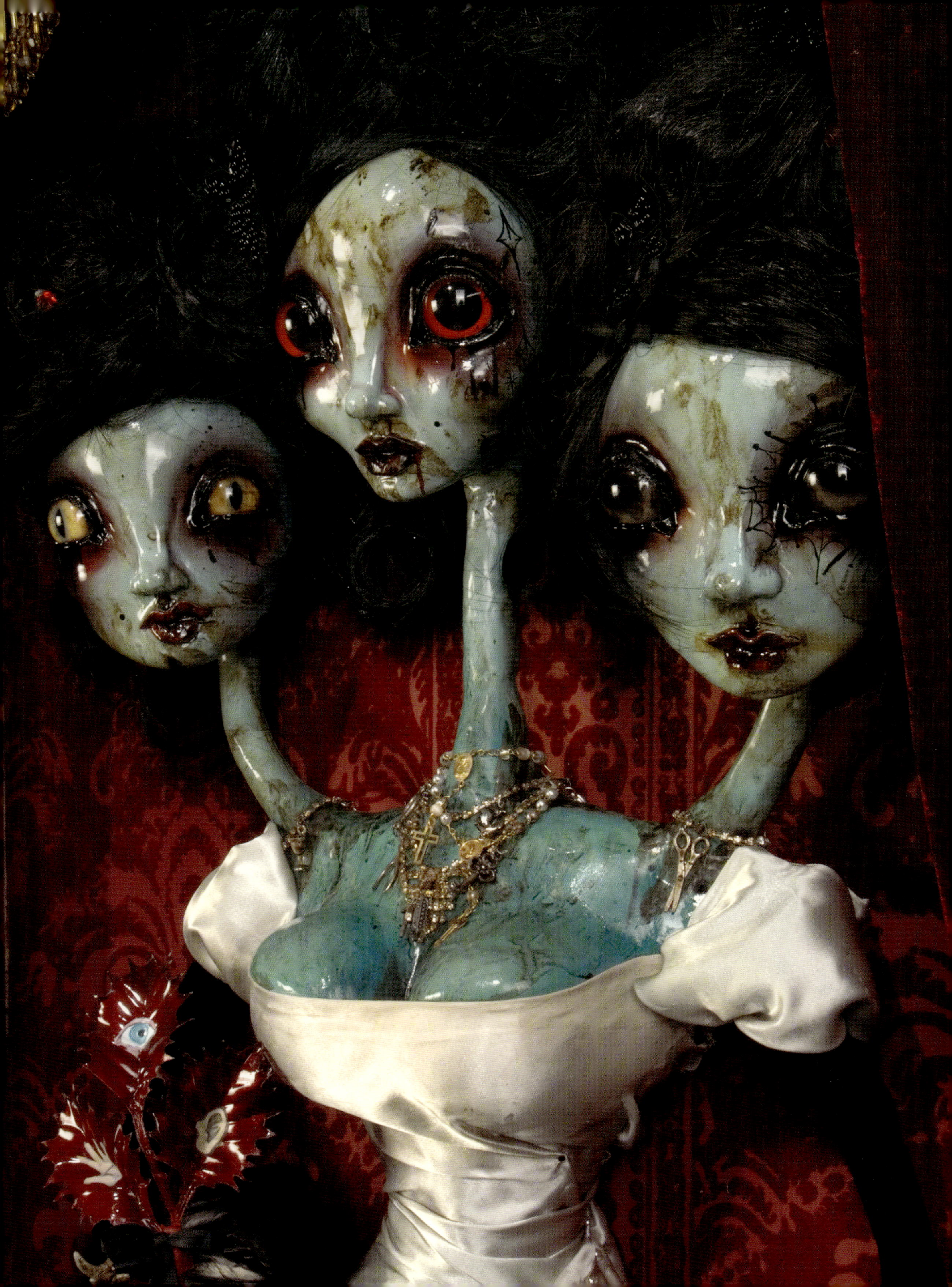

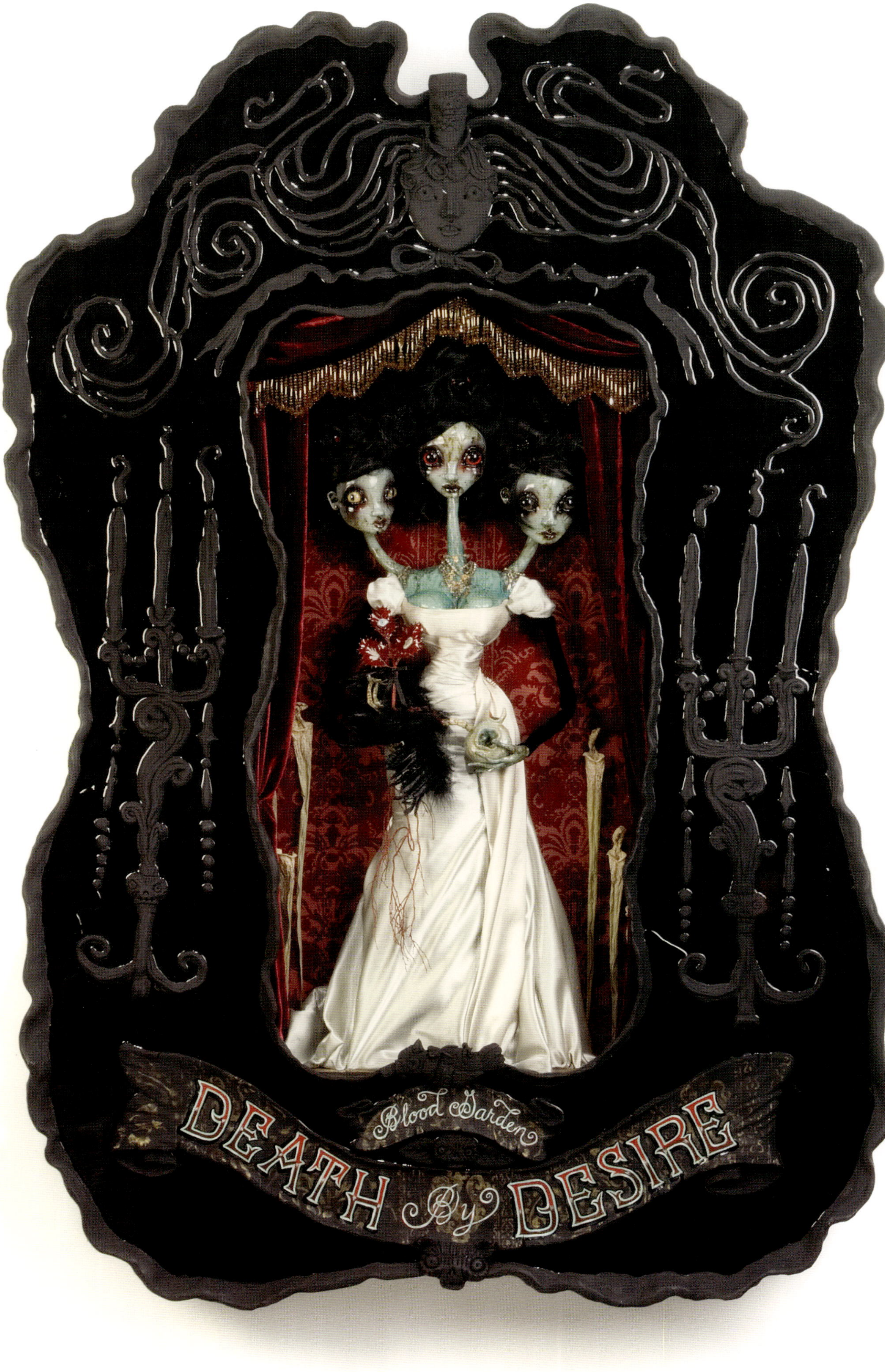
Blood Garden
DEATH By DESIRE

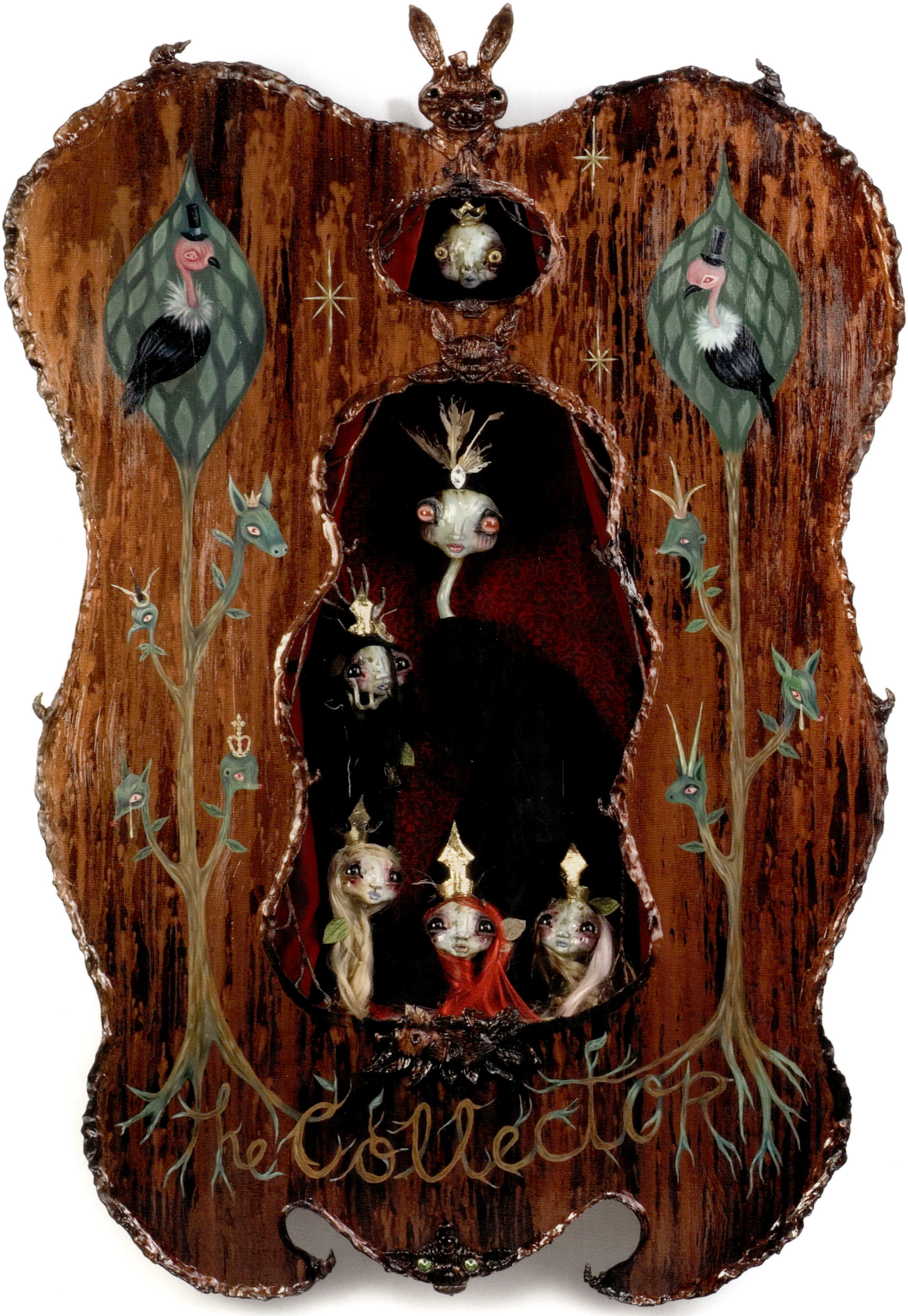
the Collector

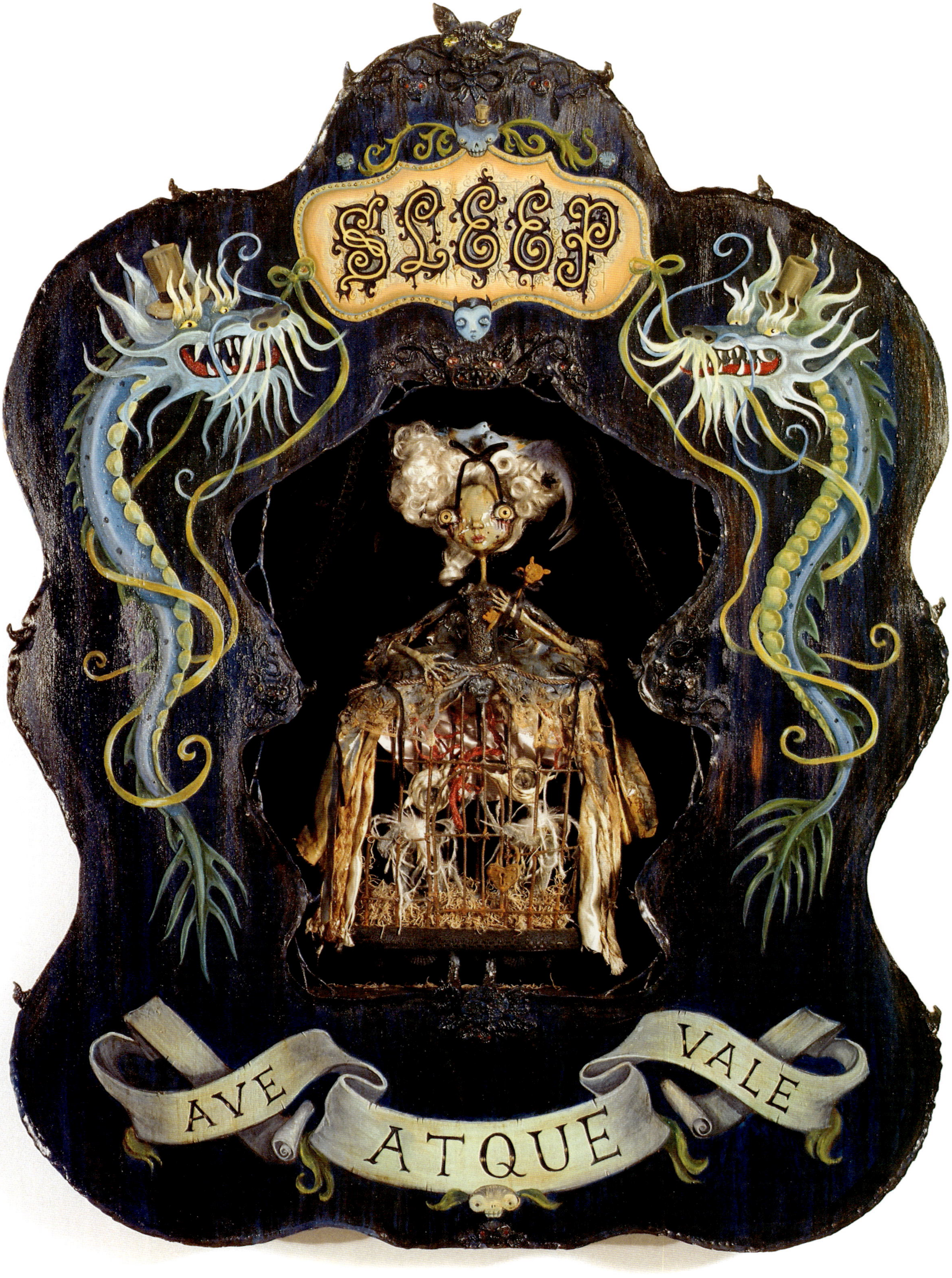
SLEEP
AVE
ATQUE
VALE

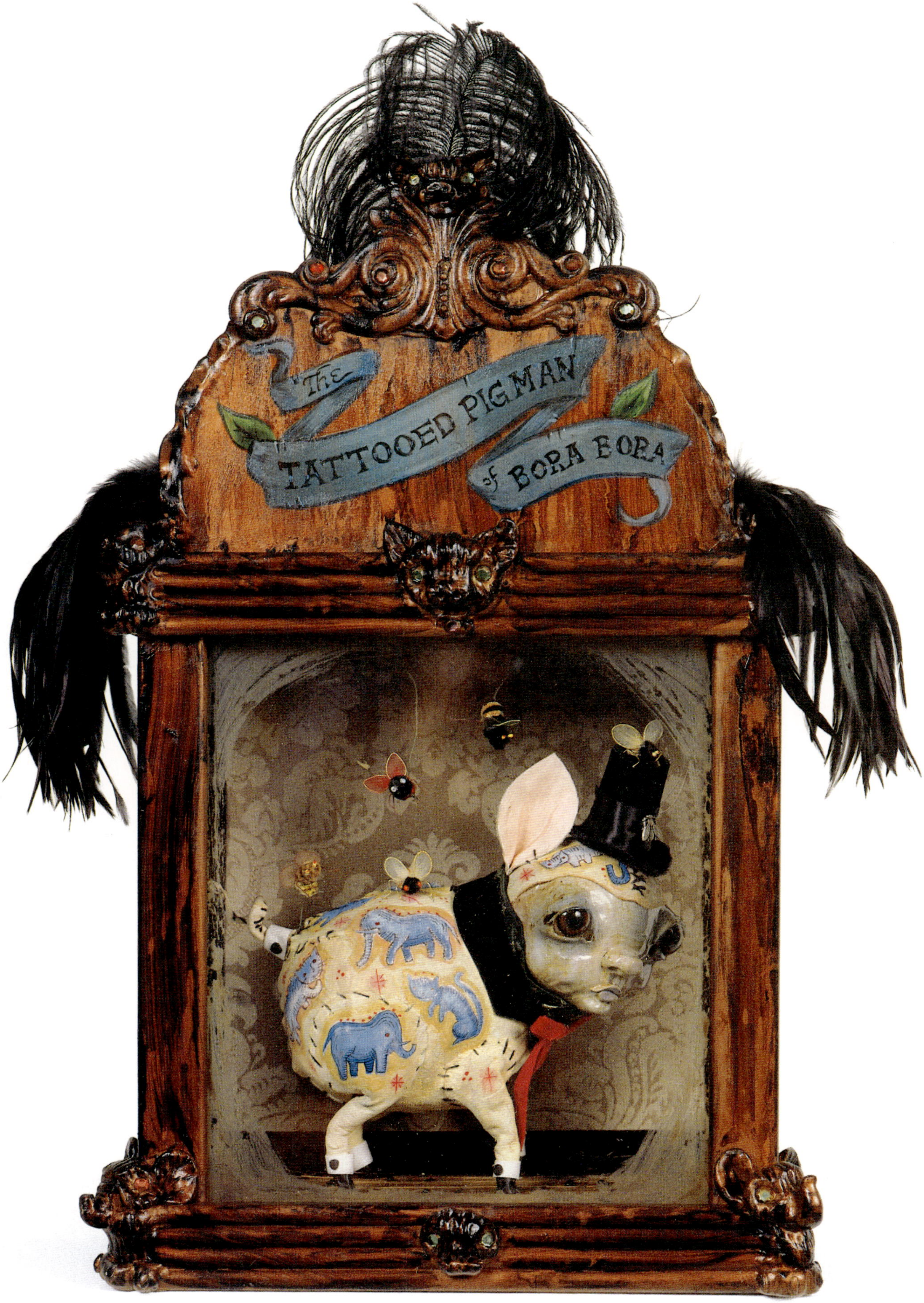
The
TATTOOED PIGMAN
of BORA BORA

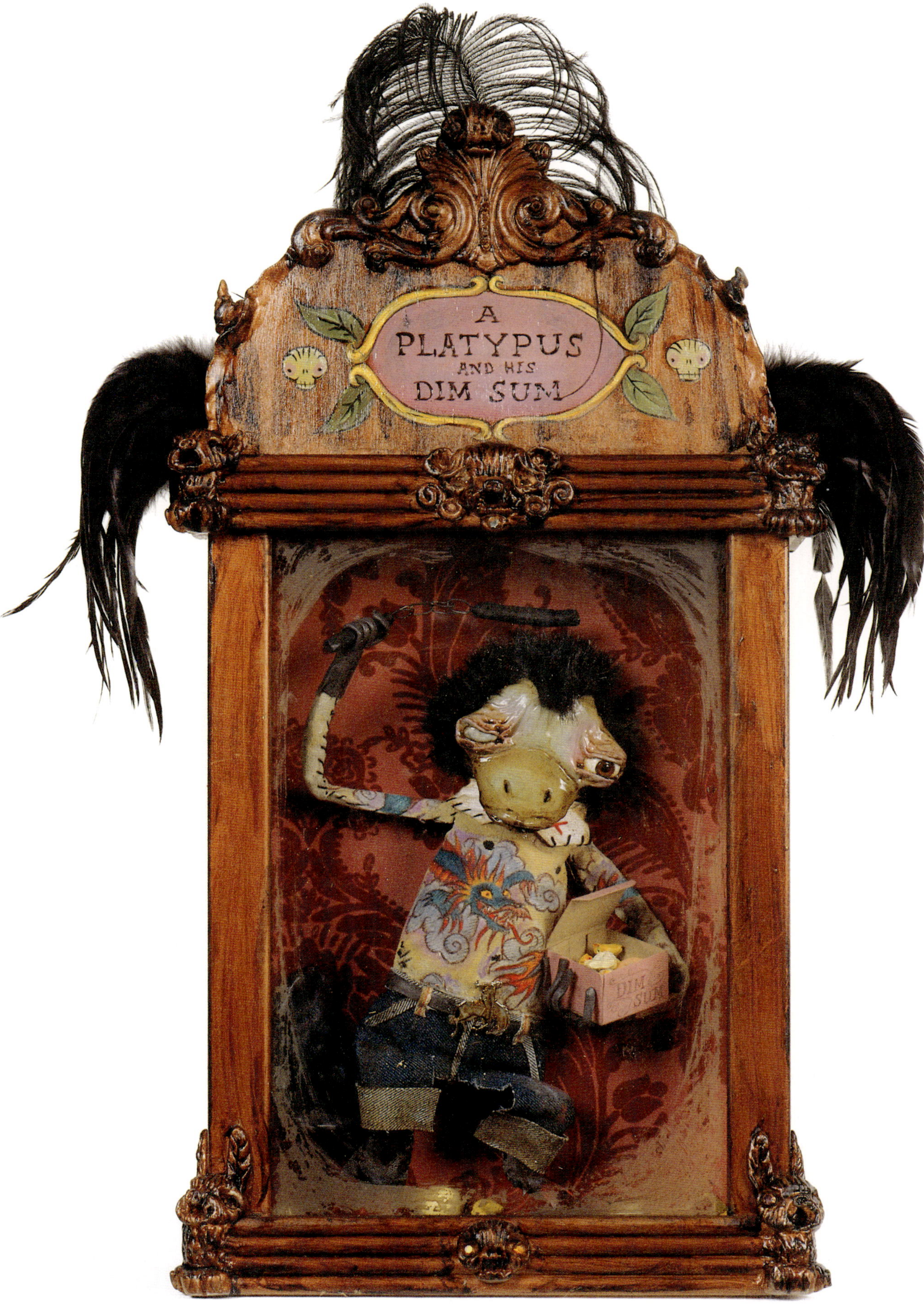
A
PLATYPUS
AND HIS
DIM SUM
DIM
SUM

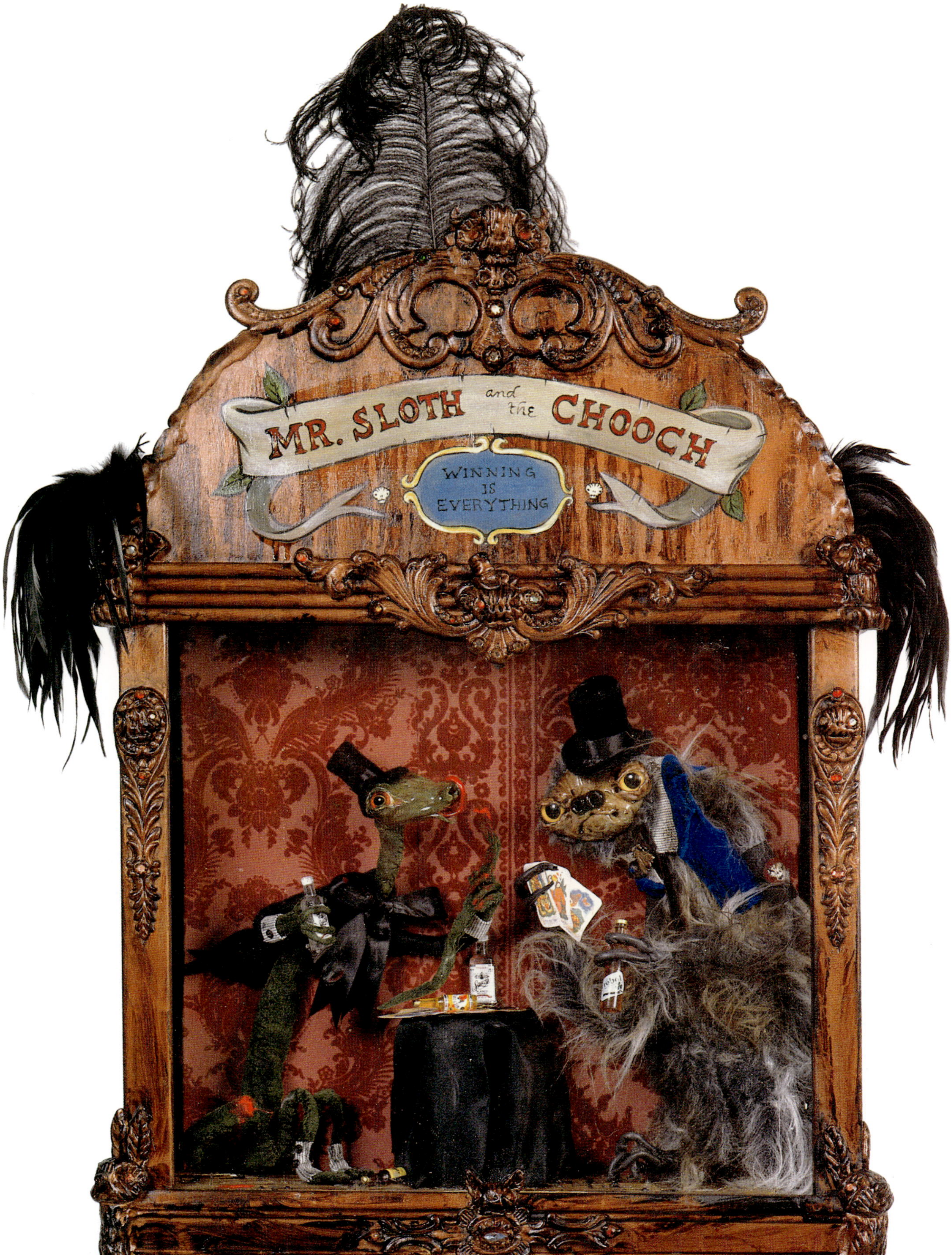
MR. SLOTH and the CHOOCH
WINNING IS EVERYTHING

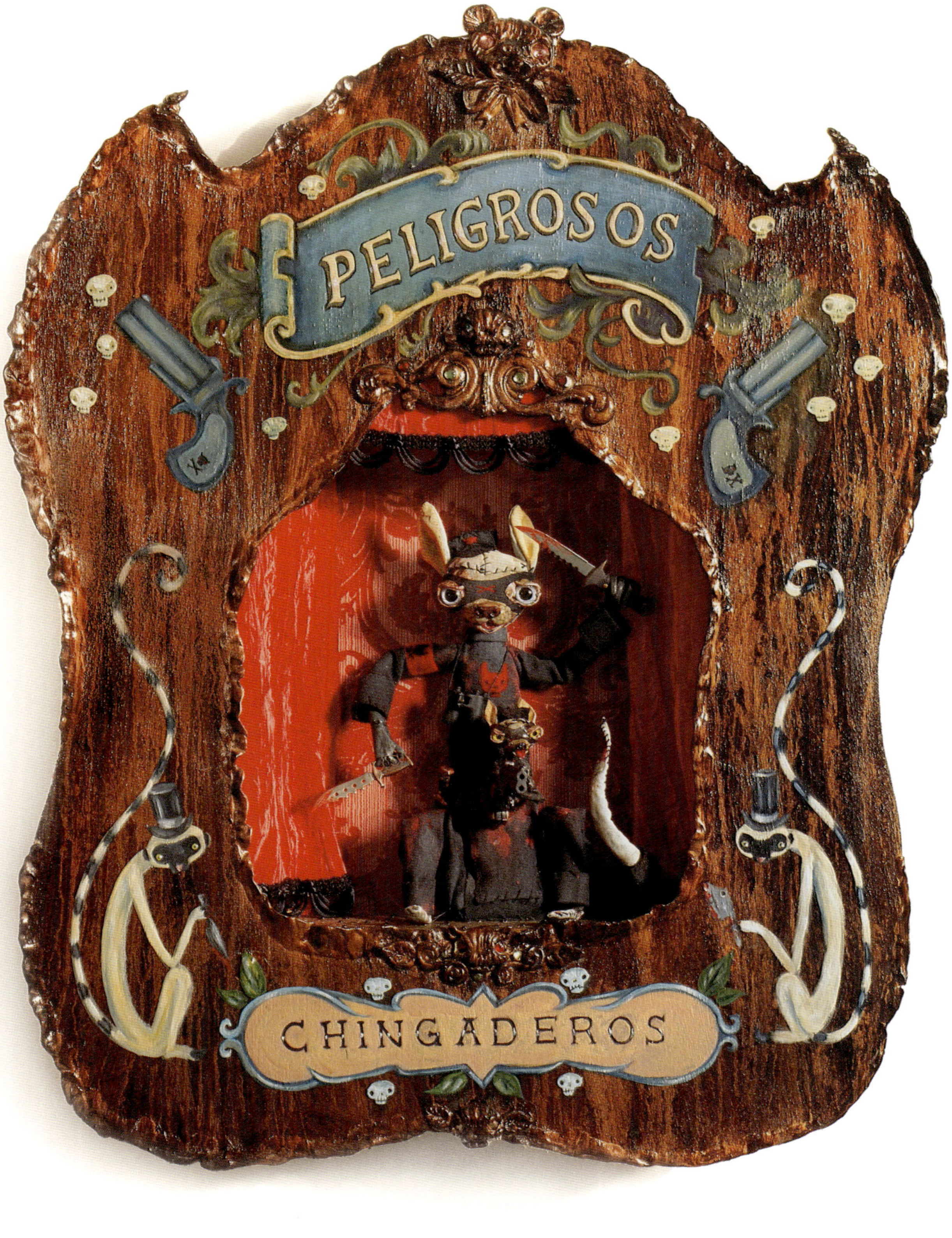
PELIGROSOS
CHINGADEROS

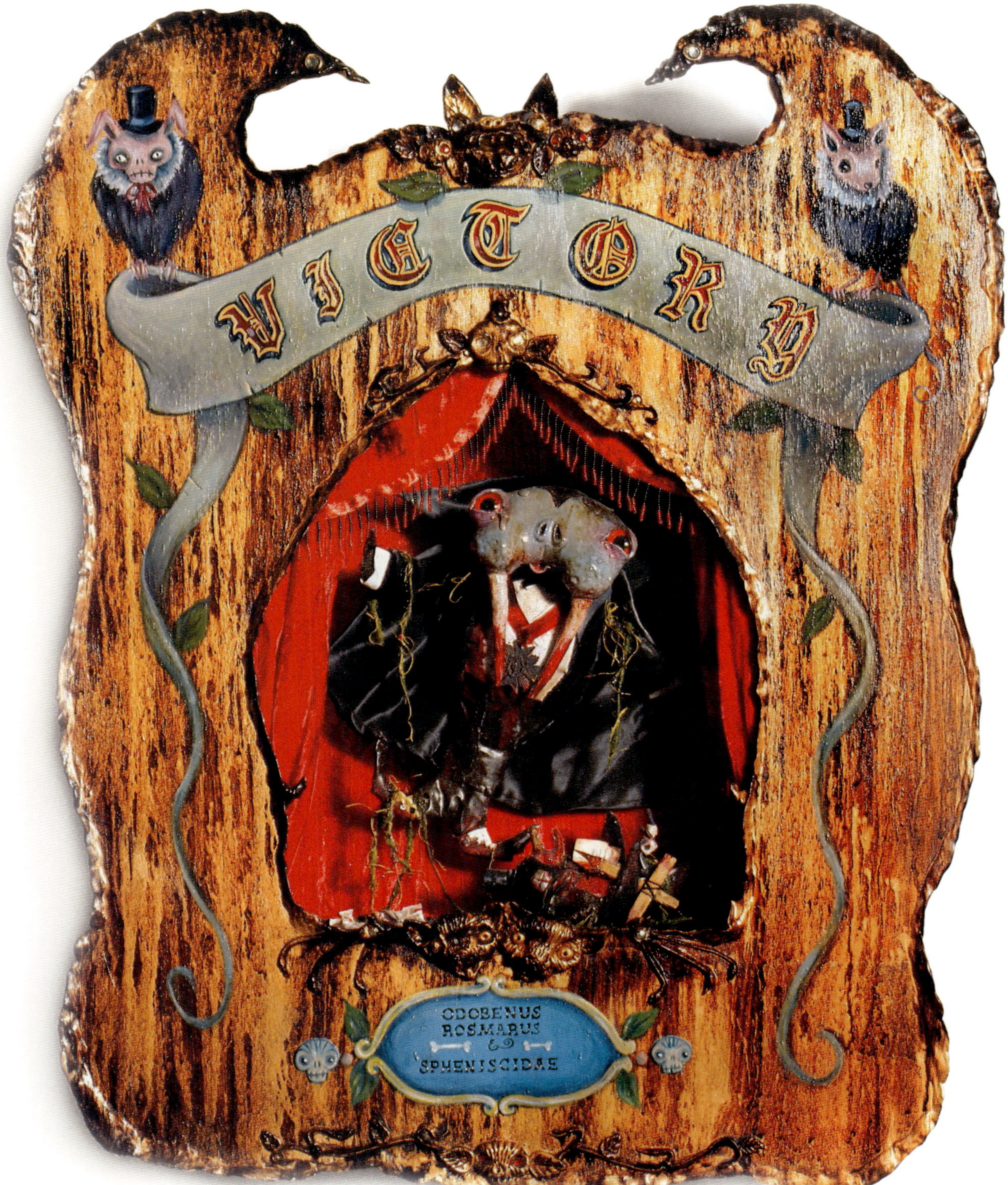
VICTORY
ODOBENUS
ROSMARUS
&
SPHENISCIDAE

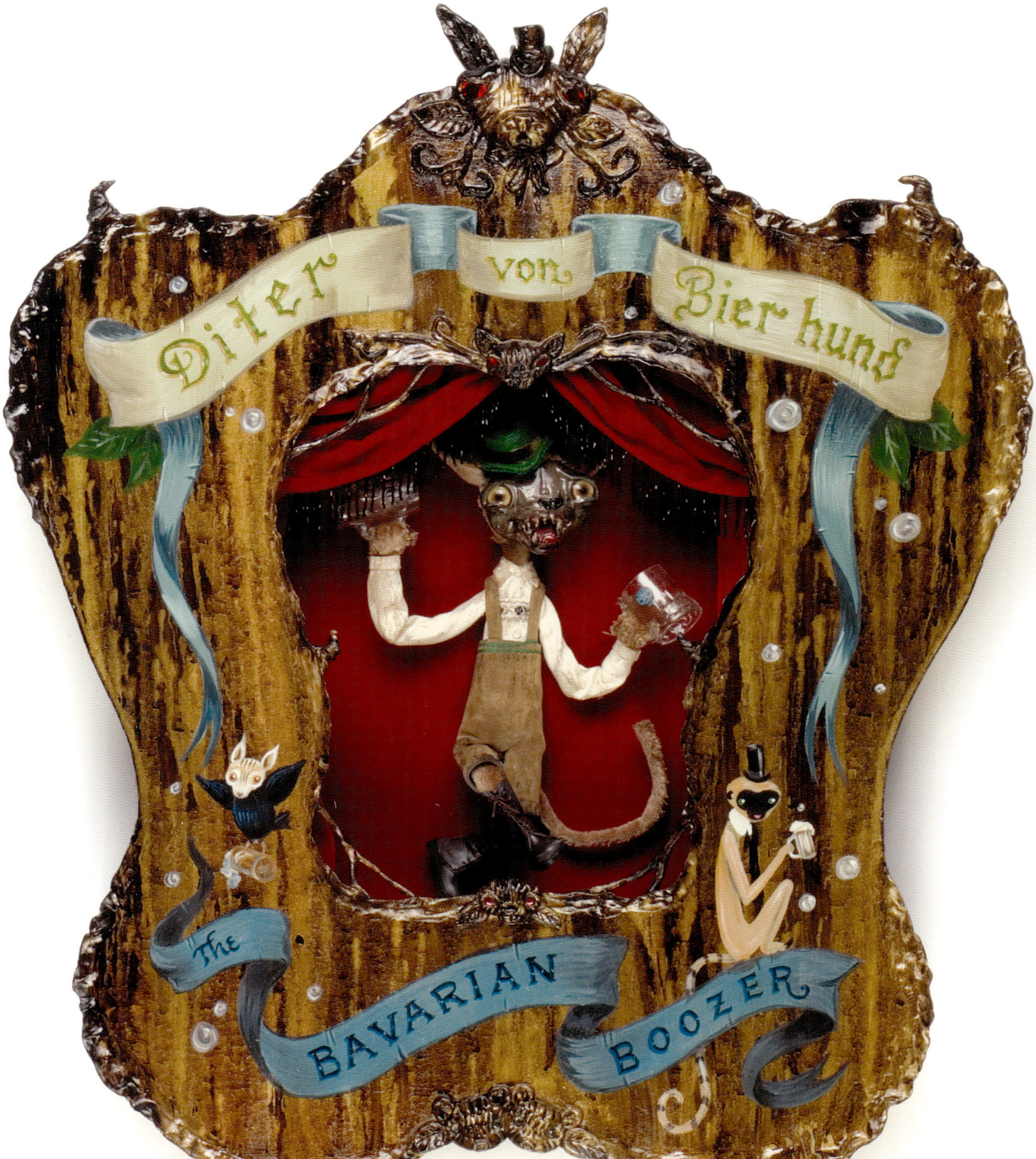
Diter von Bier hund
The
BAVARIAN
BOOZER

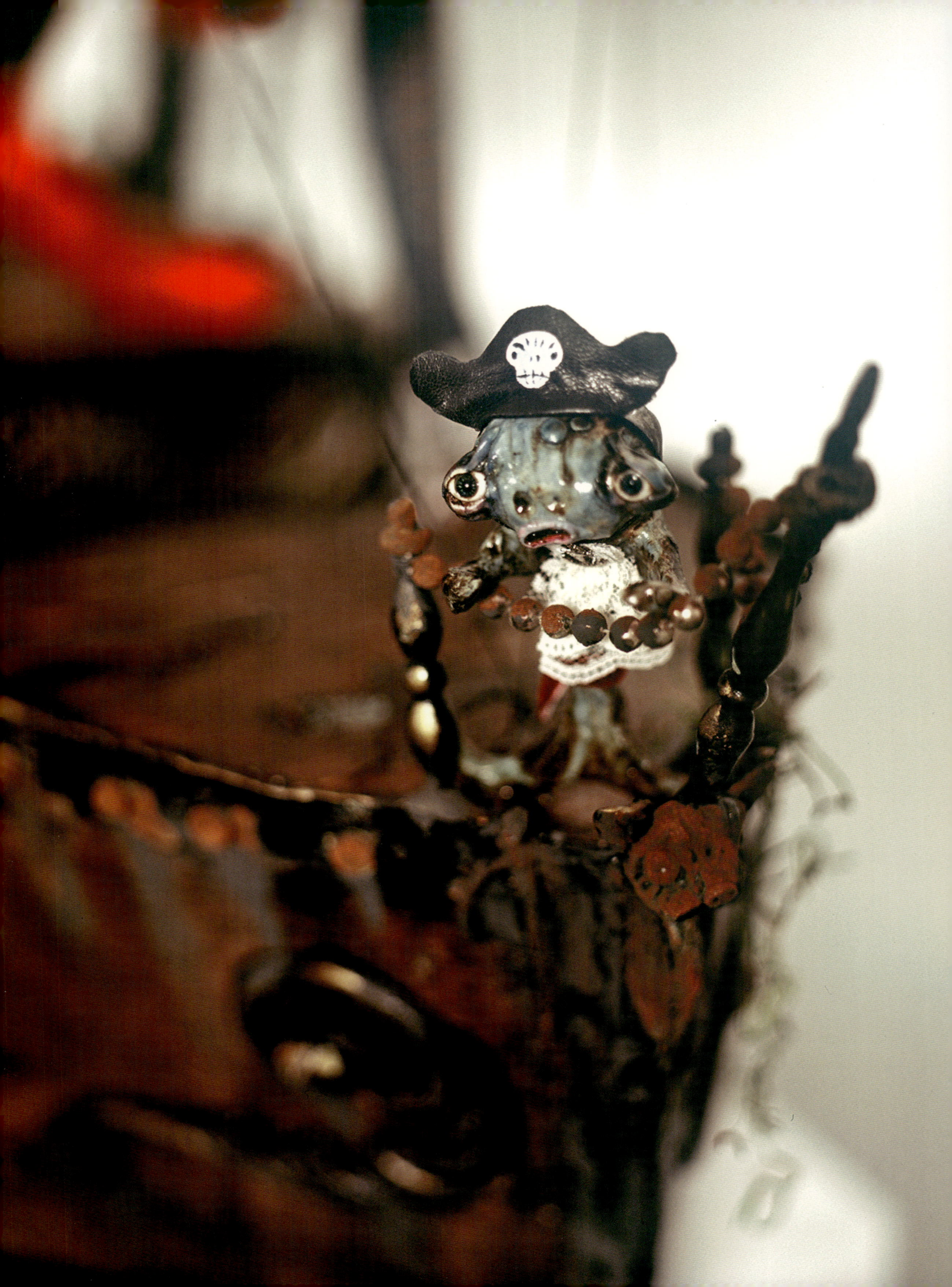

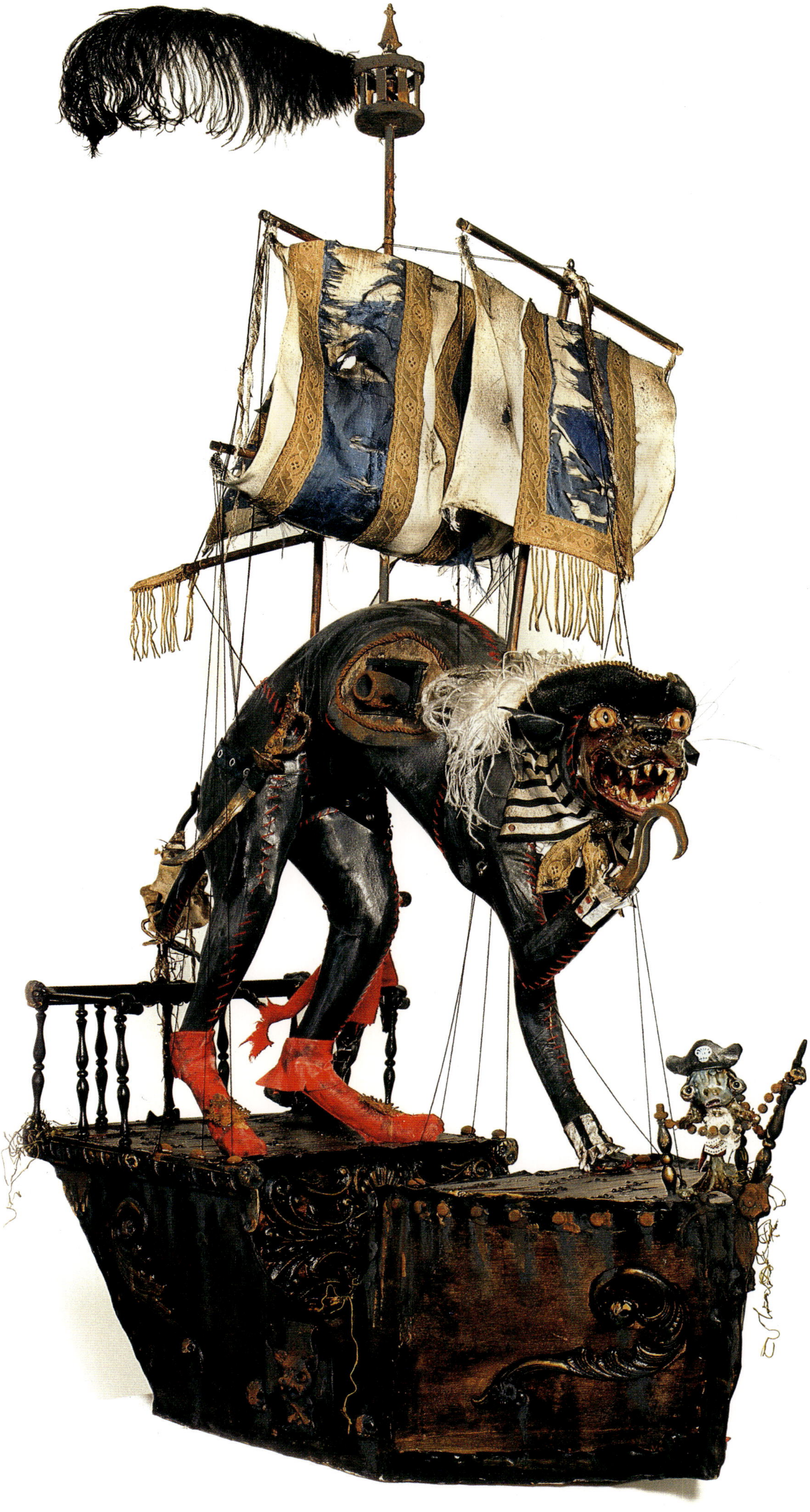

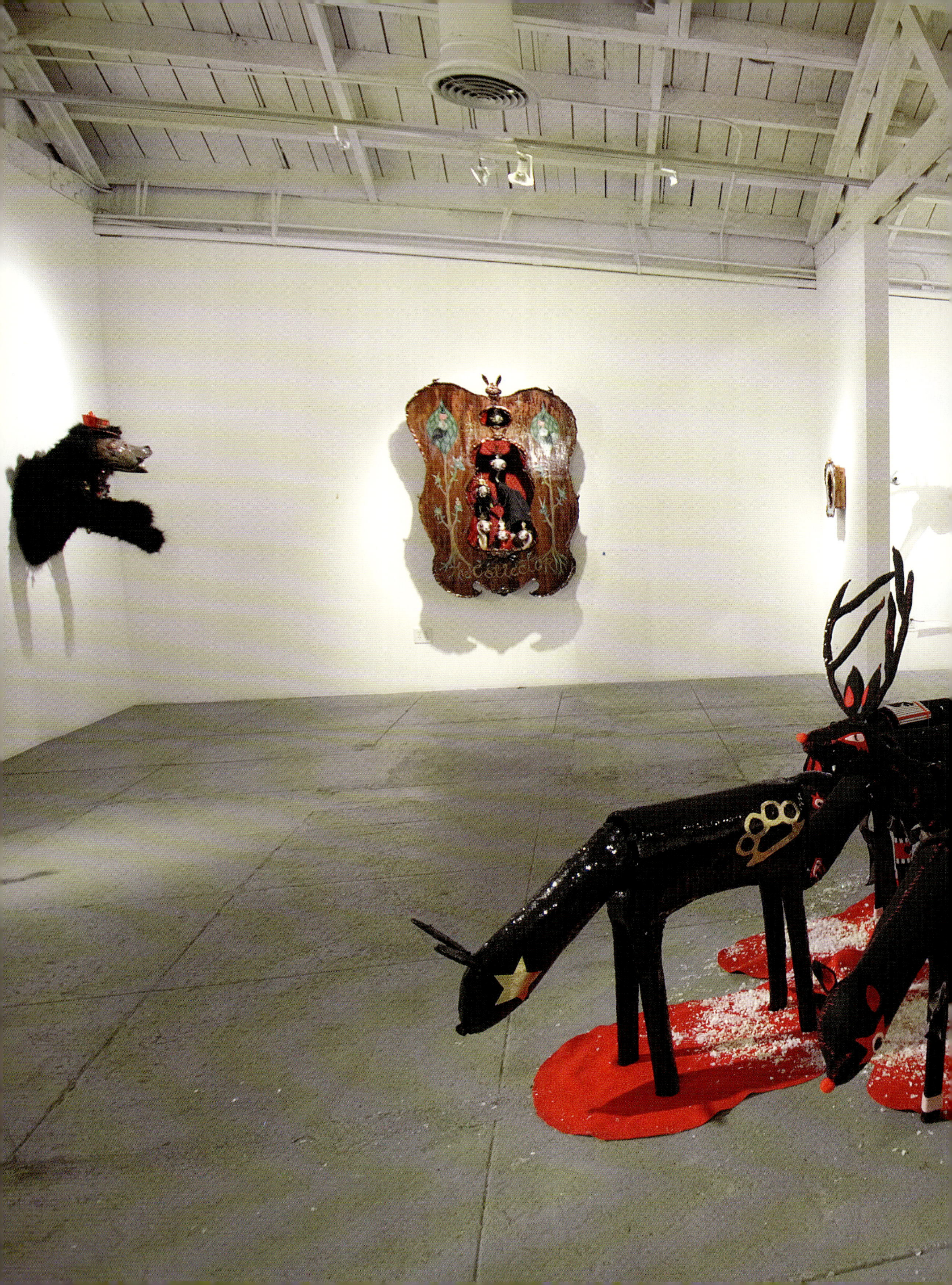

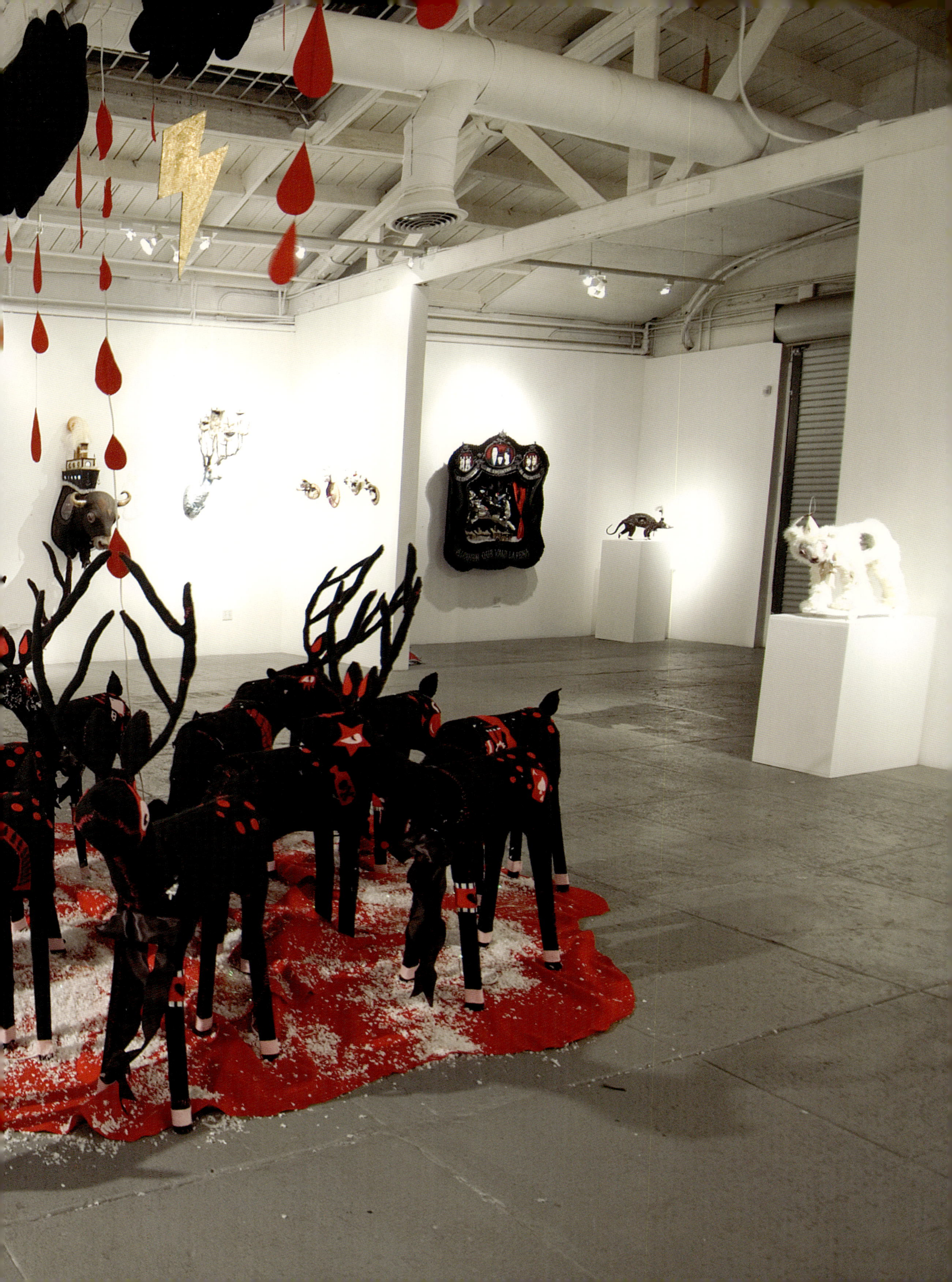

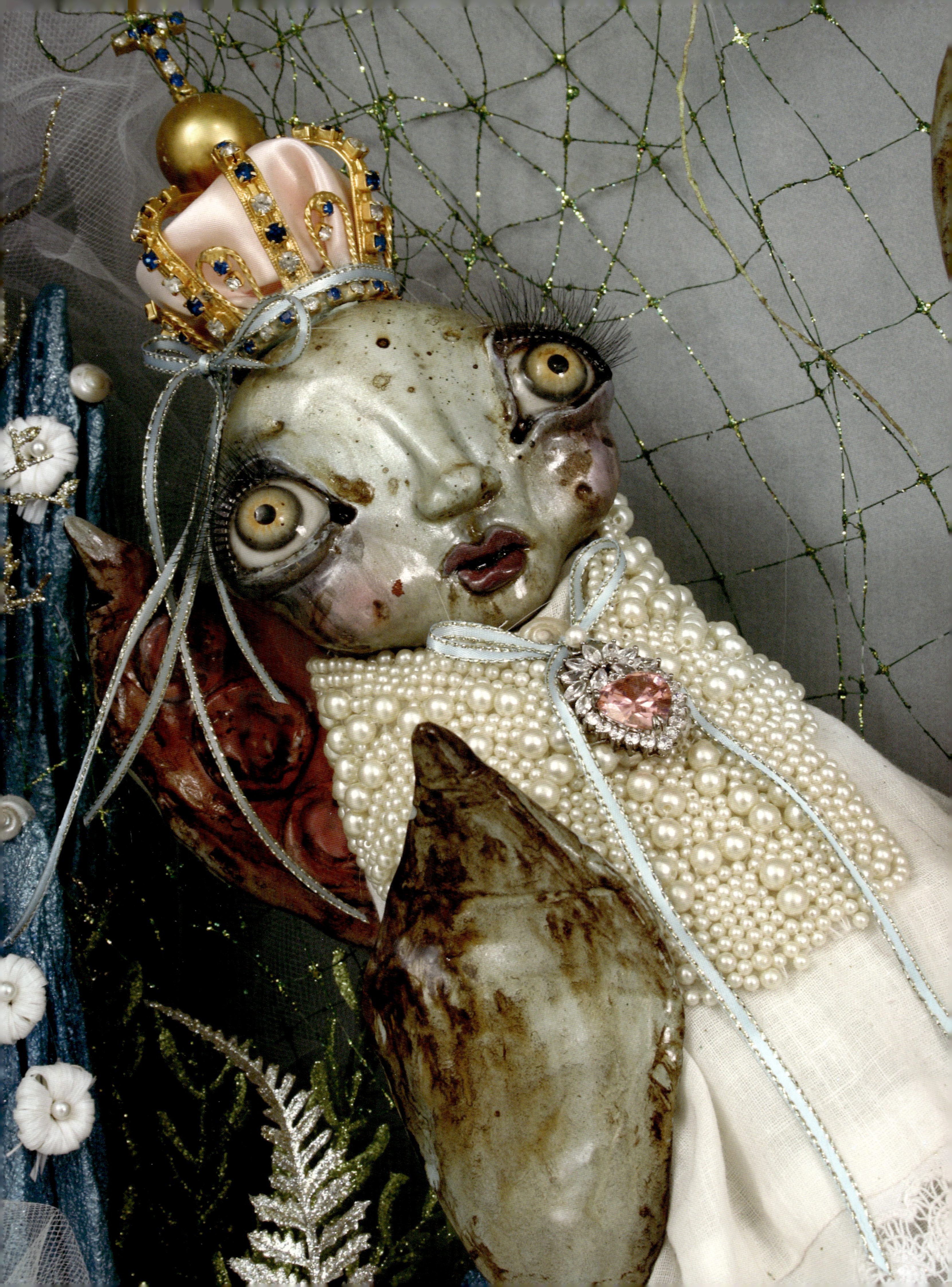

Incurable Disorder

Dead Letters: Twenty-Six Are

Without office in
This language, coffinless. The
Shape of capitals
And lower case create a
Thicket, onto which

Man's conceit has attached con-
And denotations
For decades. I brave this barb-
Tipped bramble in search
Of words, stripping stalks bone bare

My fingers drip with
Vivid truth: There is none there,
No order to my
Vocabulary of self,
No purpose. So I

Am, a hangman dangling in
Stasis, pages blank
Before me, as hungry as
Tombs. Now, here, no where
My lips rearrange themselves

To speak, a rusty-
Hinged suitcase: within, the (w)hole
Of my parts. Present
Tense, I am hand-cuffed to my
Past, to my path, a

Contagion for which there's no
Cure. I'm the symbol
Of the serpent swallowing
Its own tail, the ring
Dependent on the wearer,

The bearer. I'm a
Fugue that continually
Renews a refrain:
What's at the core; what's
At the core; what's at the core

Clint Catalyst

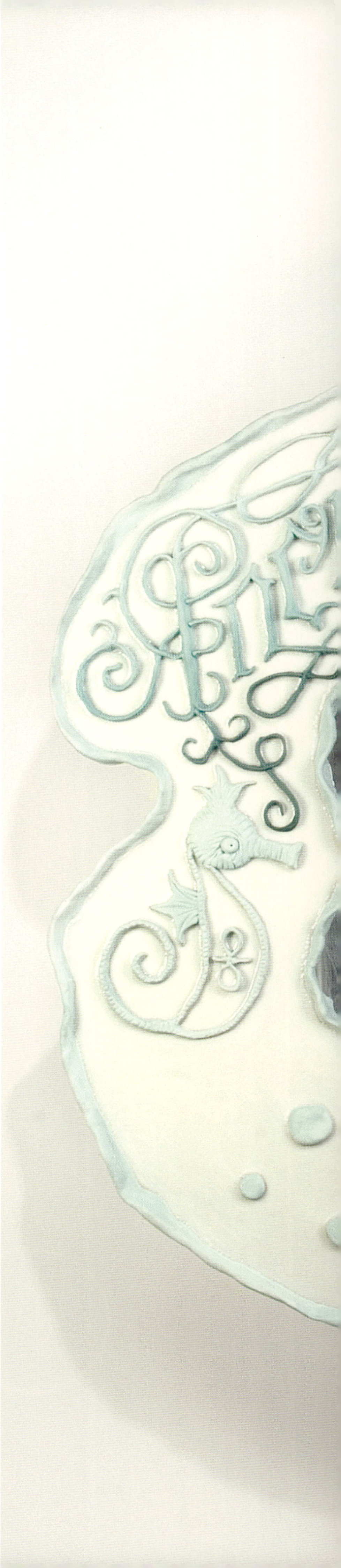

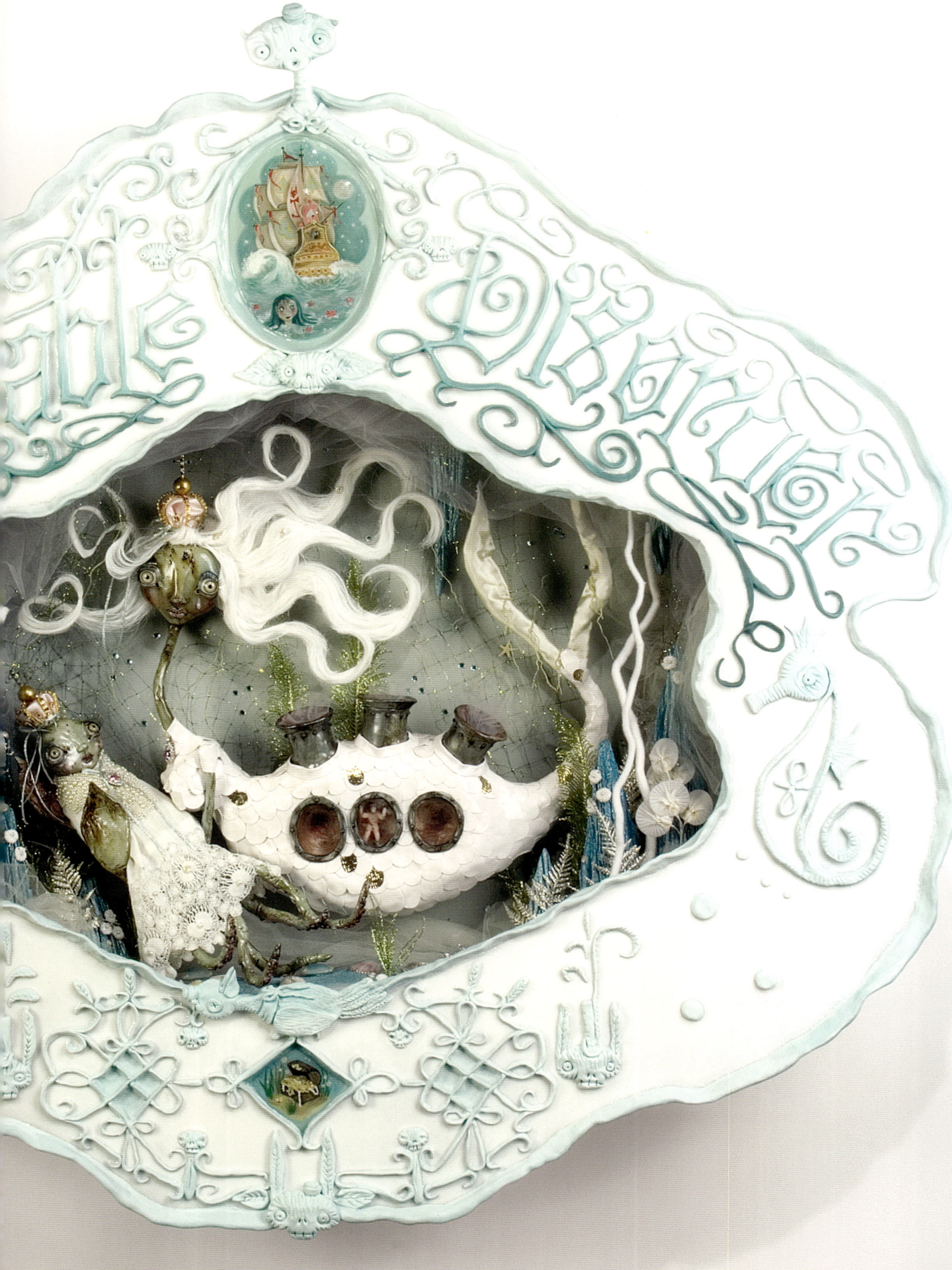

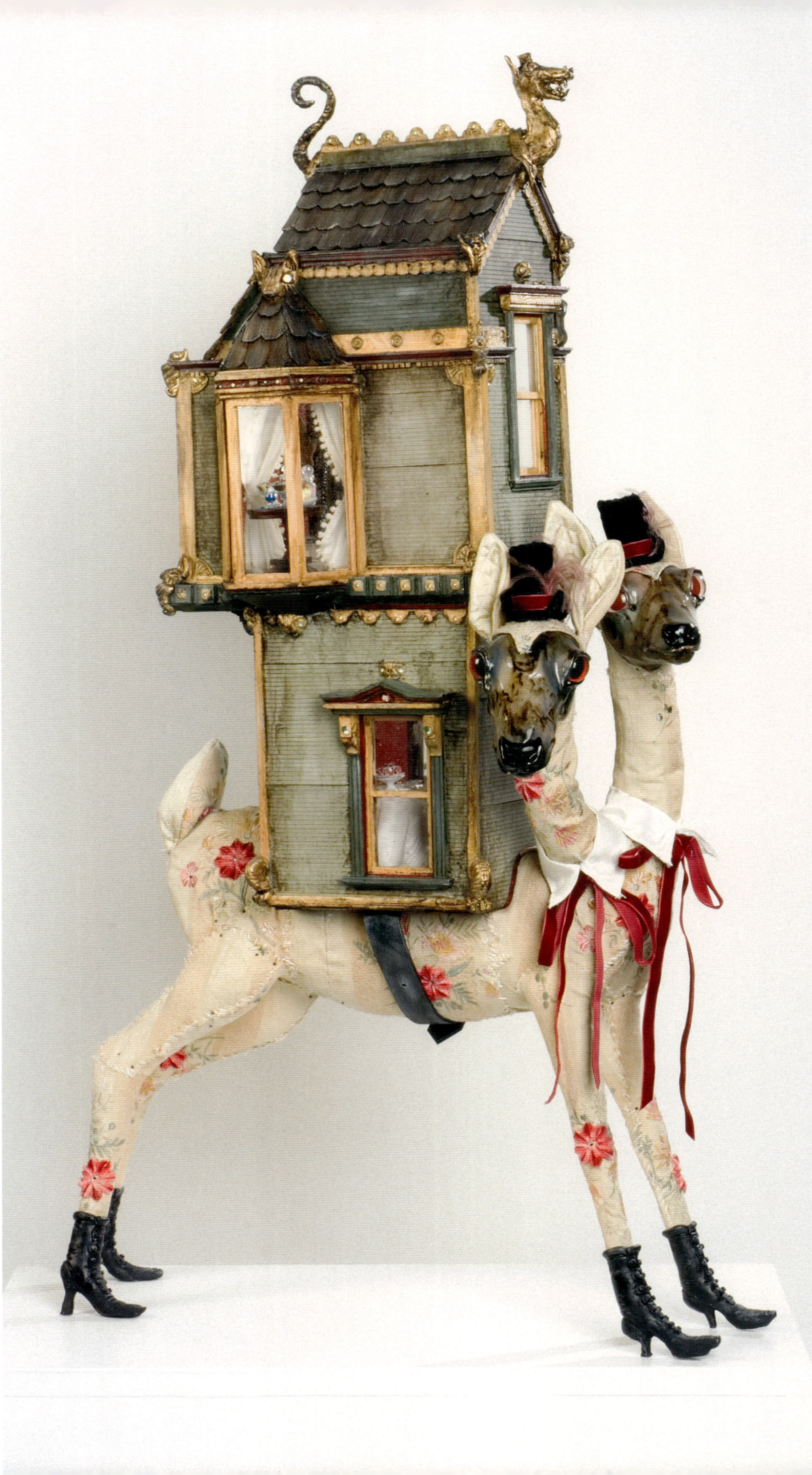

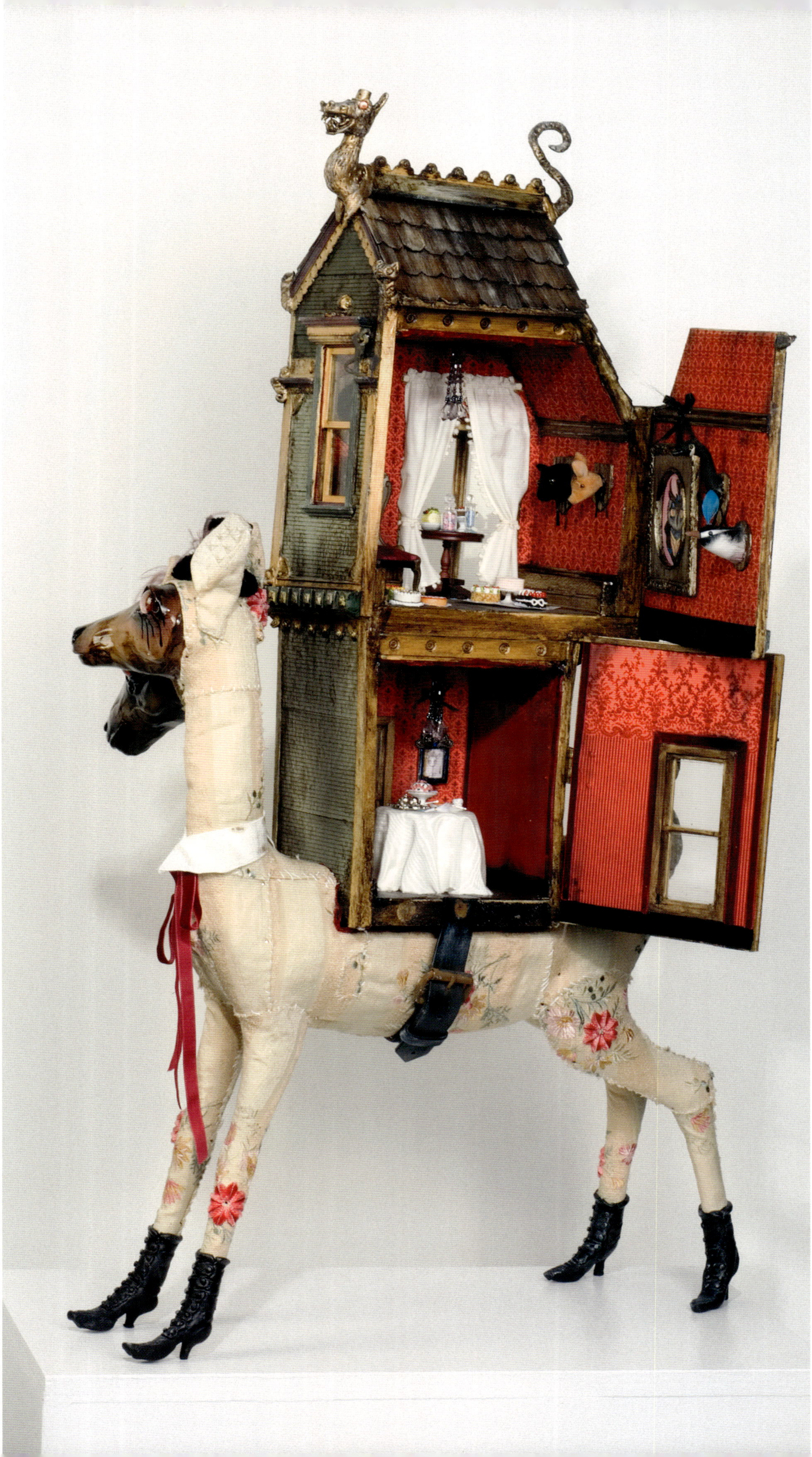

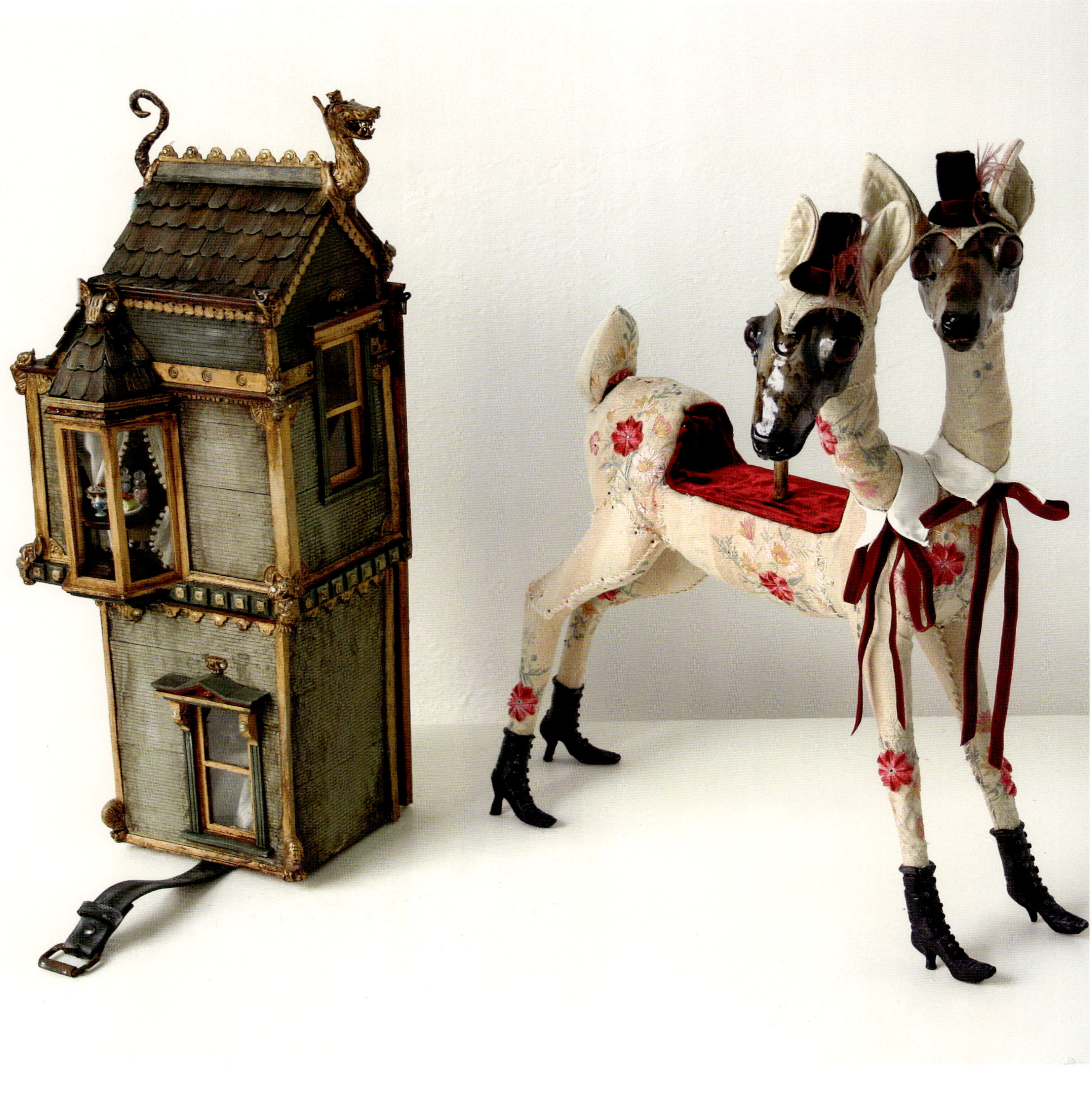

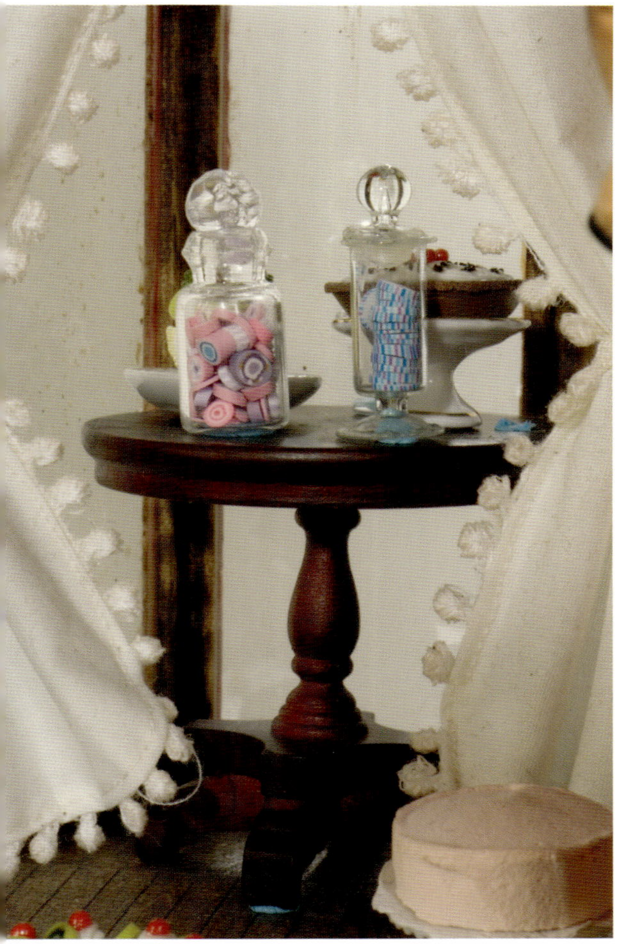

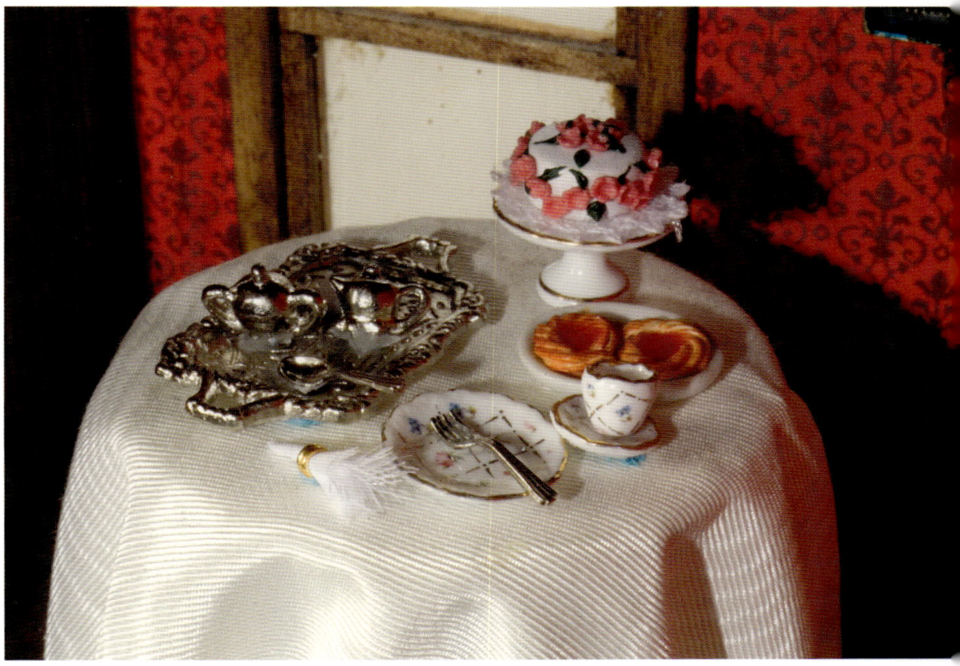

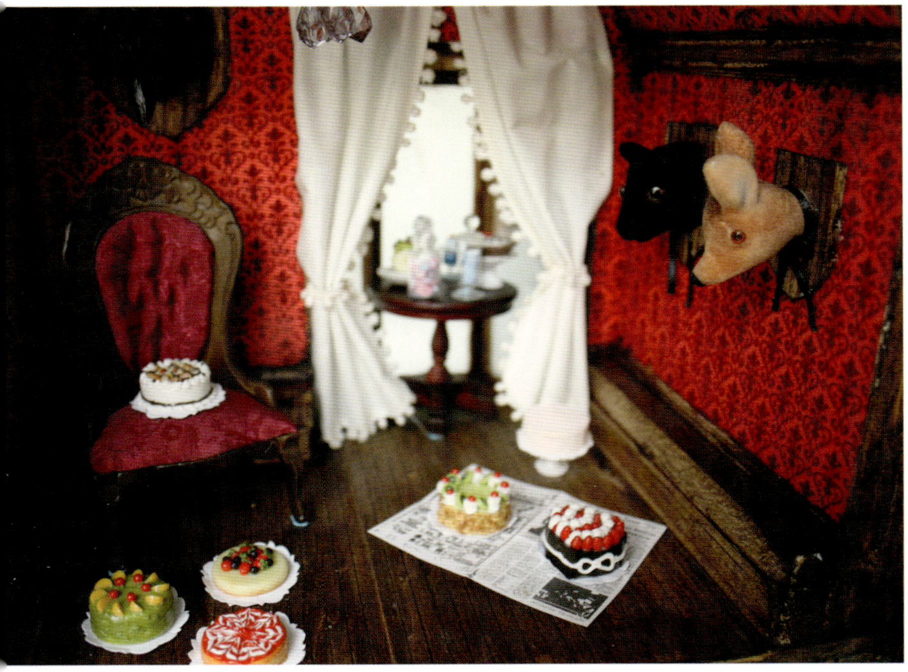

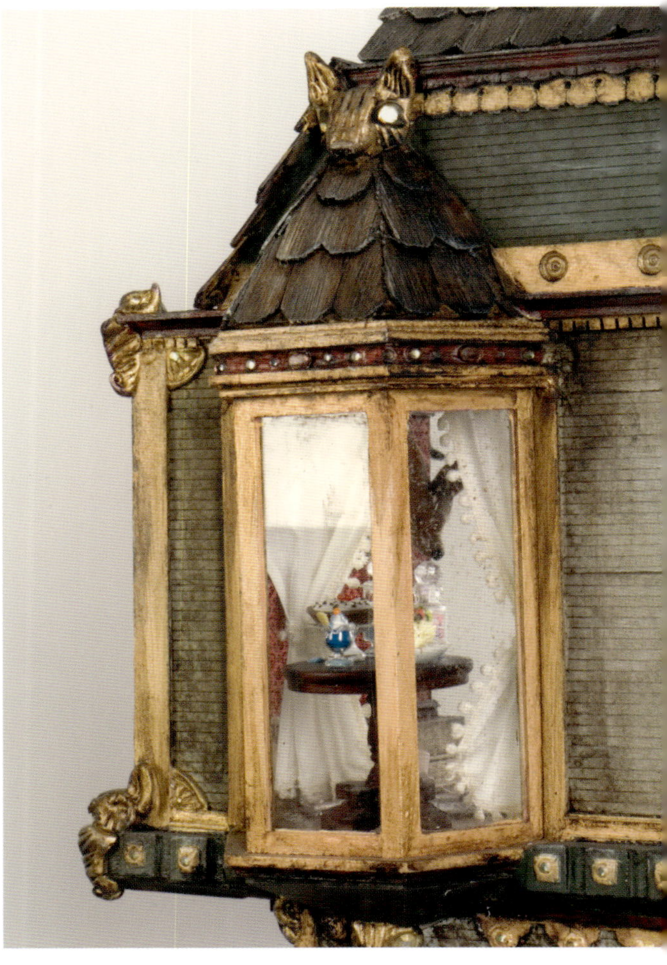

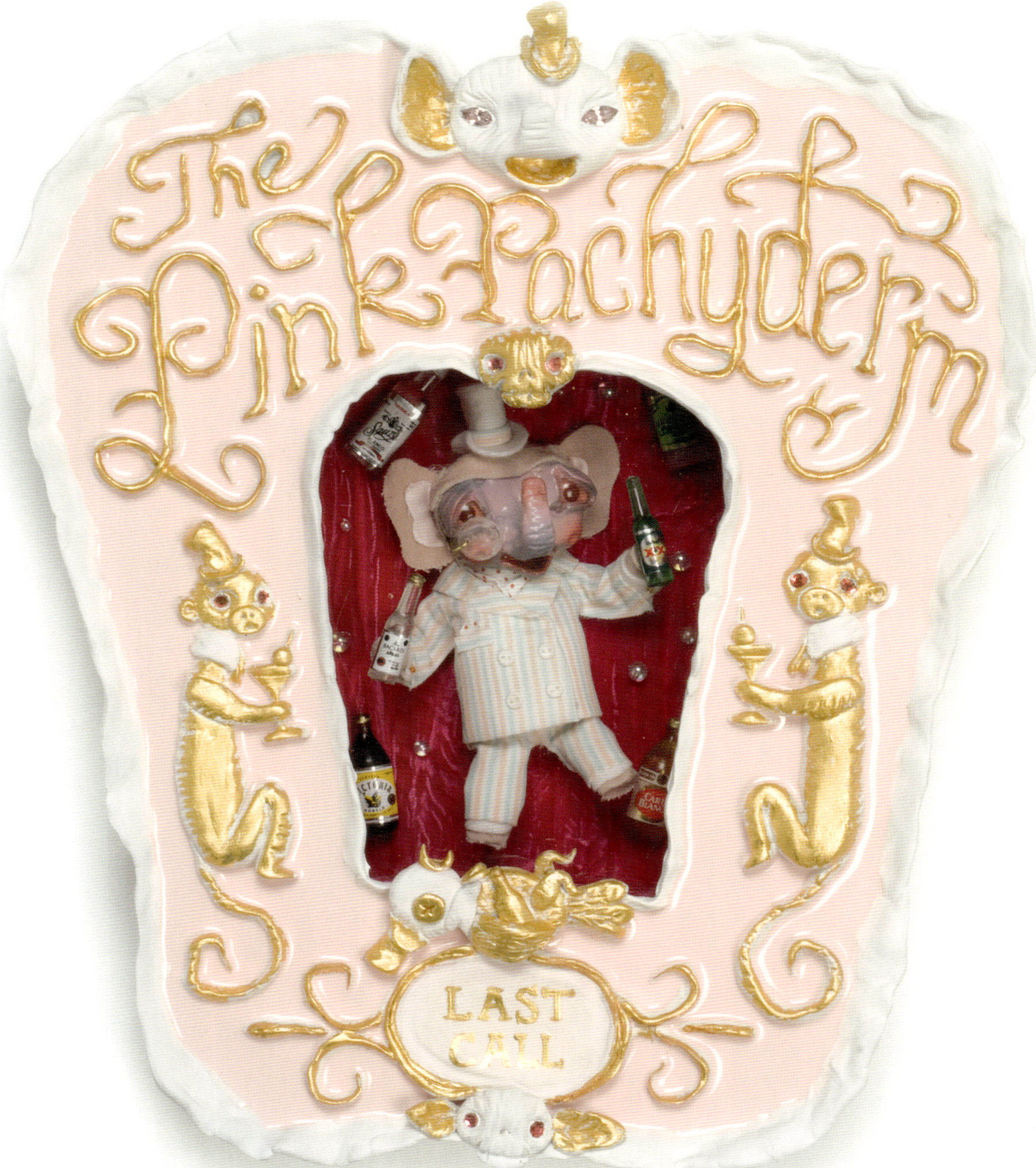

Santa Ana winds in a pint glass over ice, 2oz helicopter fuel or French brandy, the juice from several concord grapes, fresh lime to taste. Combine all and transfer into a rainbow trout, shake, then pour into a champagne flute. Enjoy!

Erik Cantu

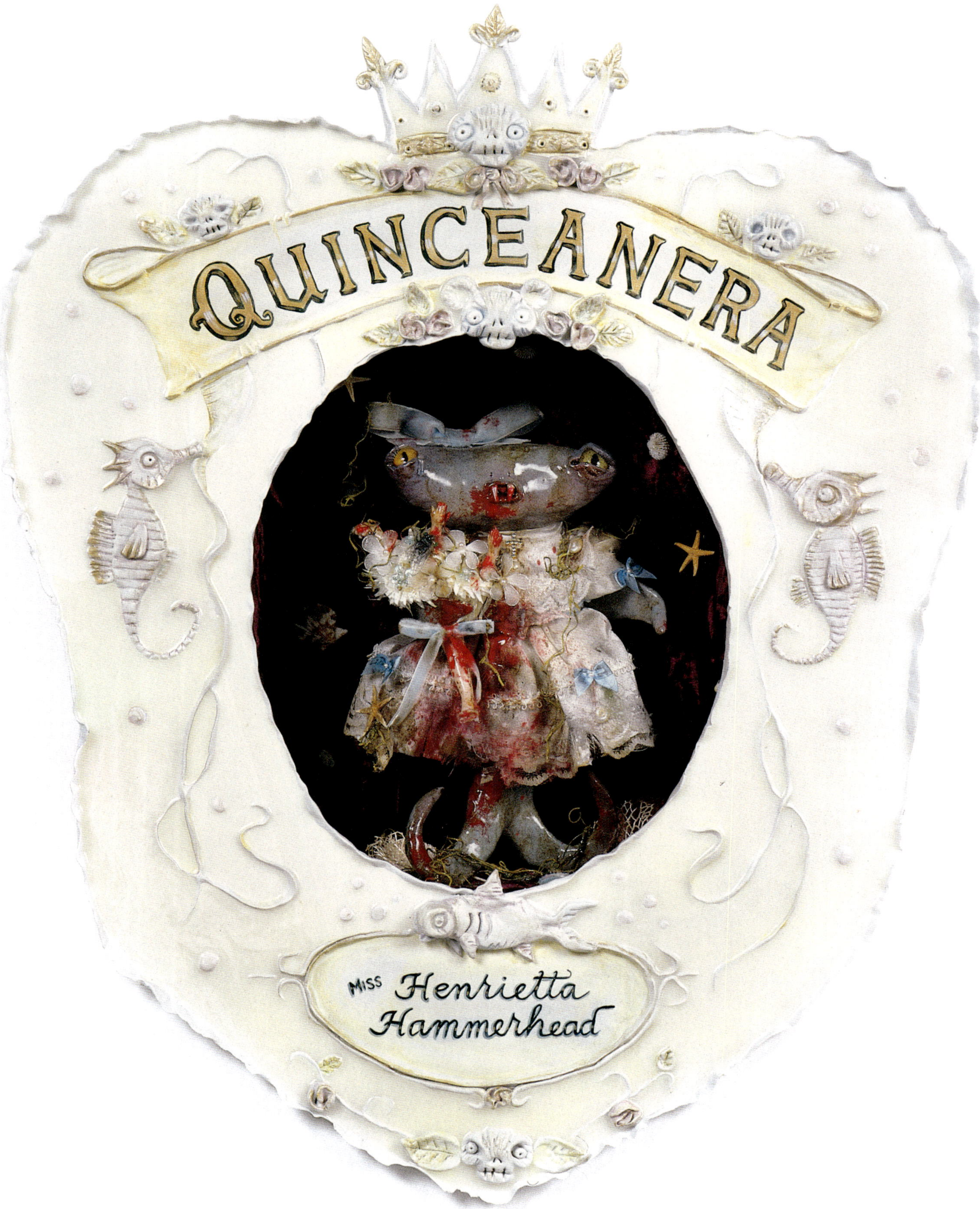
QUINCEANERA
MISS Henrietta Hammerhead

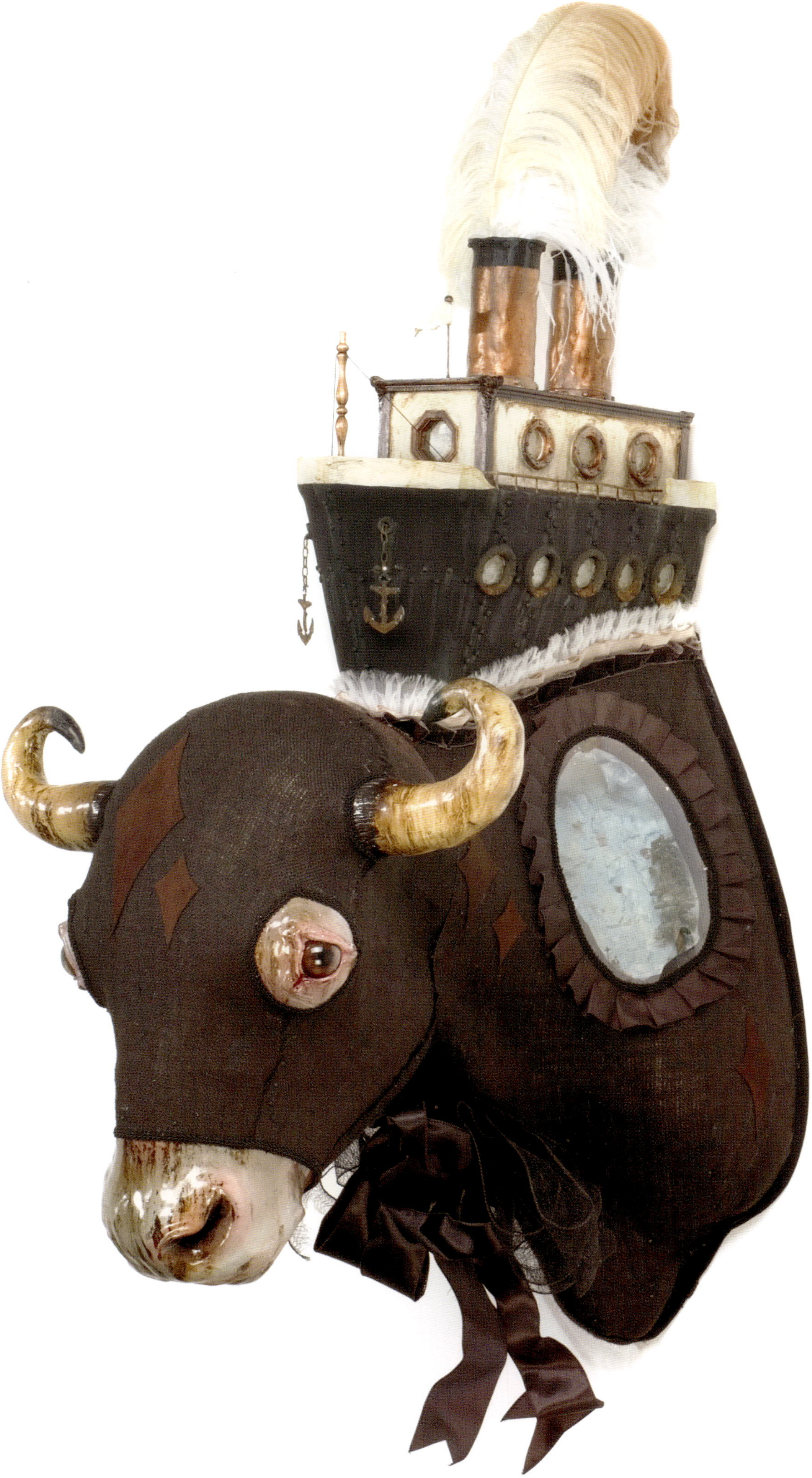

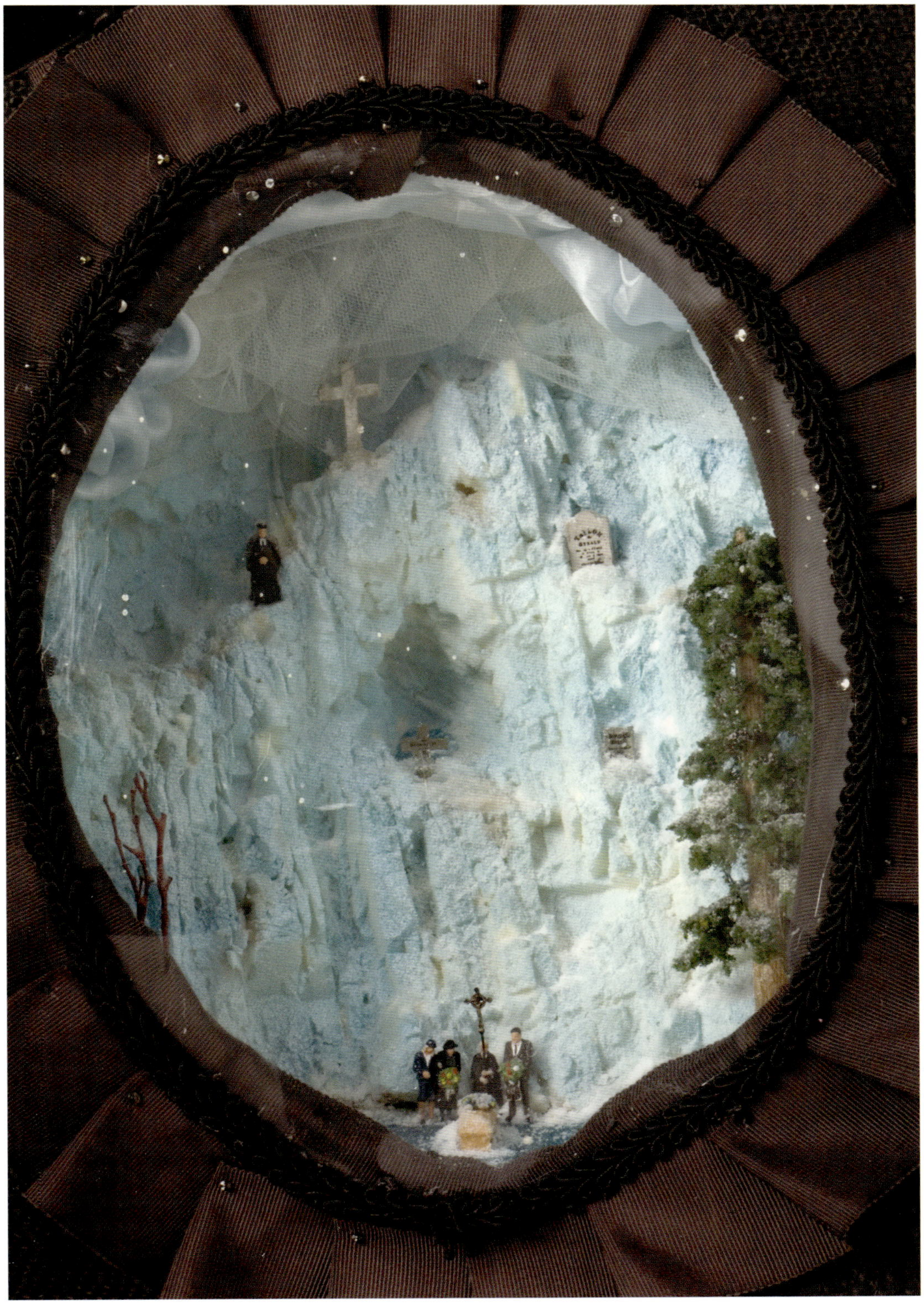

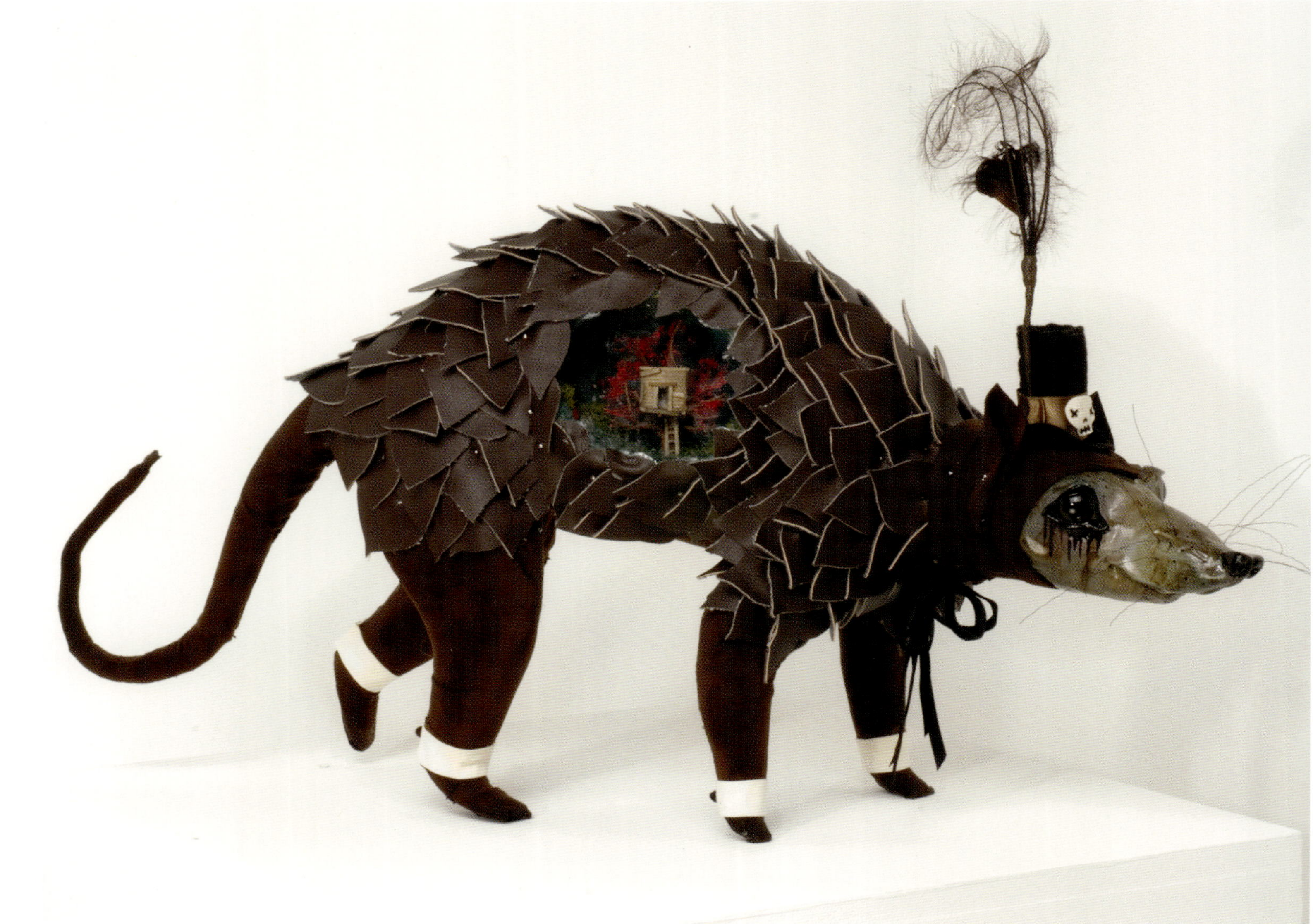

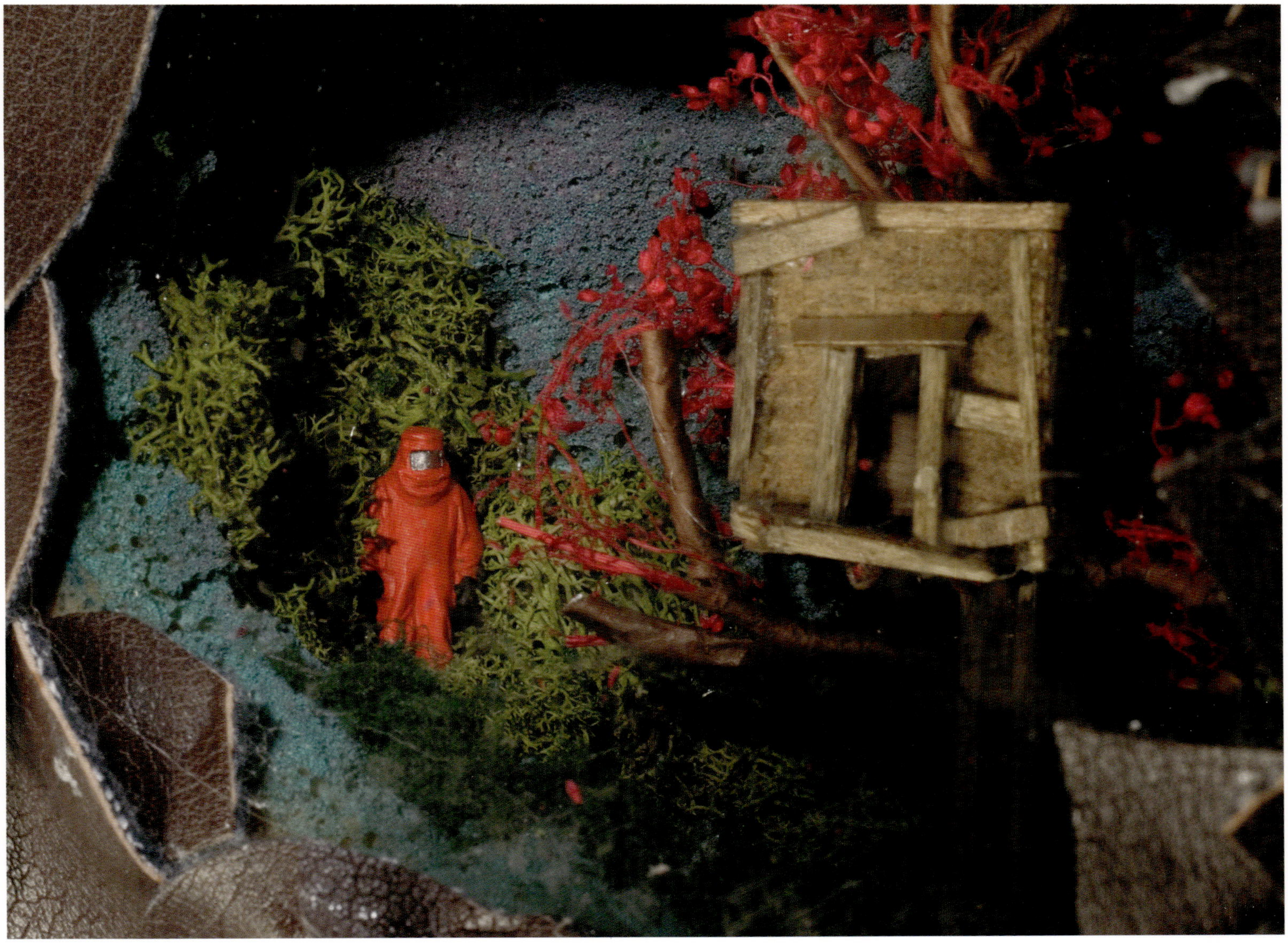

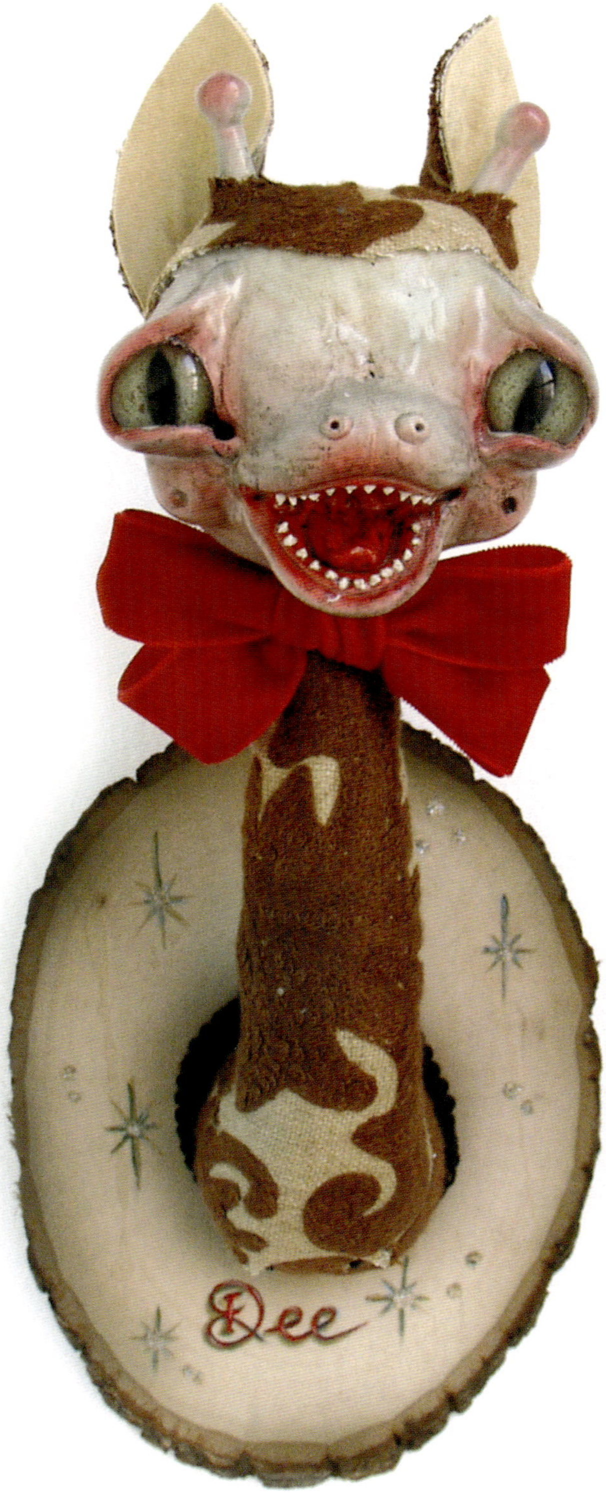
Dee

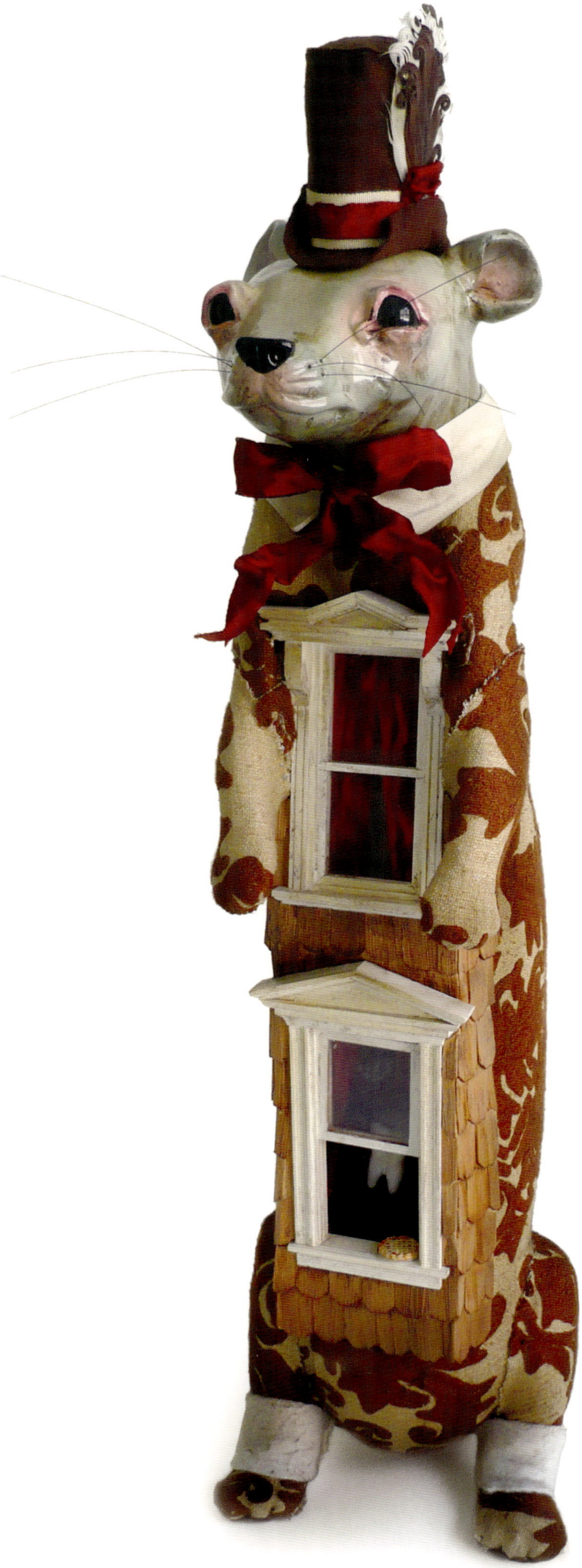

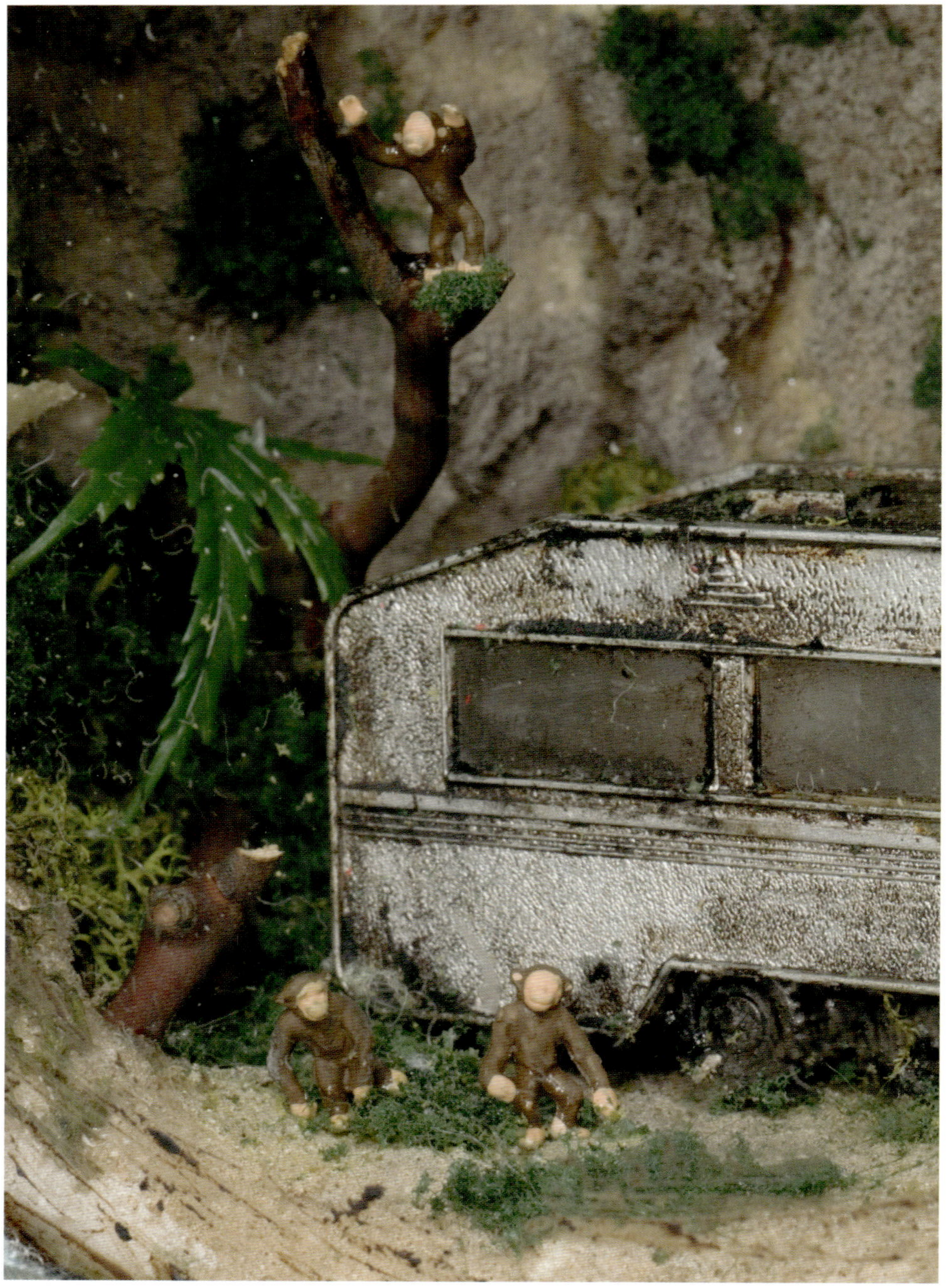

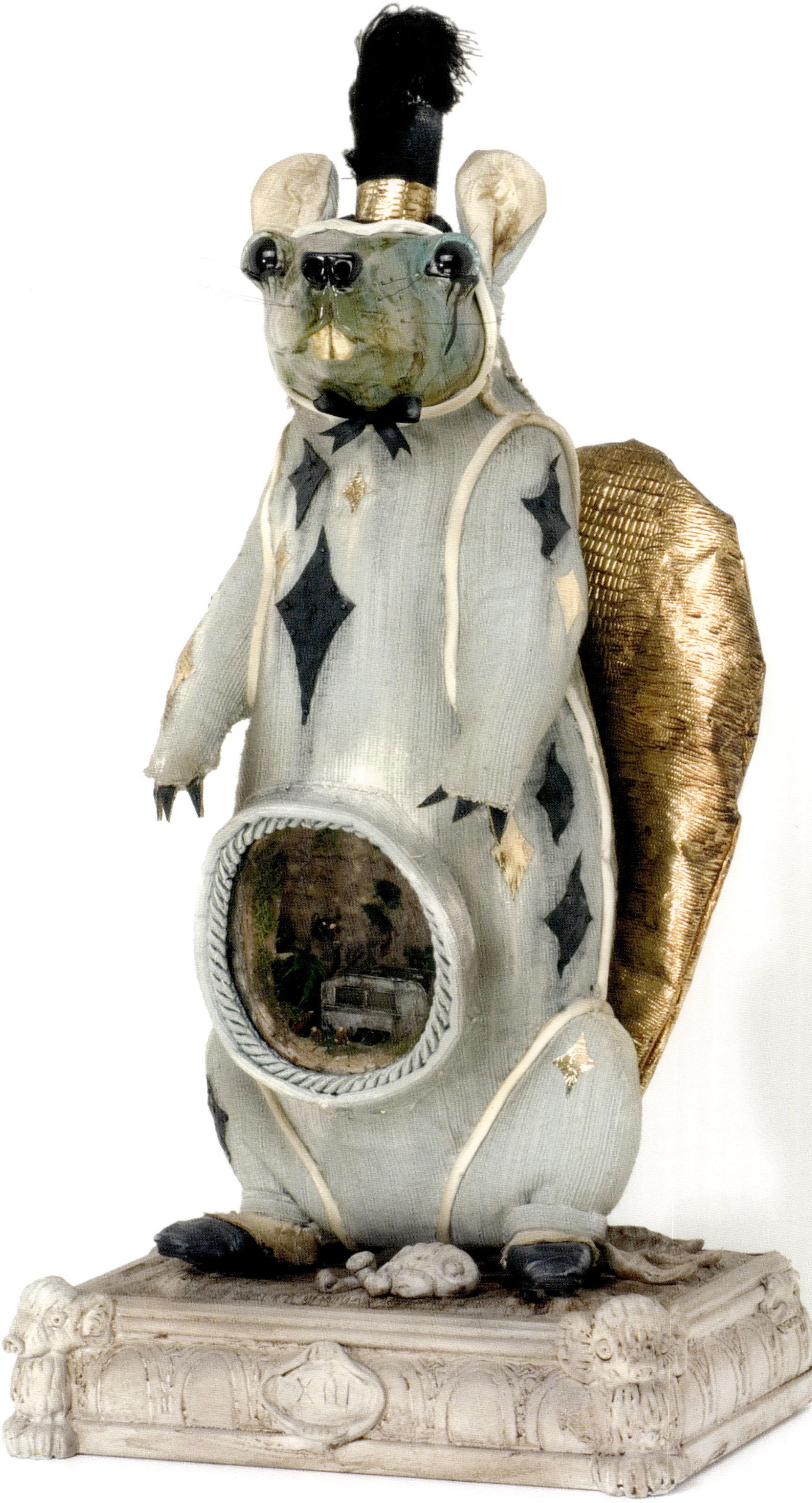

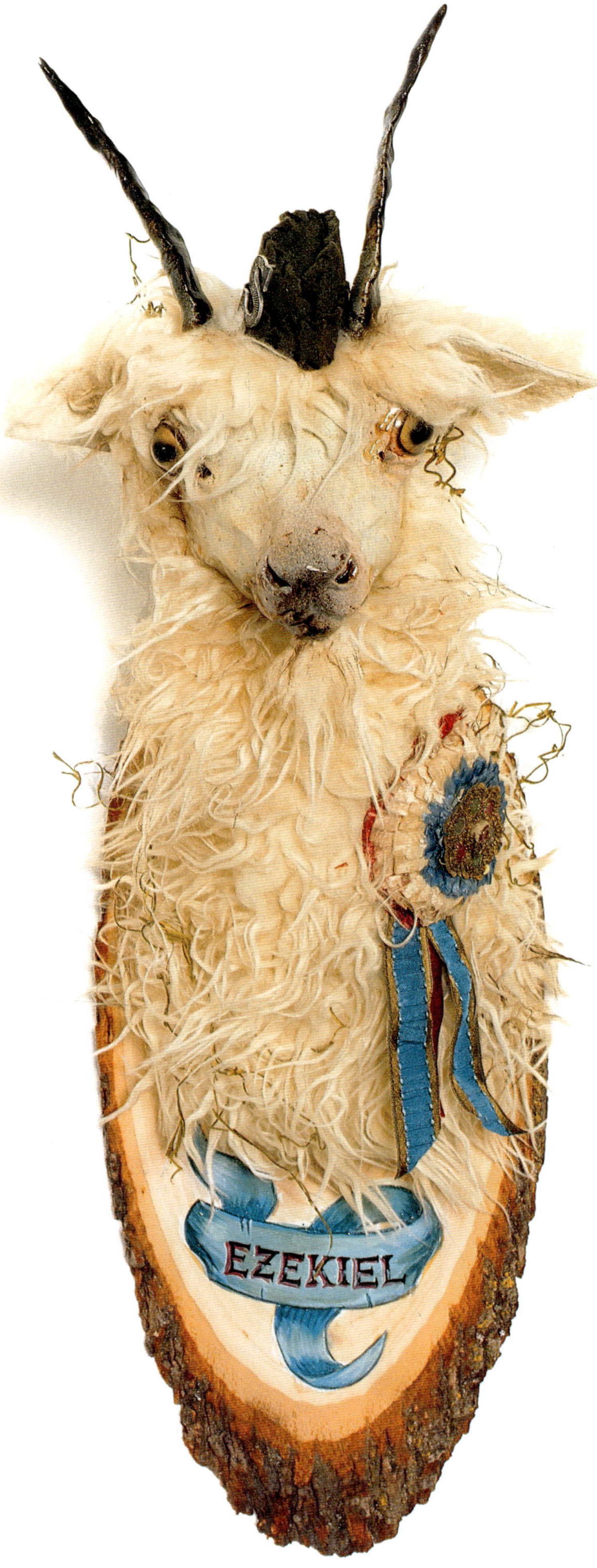
EZEKIEL

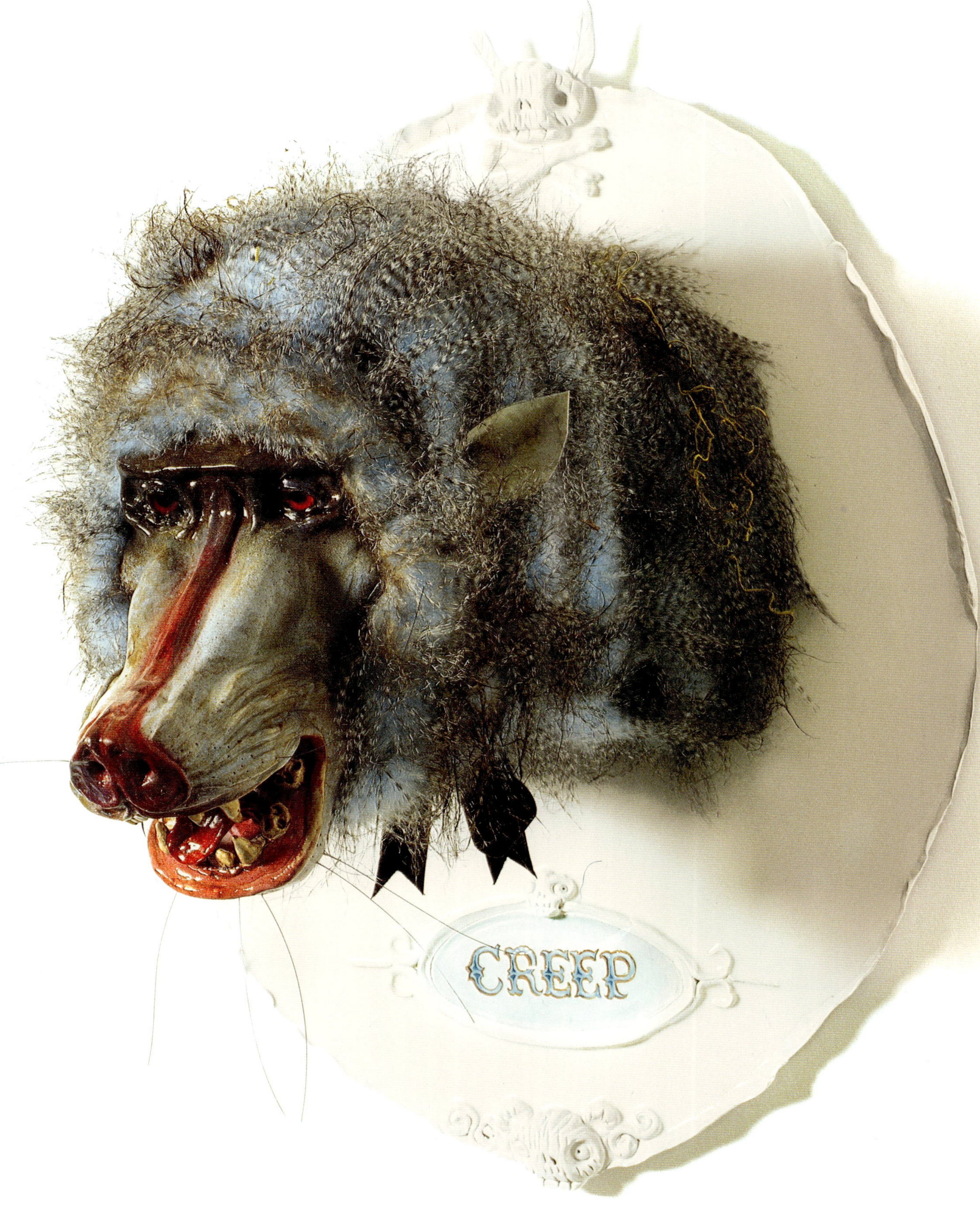
CREEP

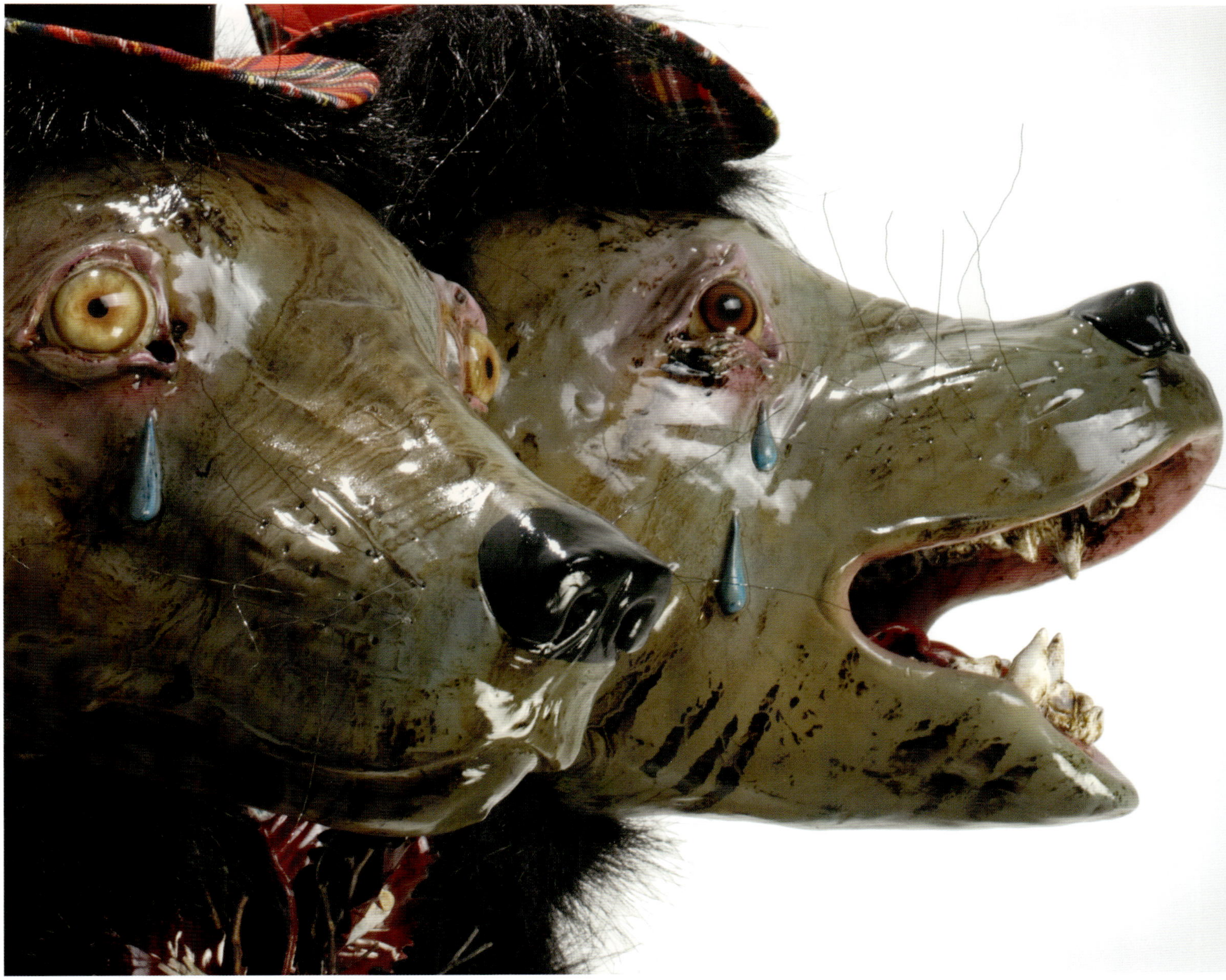

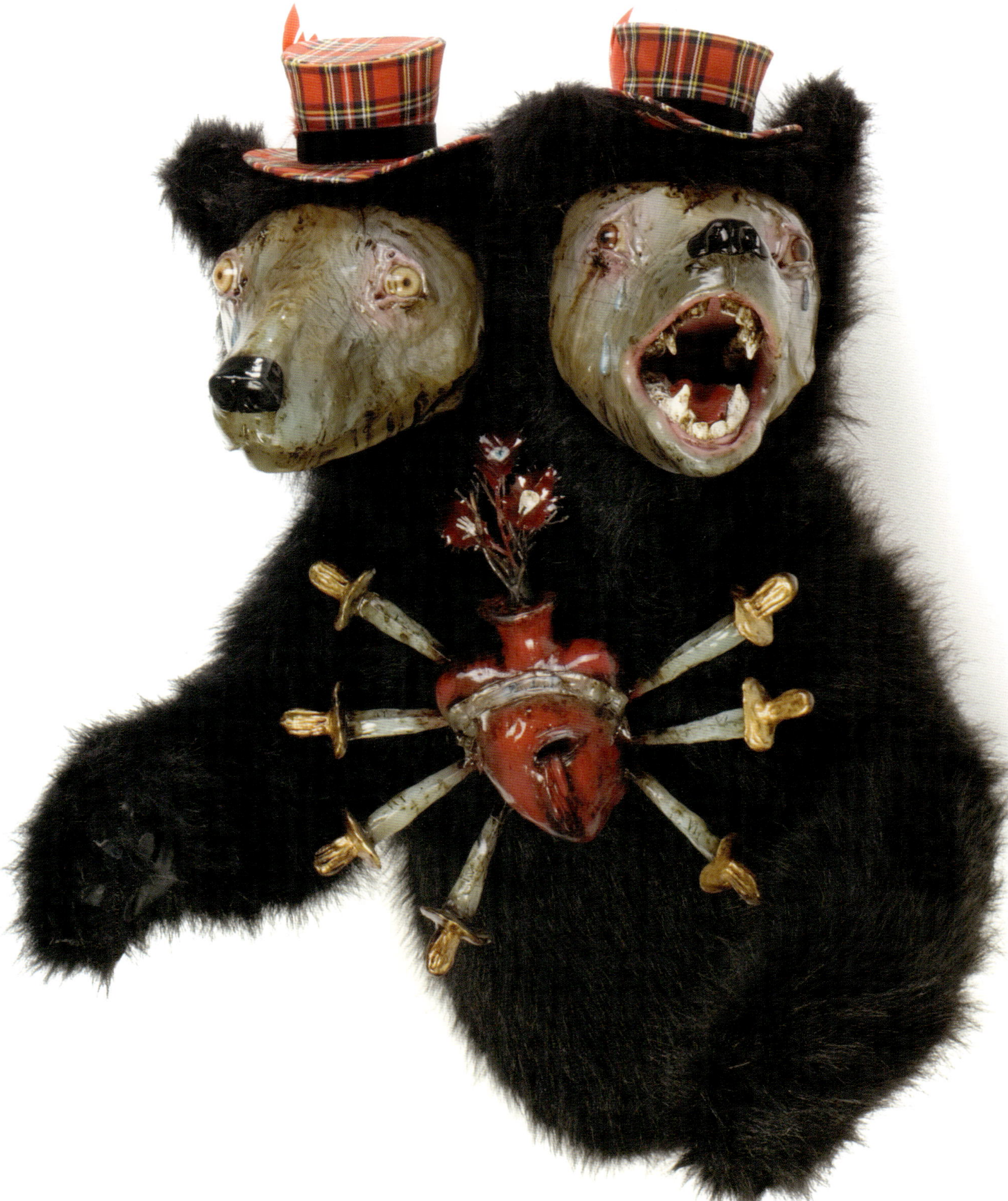

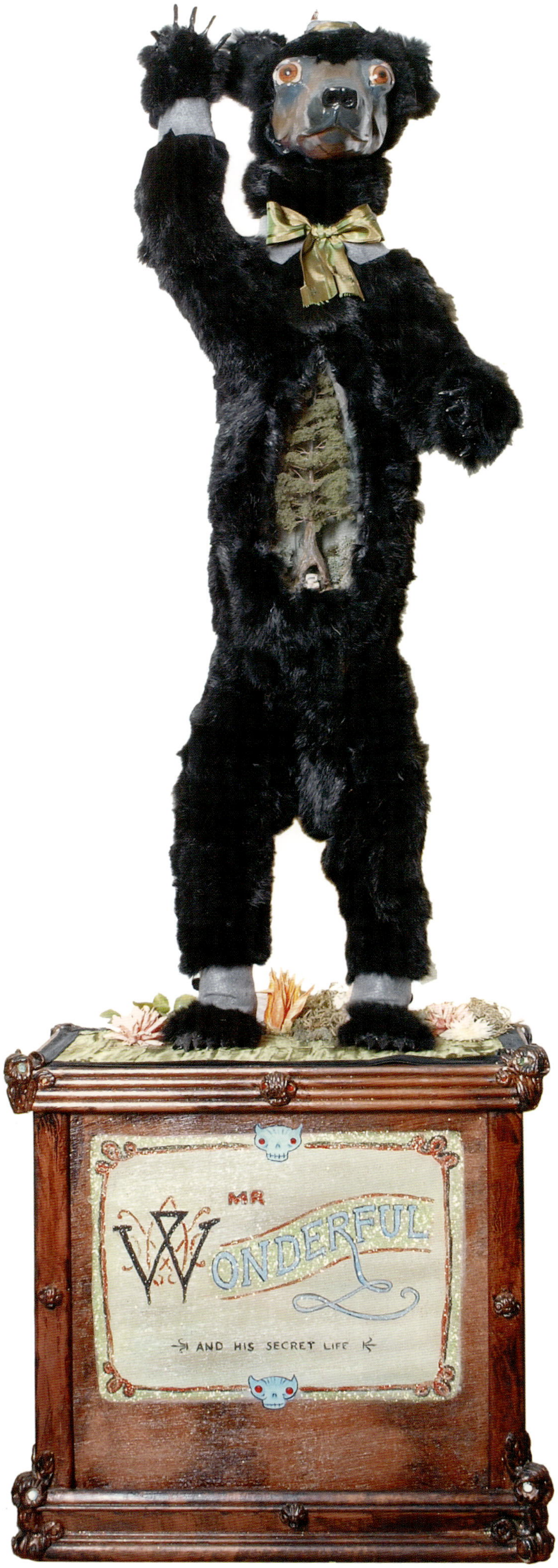
MR
WONDERFUL
AND HIS SECRET LIFE

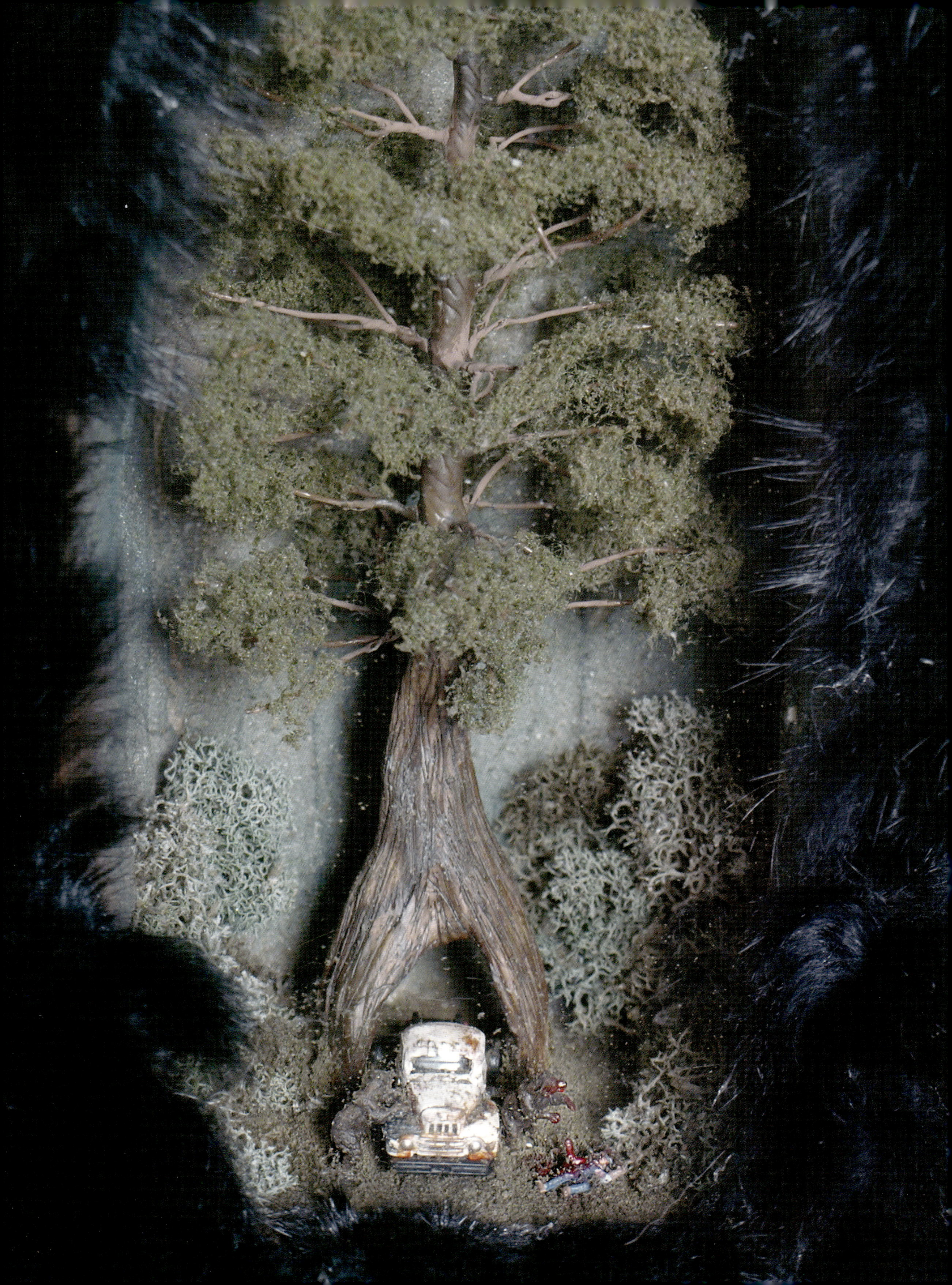

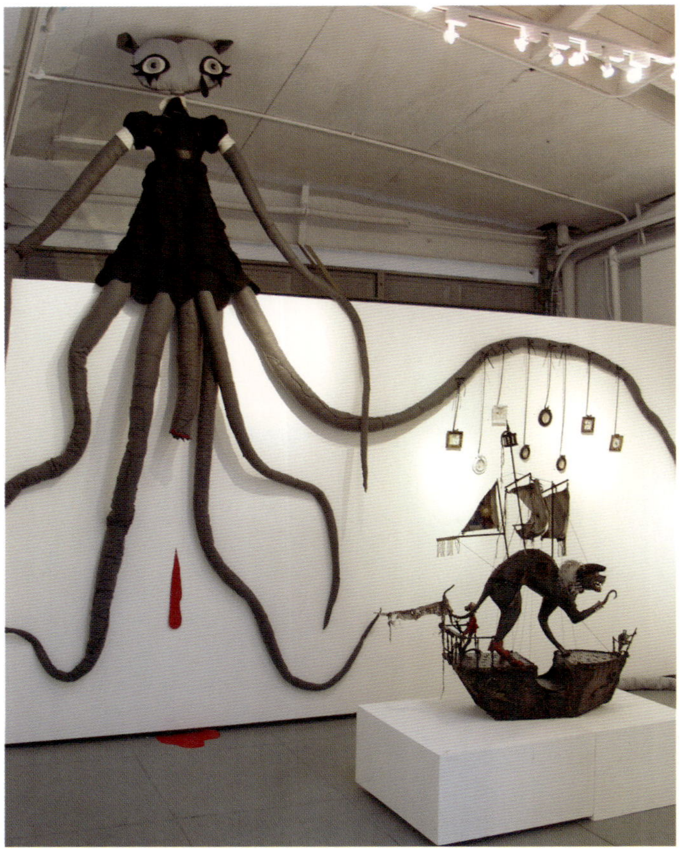

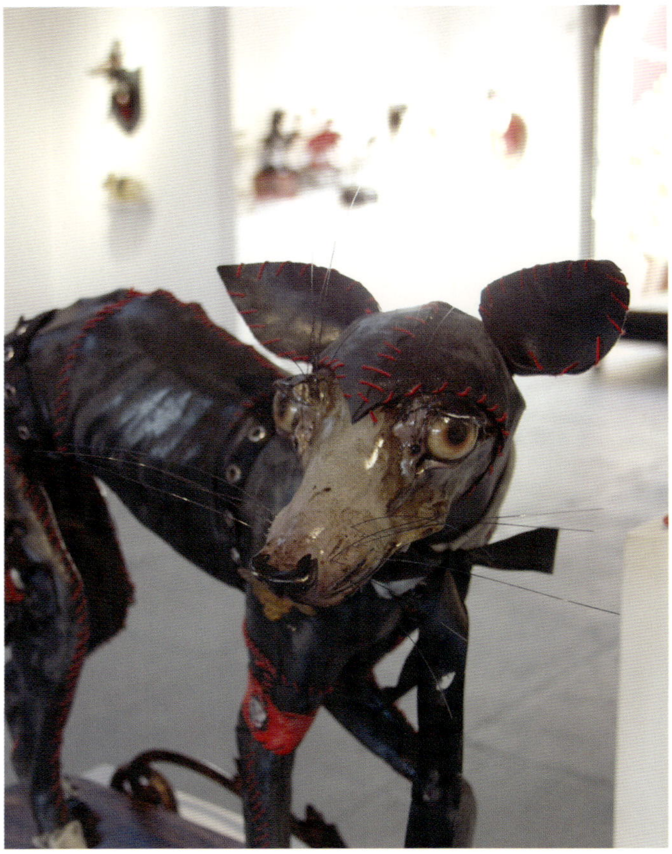

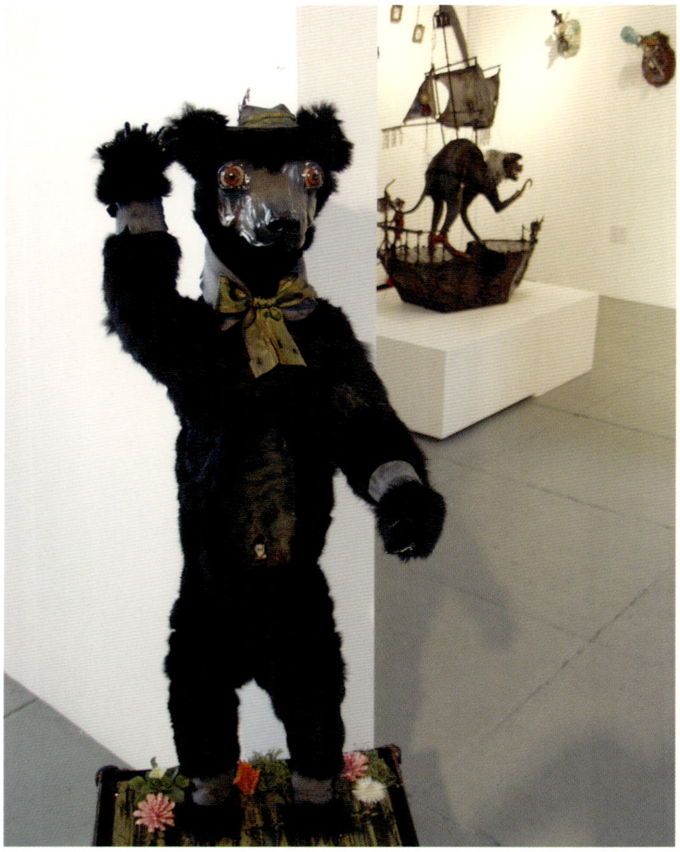

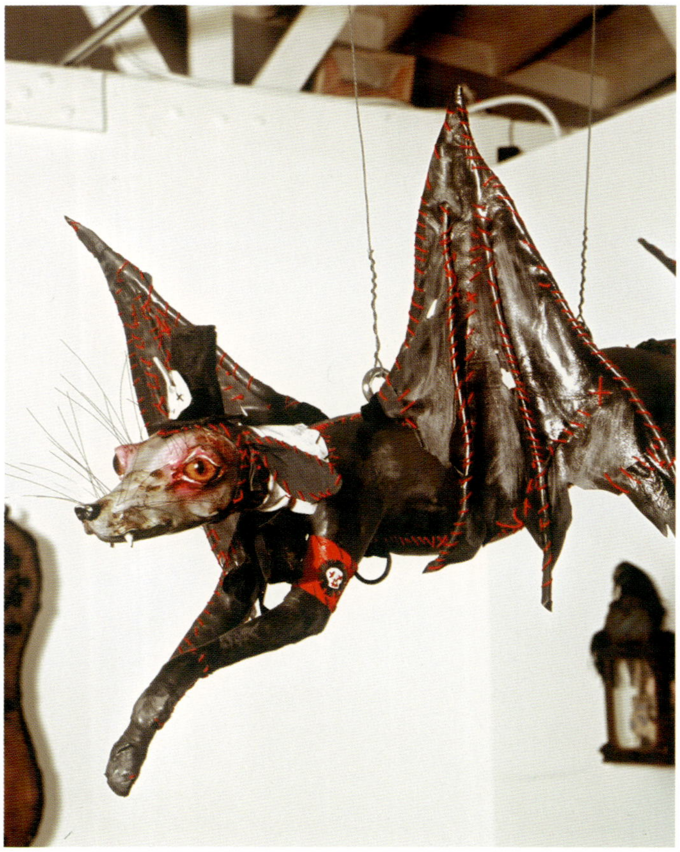

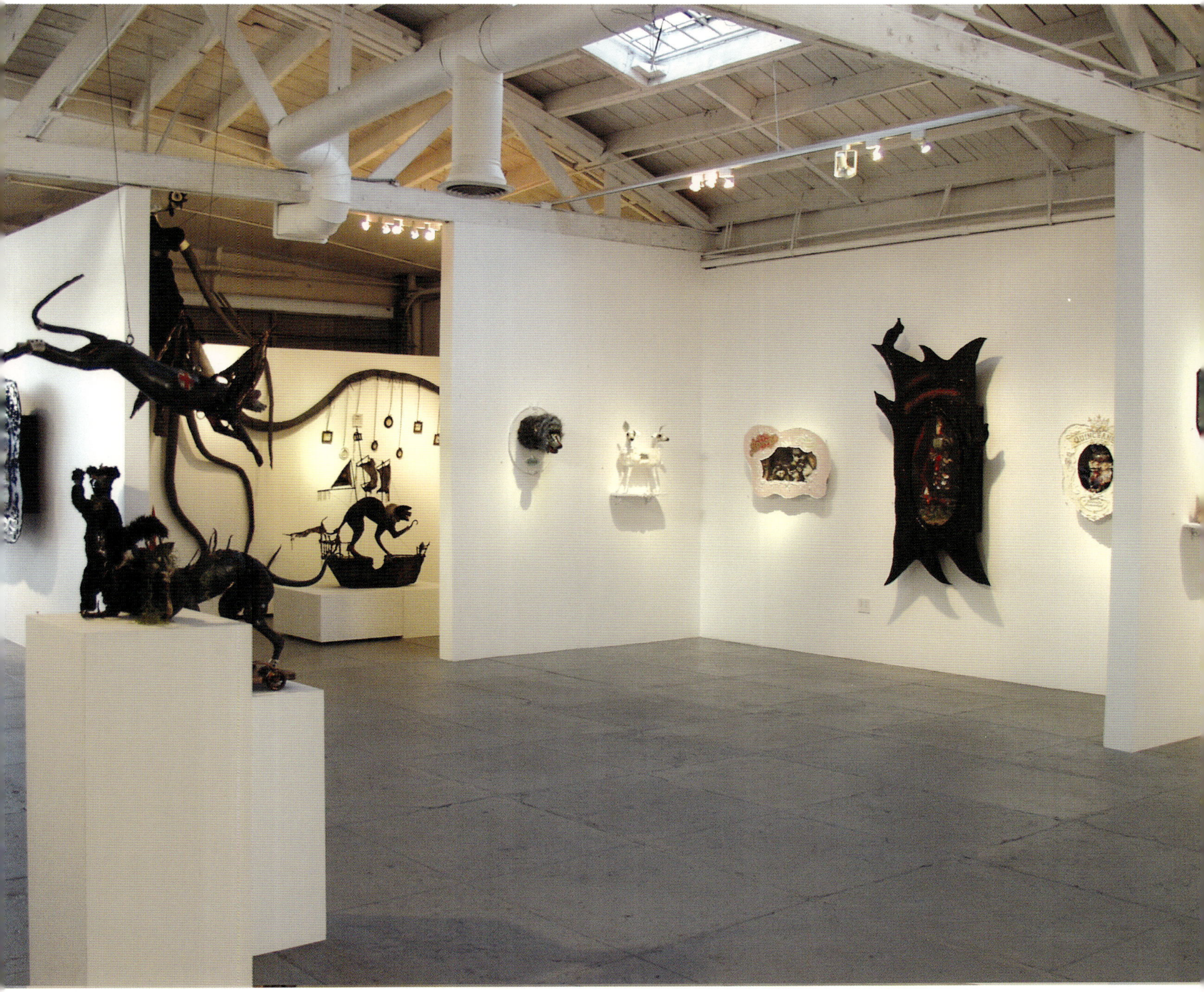

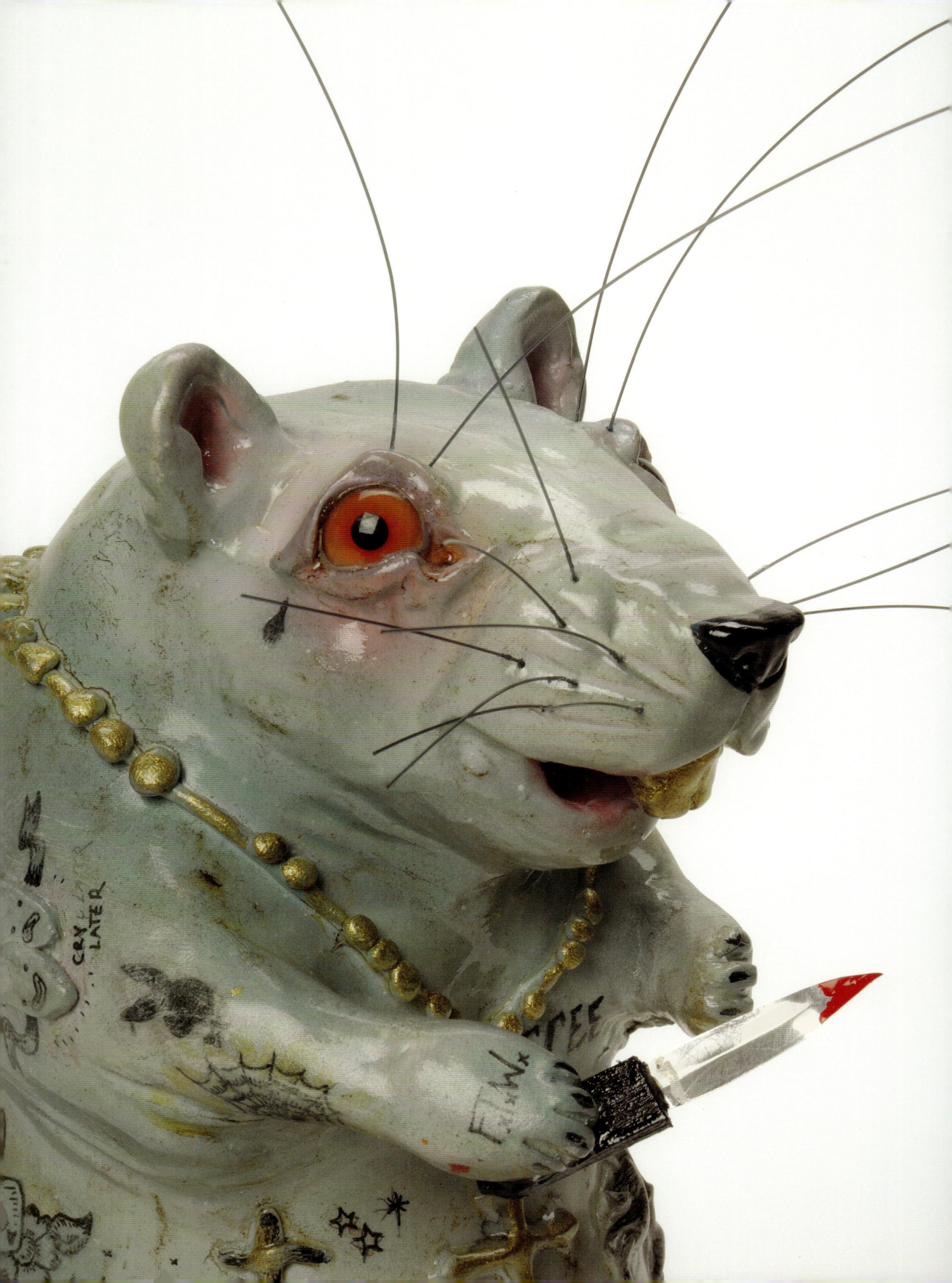
CRY LATER

American Animals

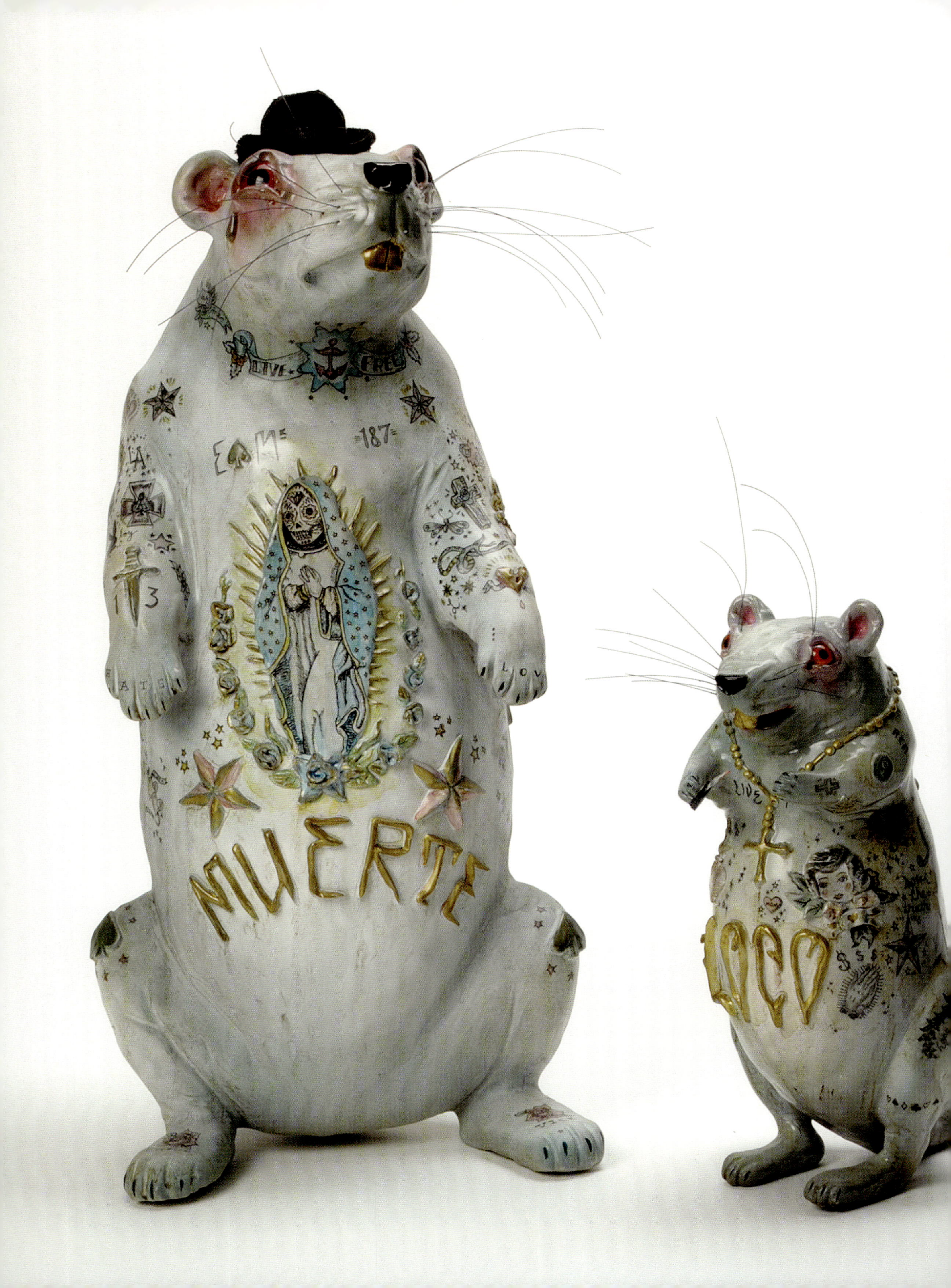
LIVE FREE
187
MUERTE
LOCO

There are gods in Alabama:
Jack Daniel's, high school quarterbacks,
trucks, big tits, and also Jesus."

Excerpt from
"Gods In Alabama"
JOSHILYN JACKSON

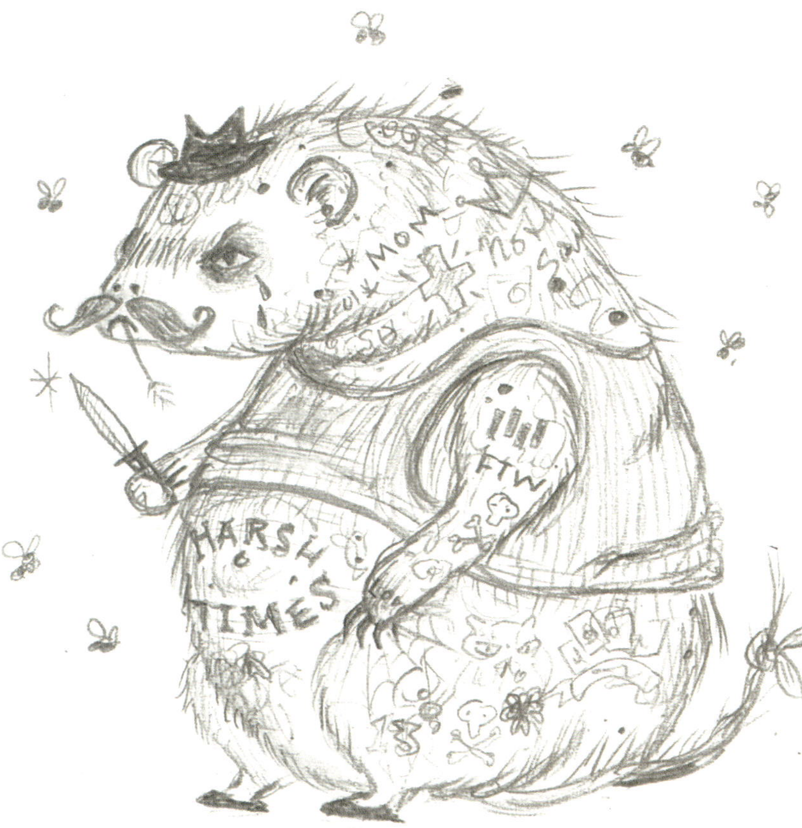

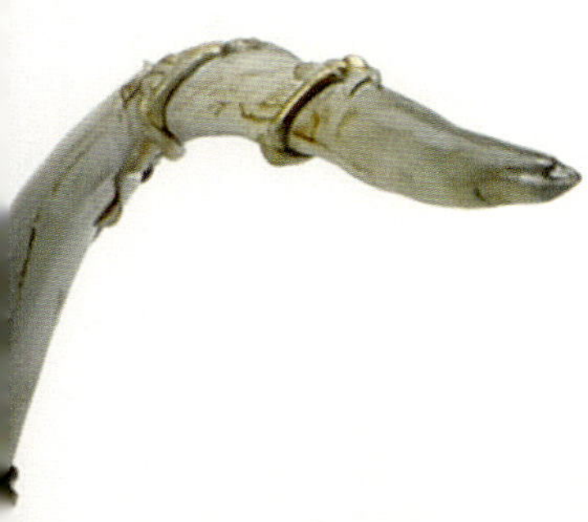

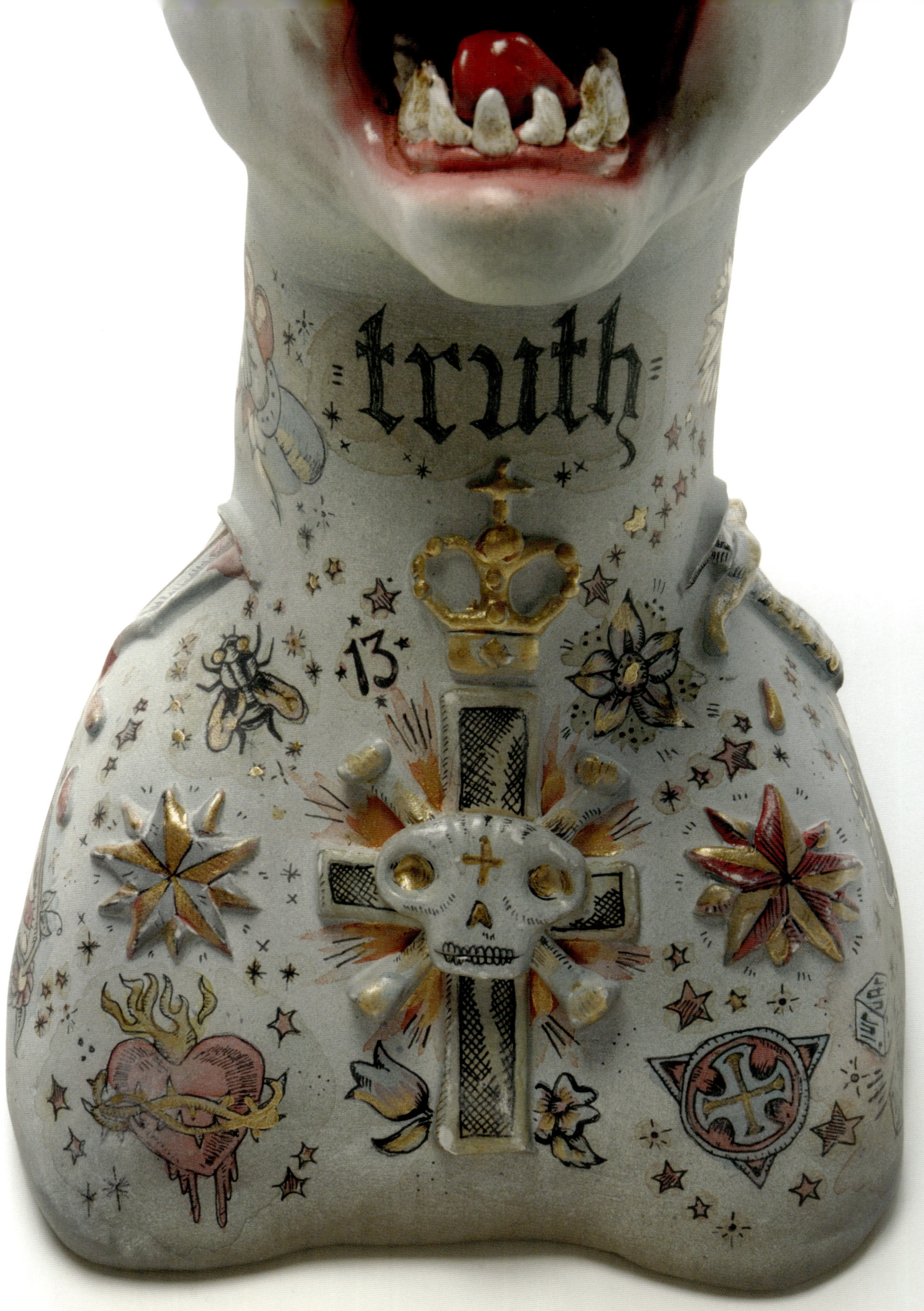
truth
13

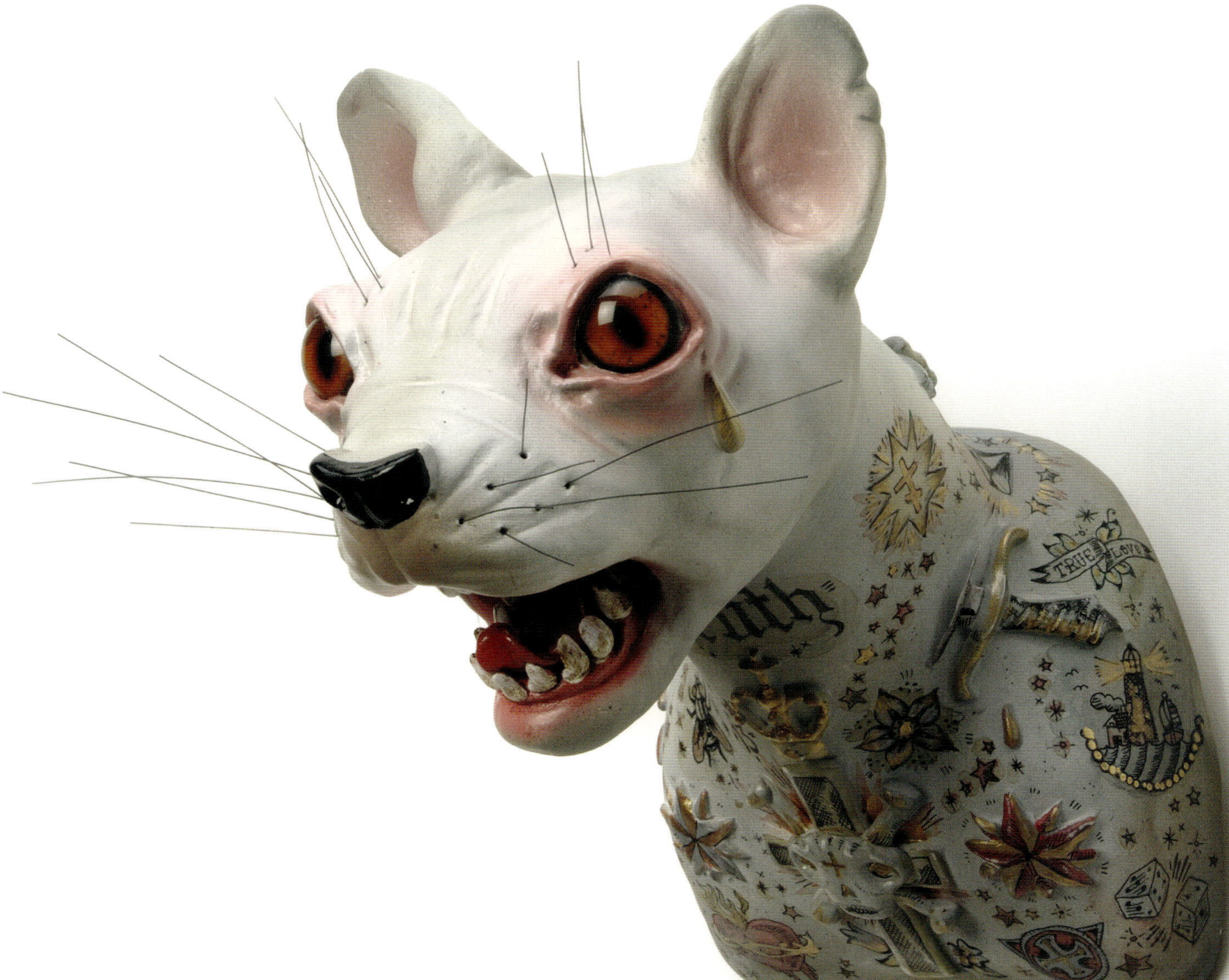
TRUE LOVE

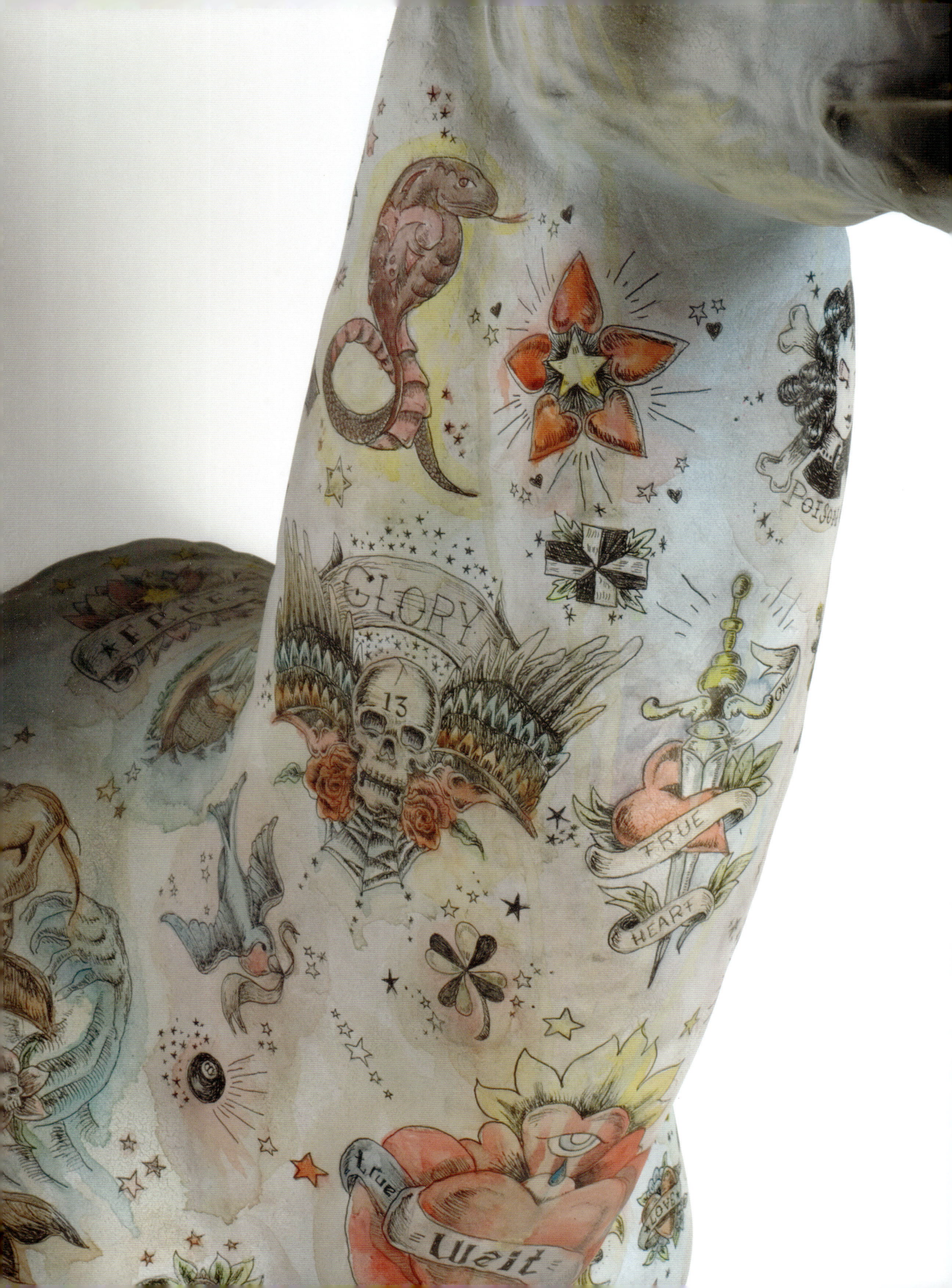

GLORY
13
ONE
TRUE
HEART
True
LOVE

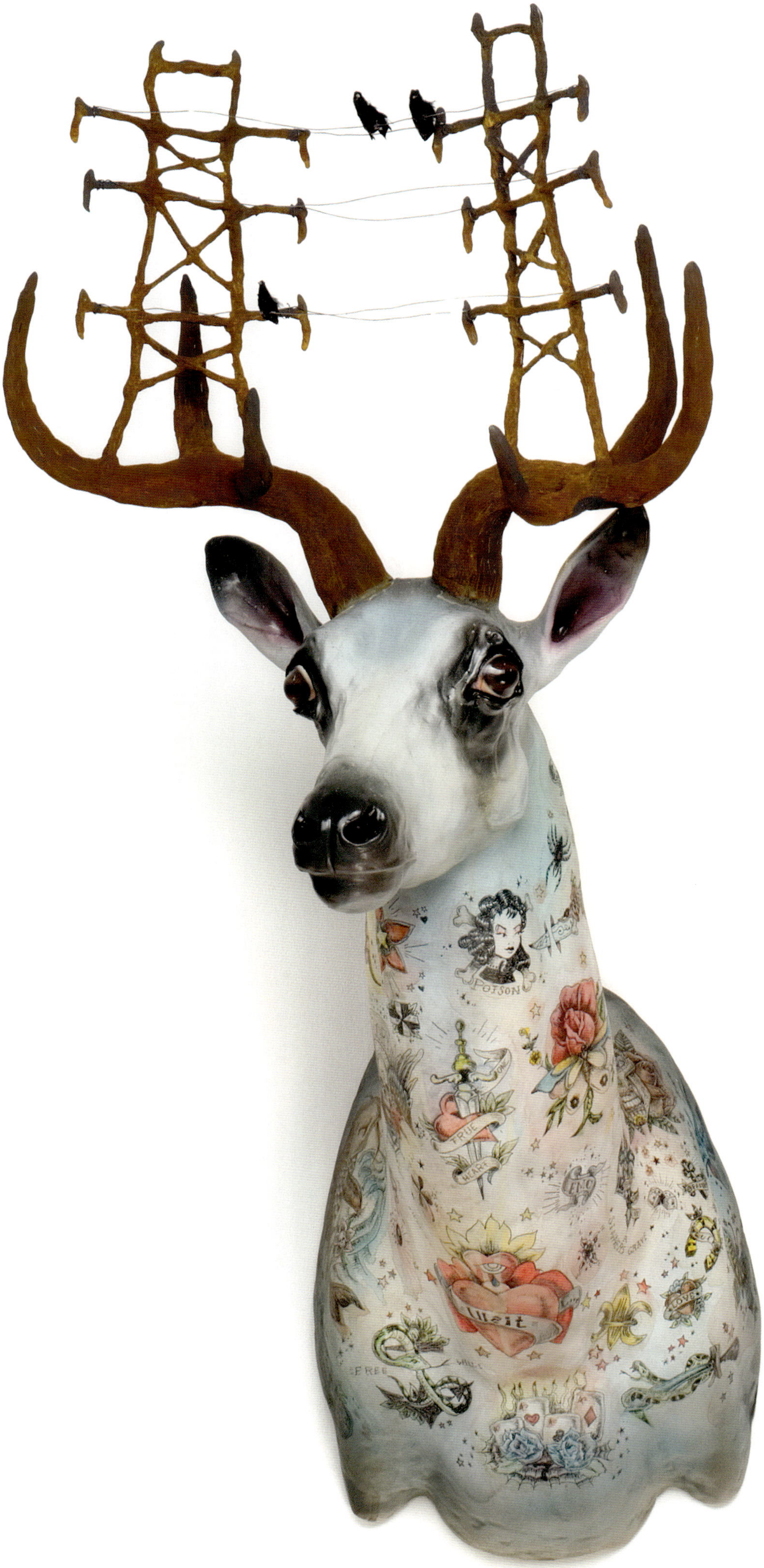
POISON

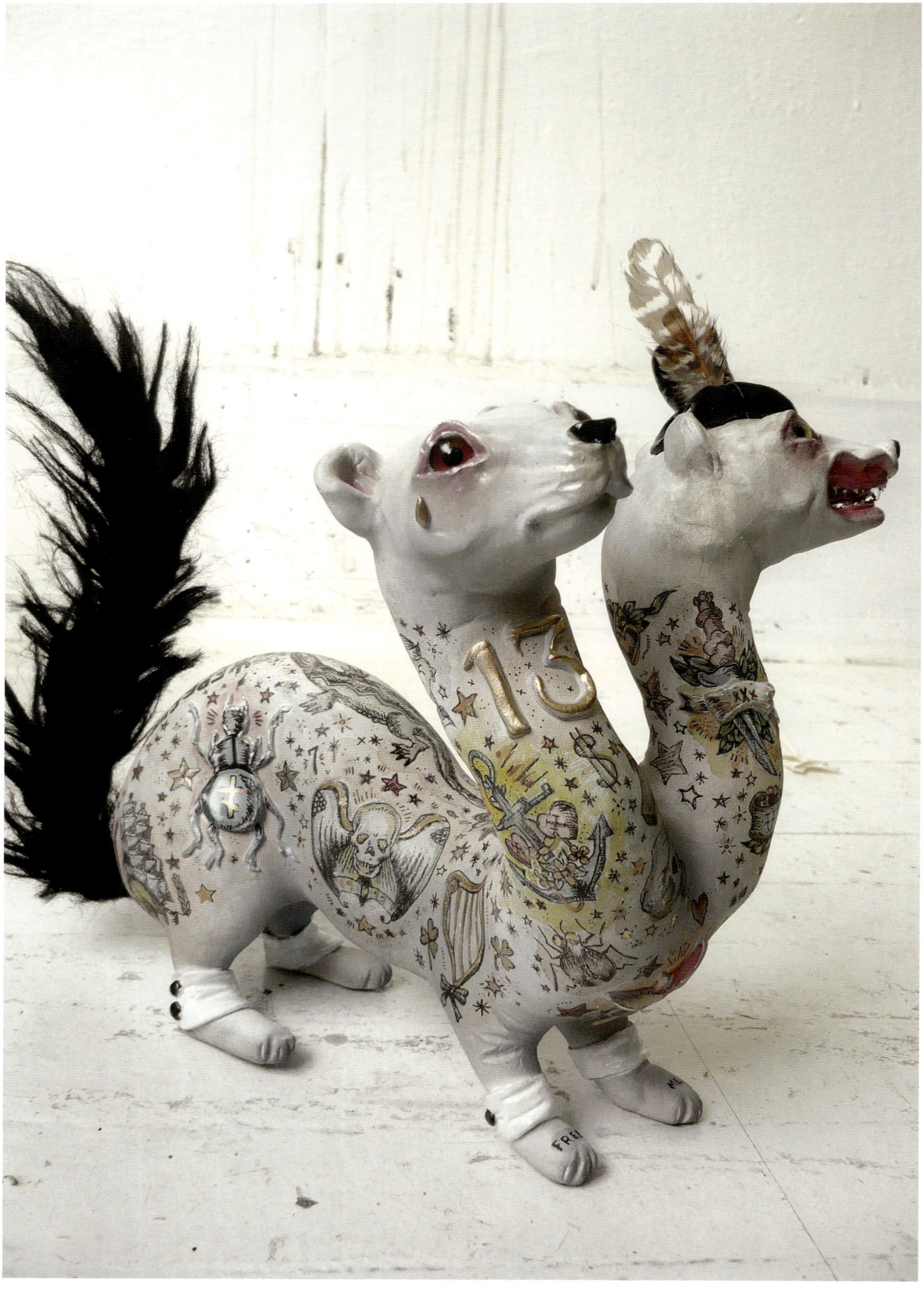

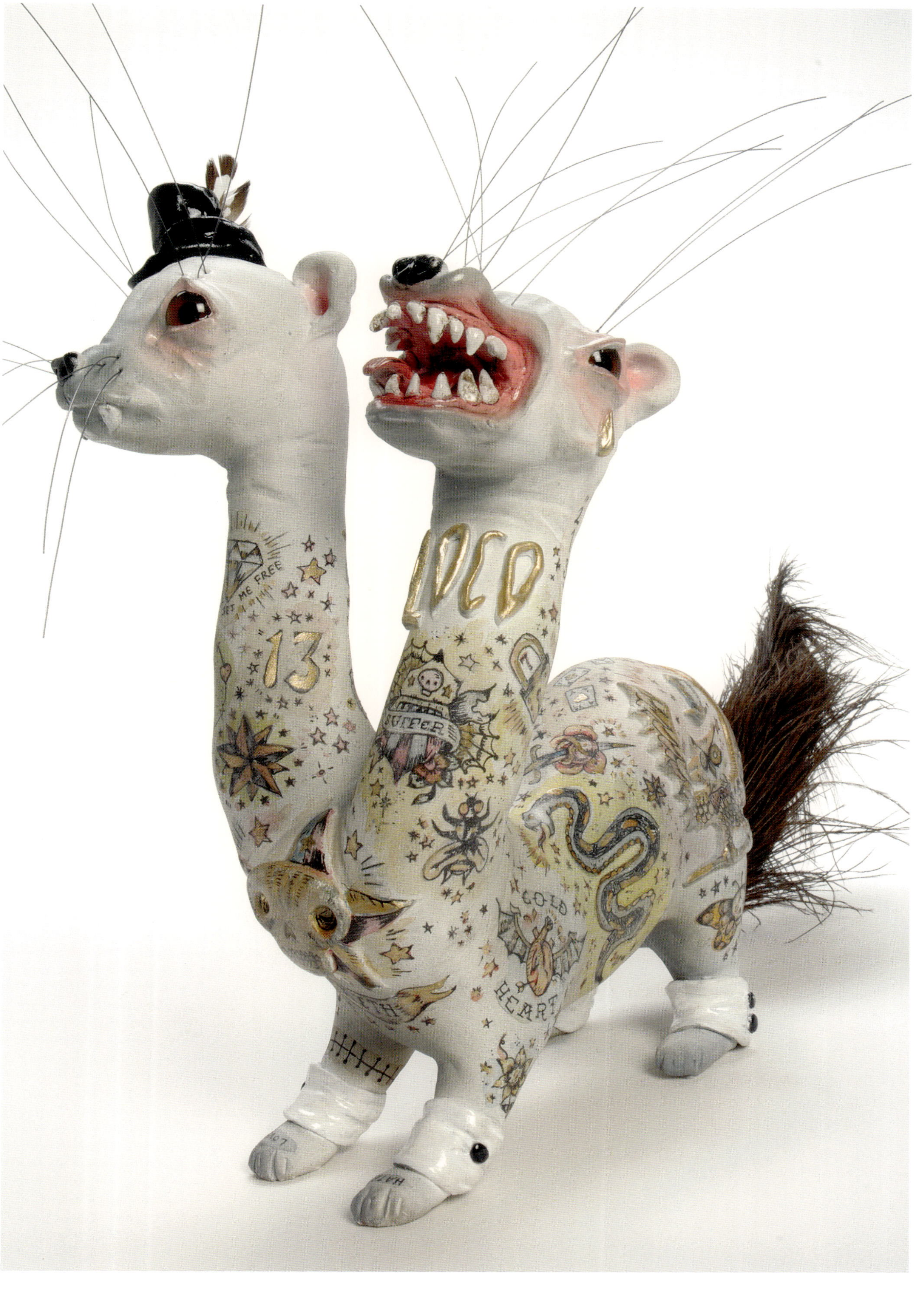
13
LOCO
COLD
HEART

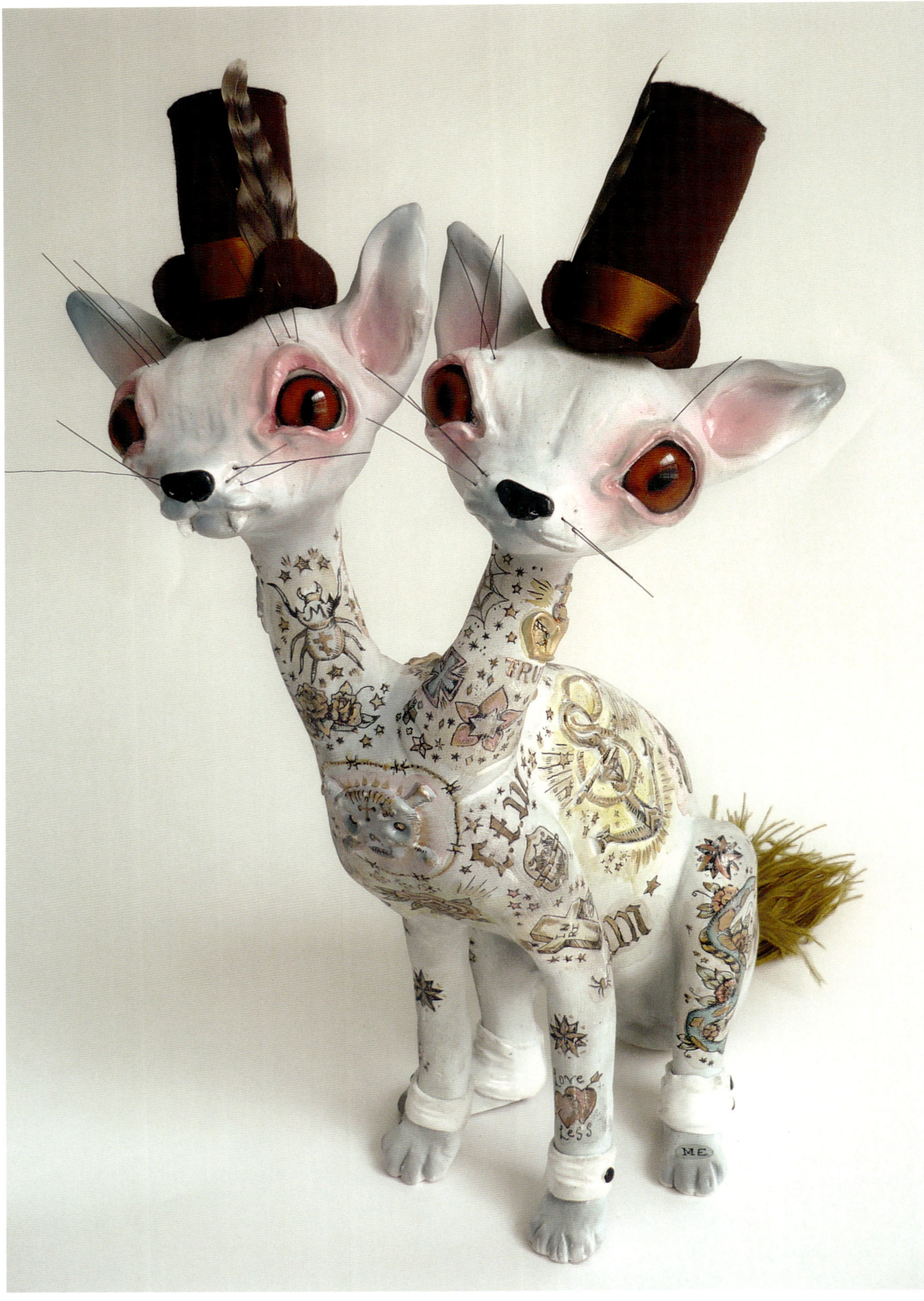
Love
Less
ME

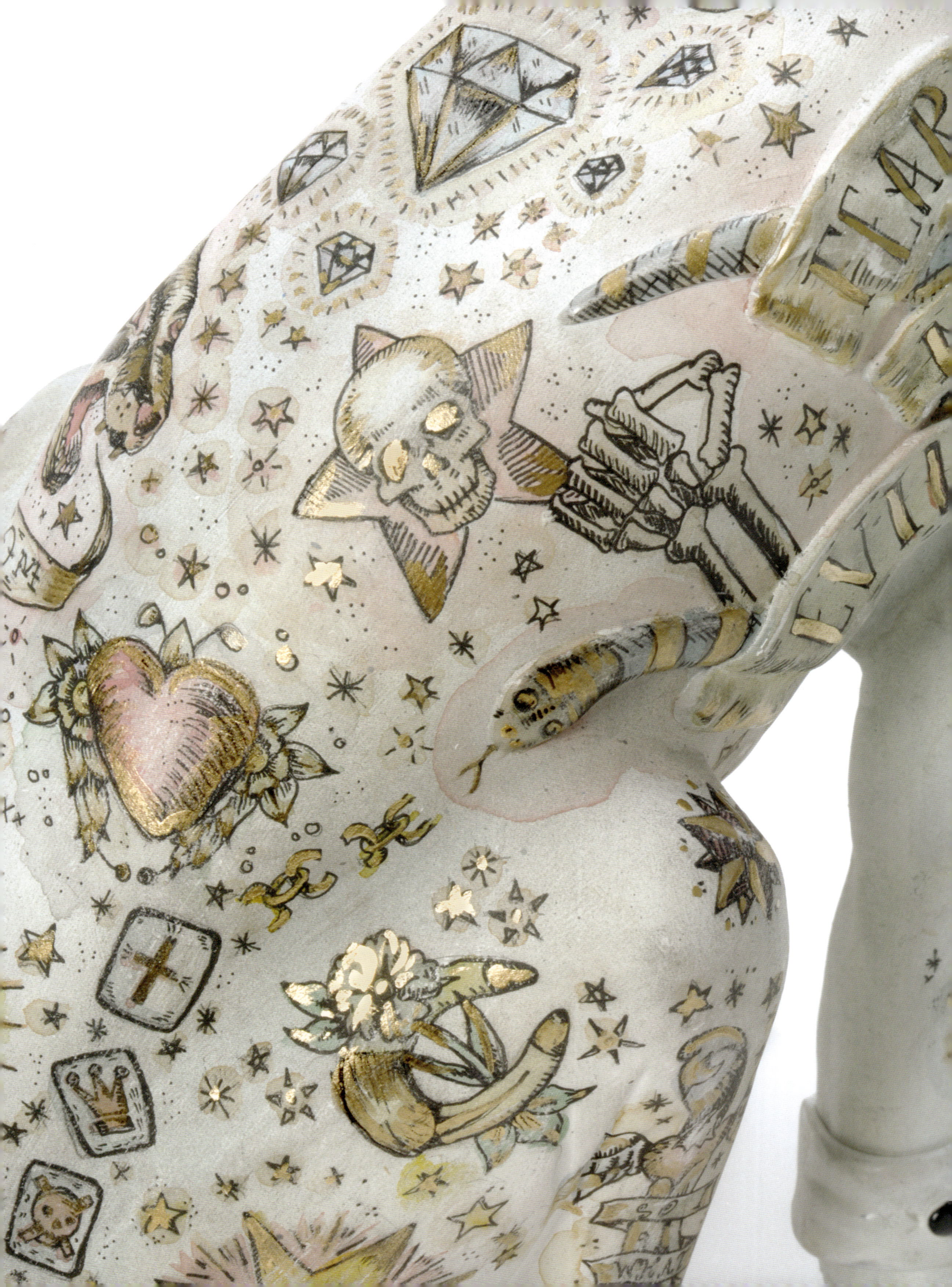

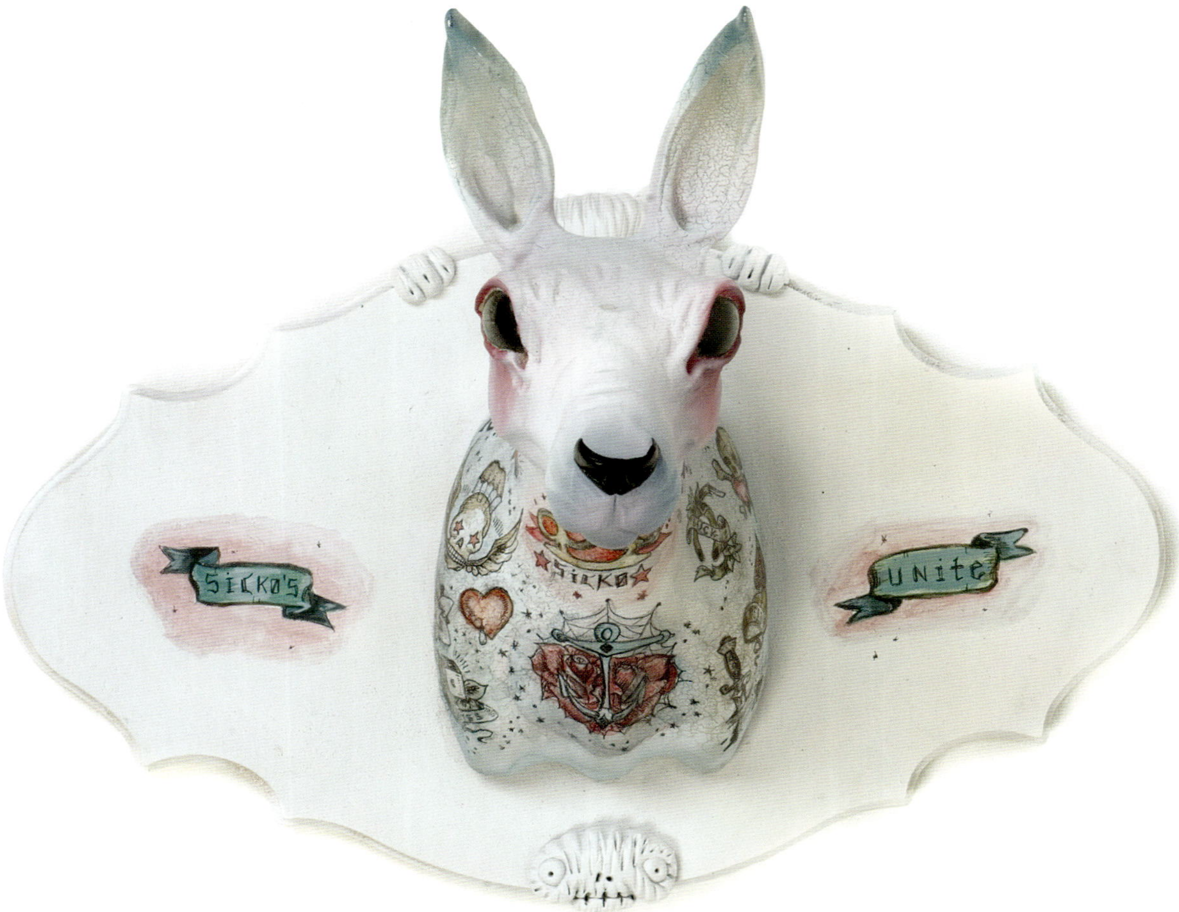
Sicko's
unite

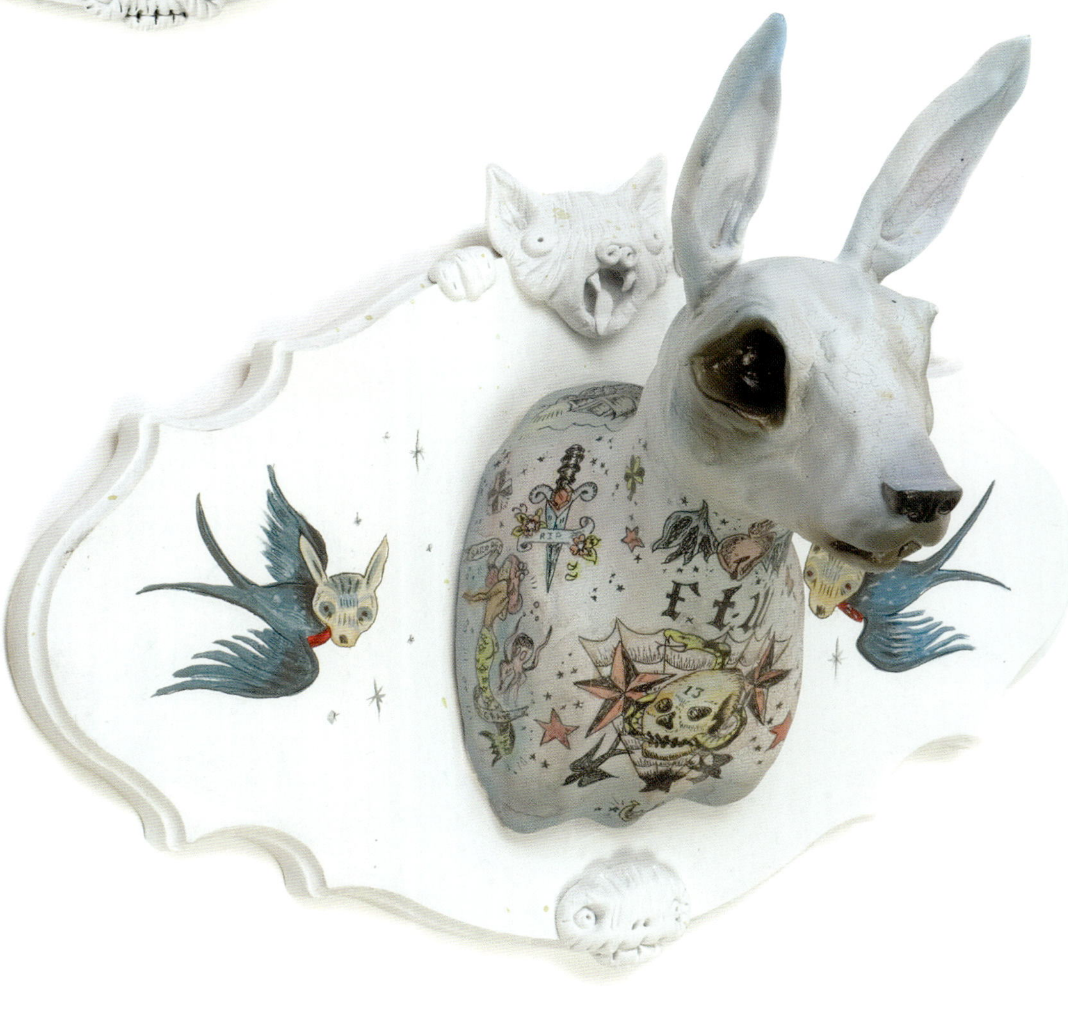

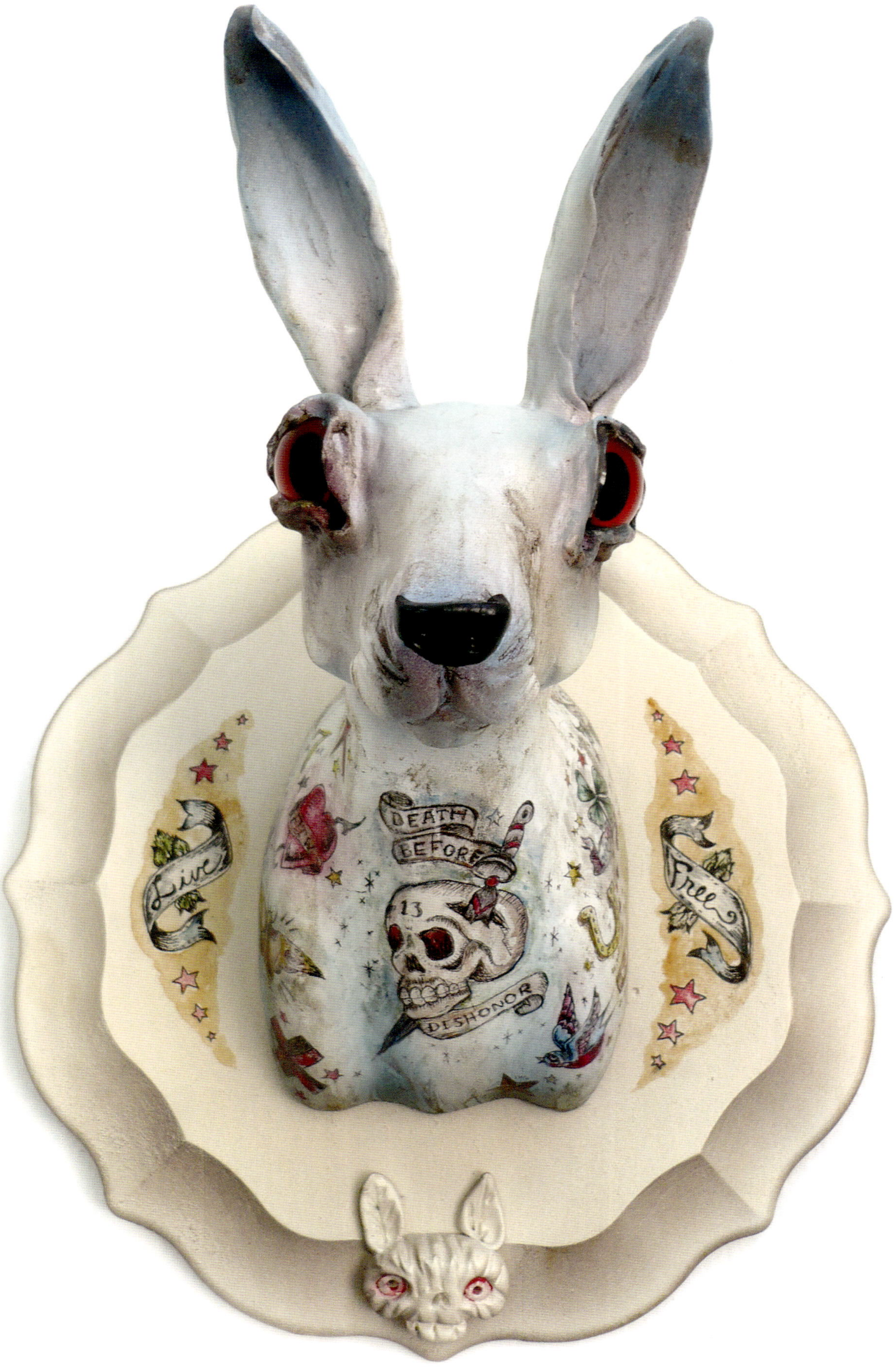
Live
DEATH
BEFORE
13
DISHONOR
Free

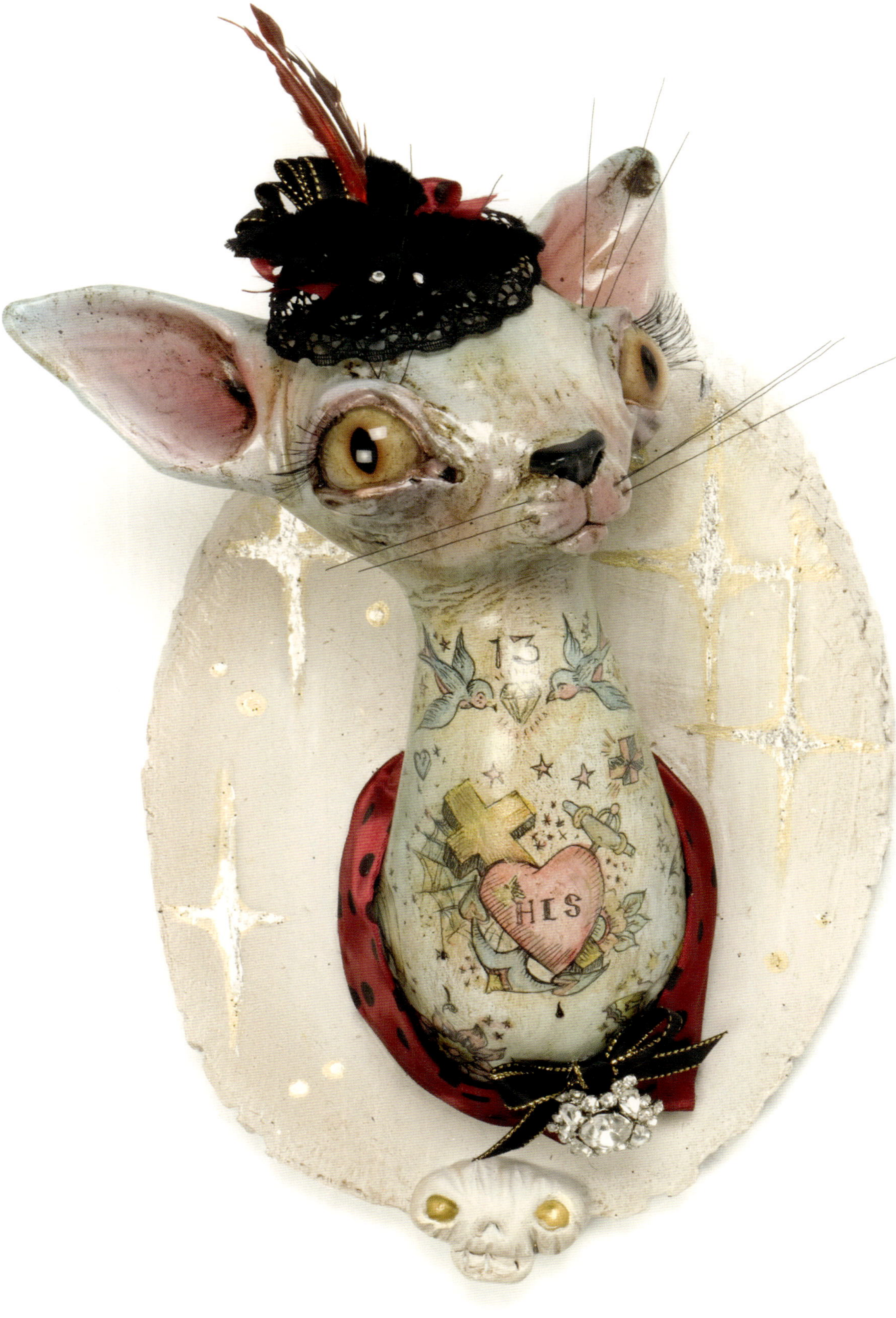
13
HIS

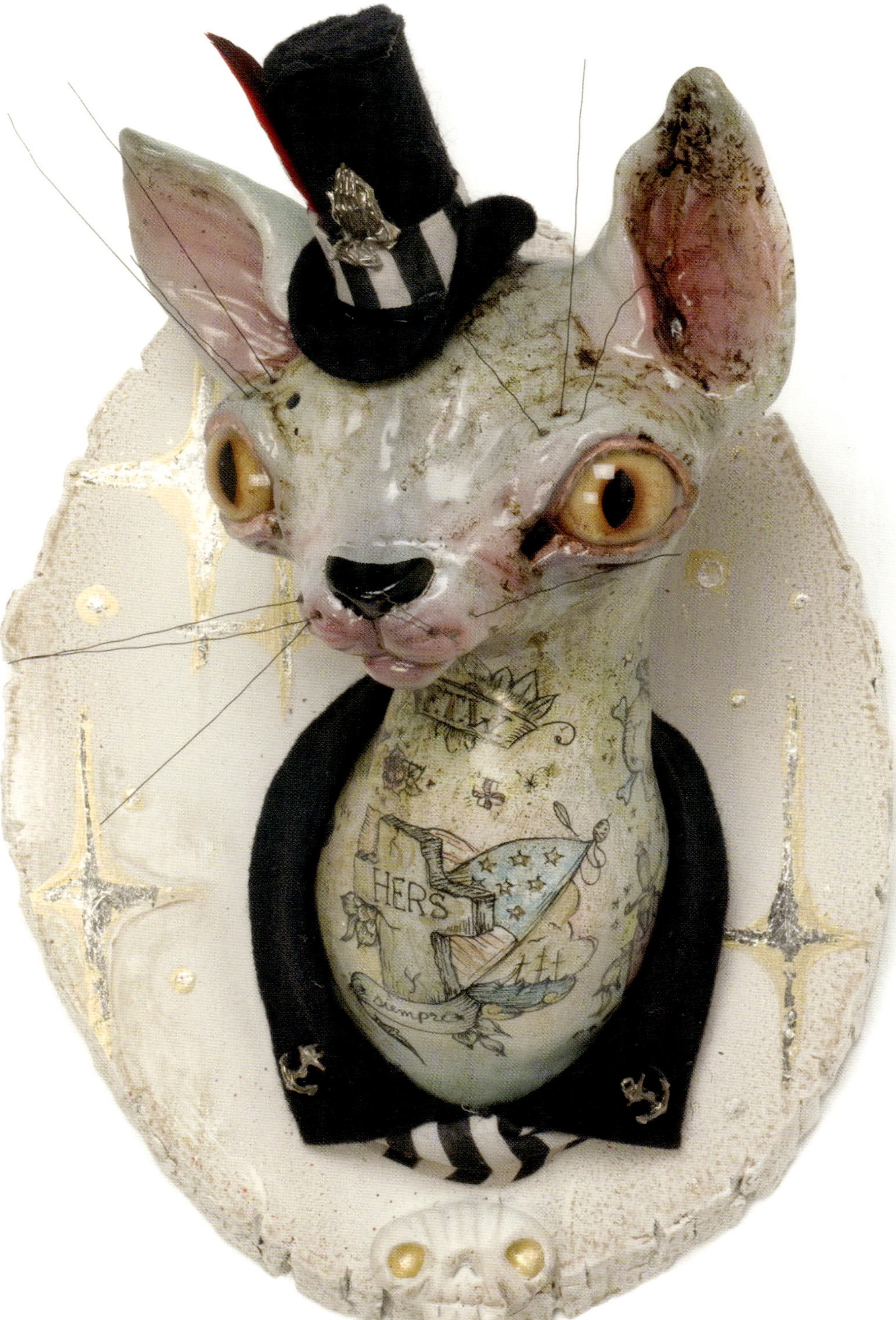
HERS
siempre

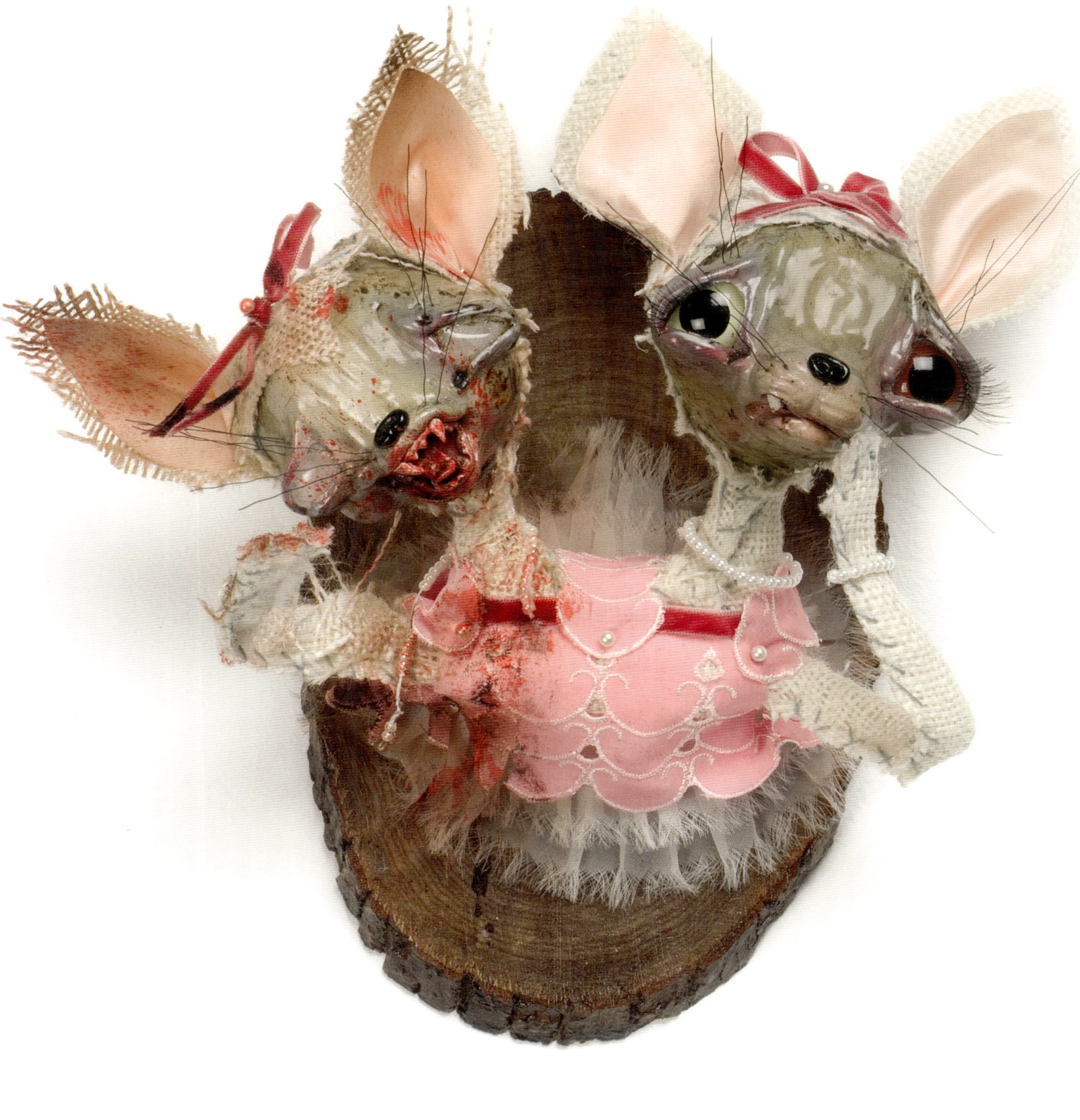

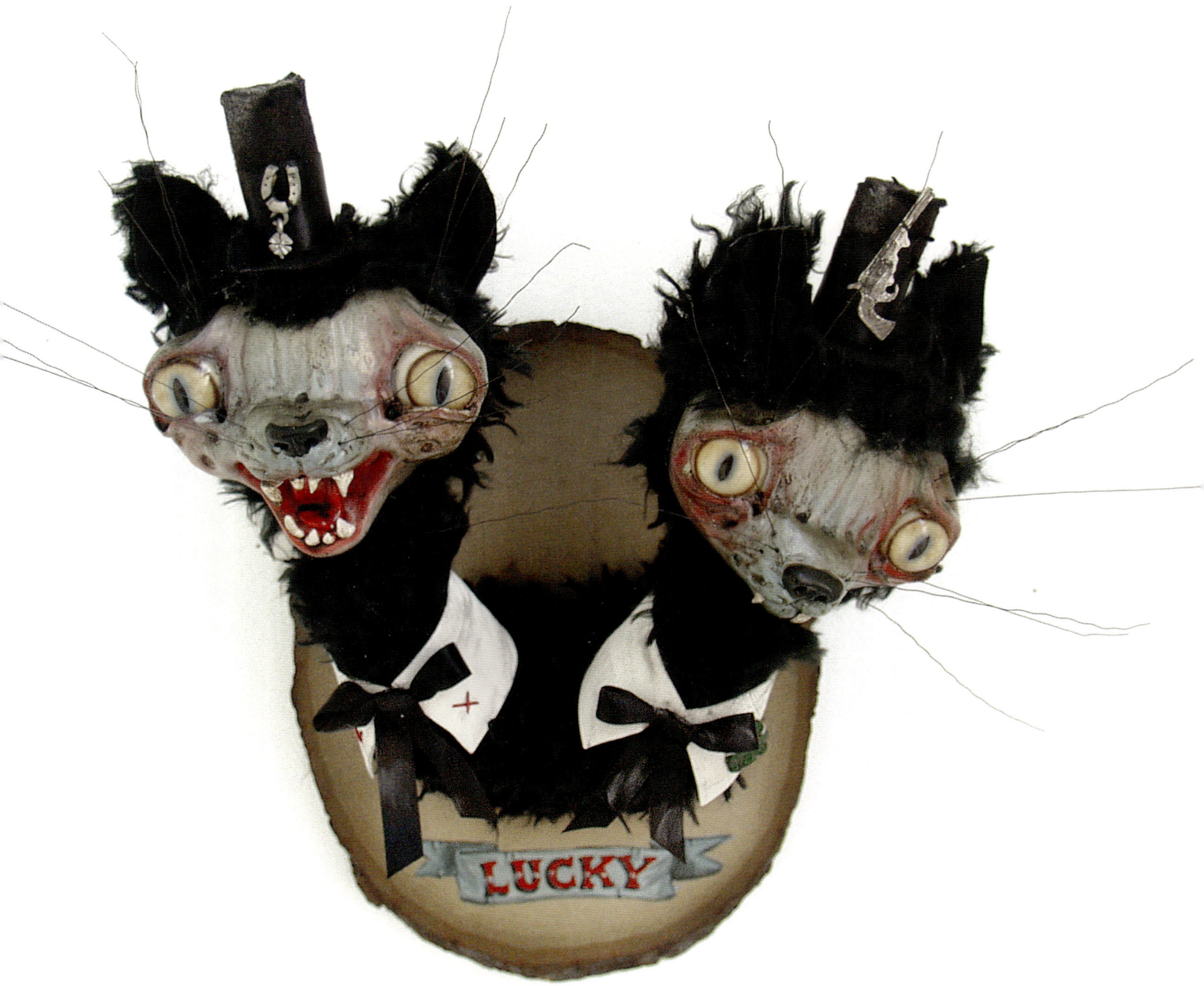
LUCKY

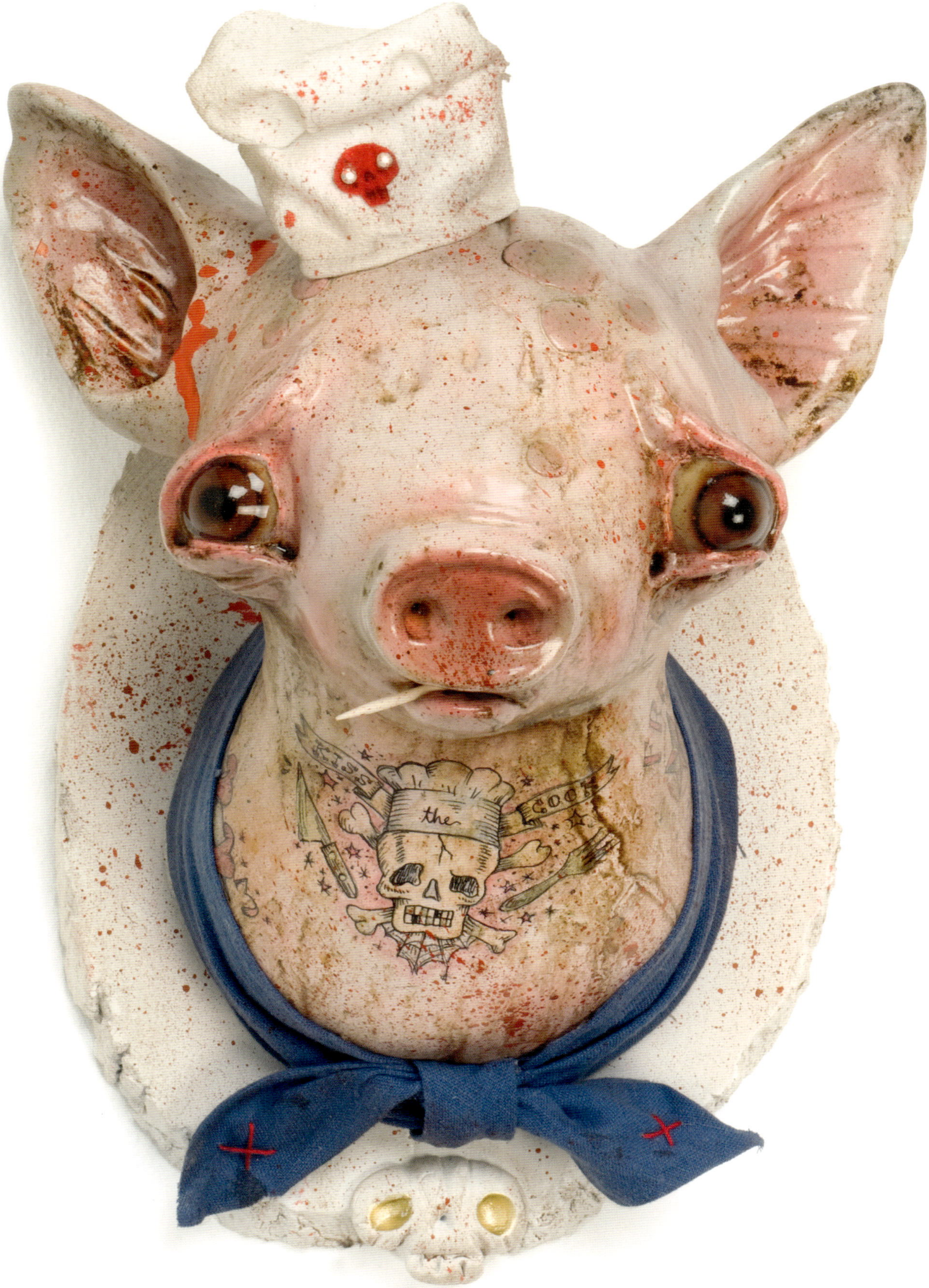
KISS
the

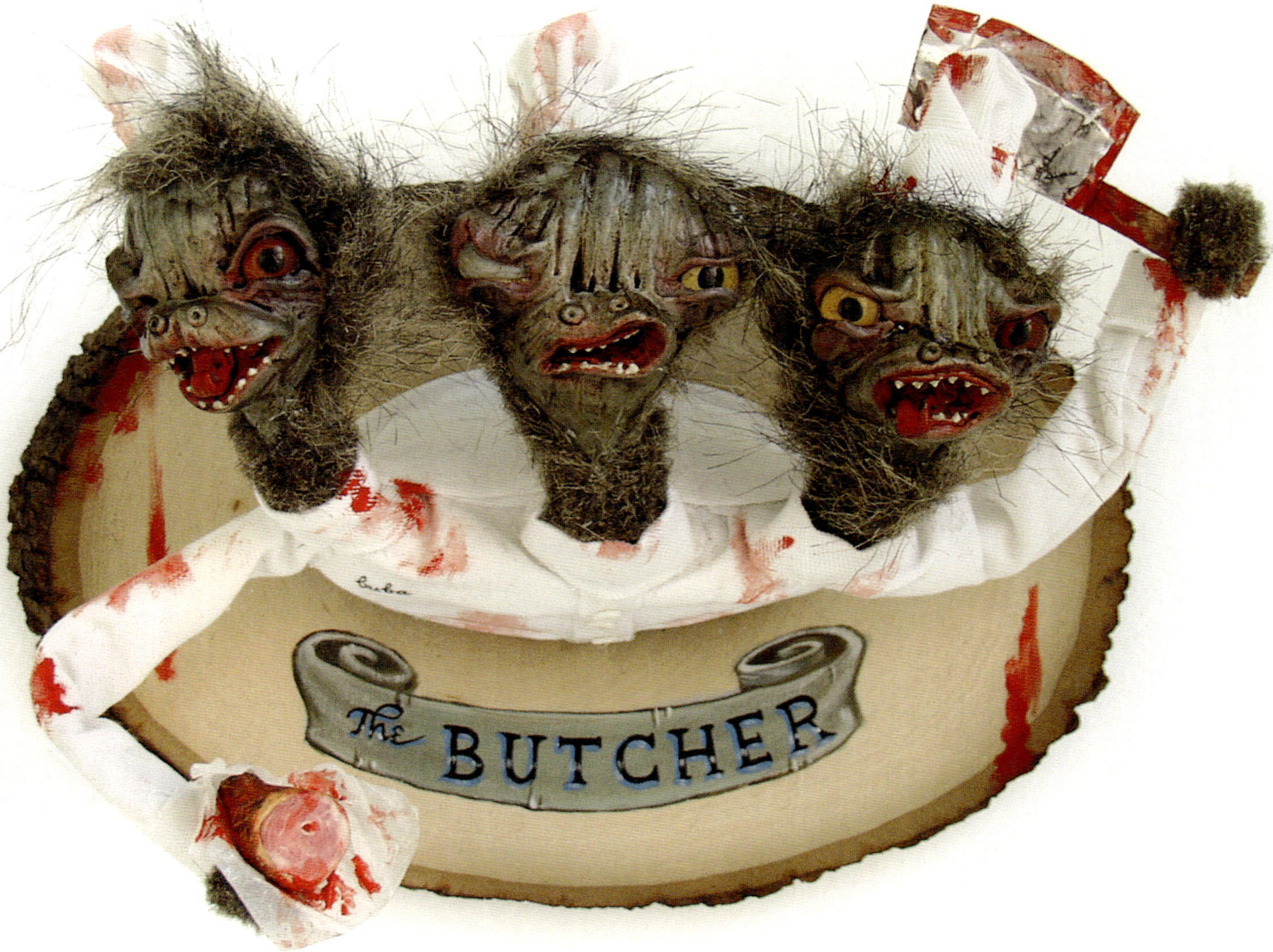
The BUTCHER

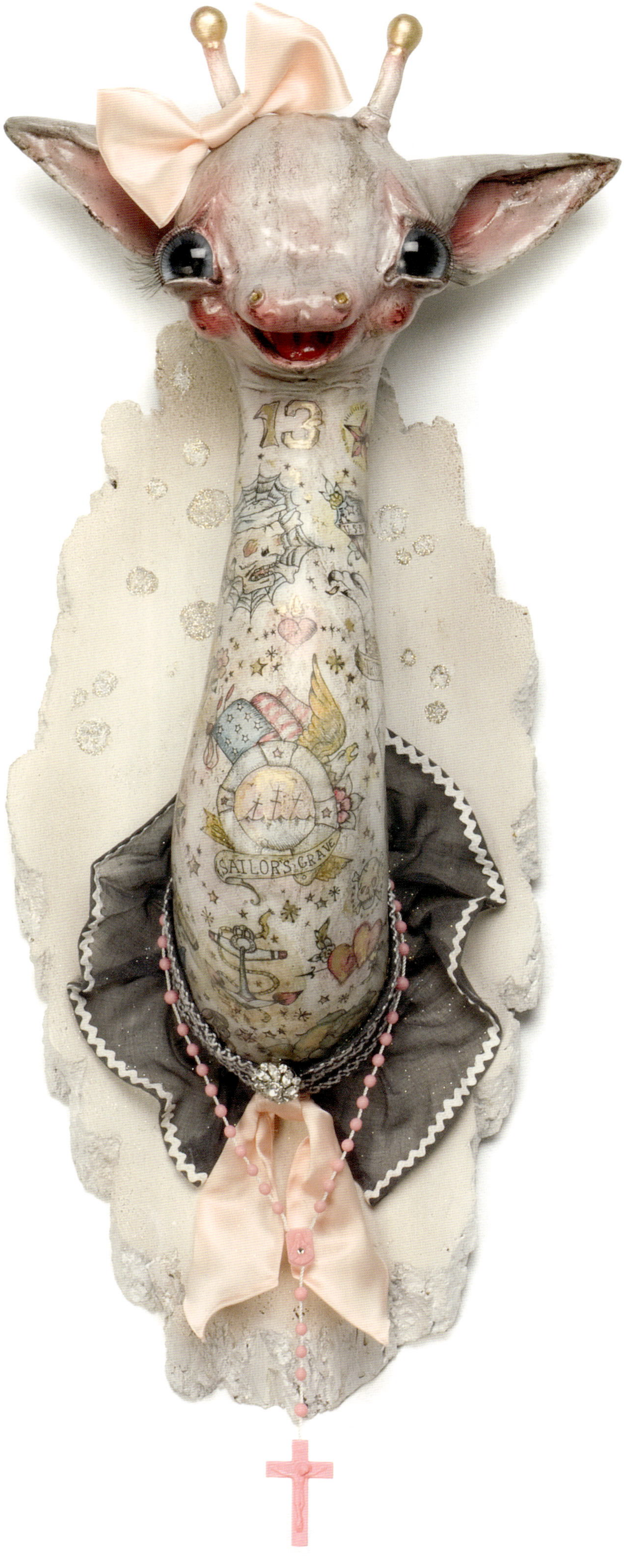
13
SAILOR'S GRAVE

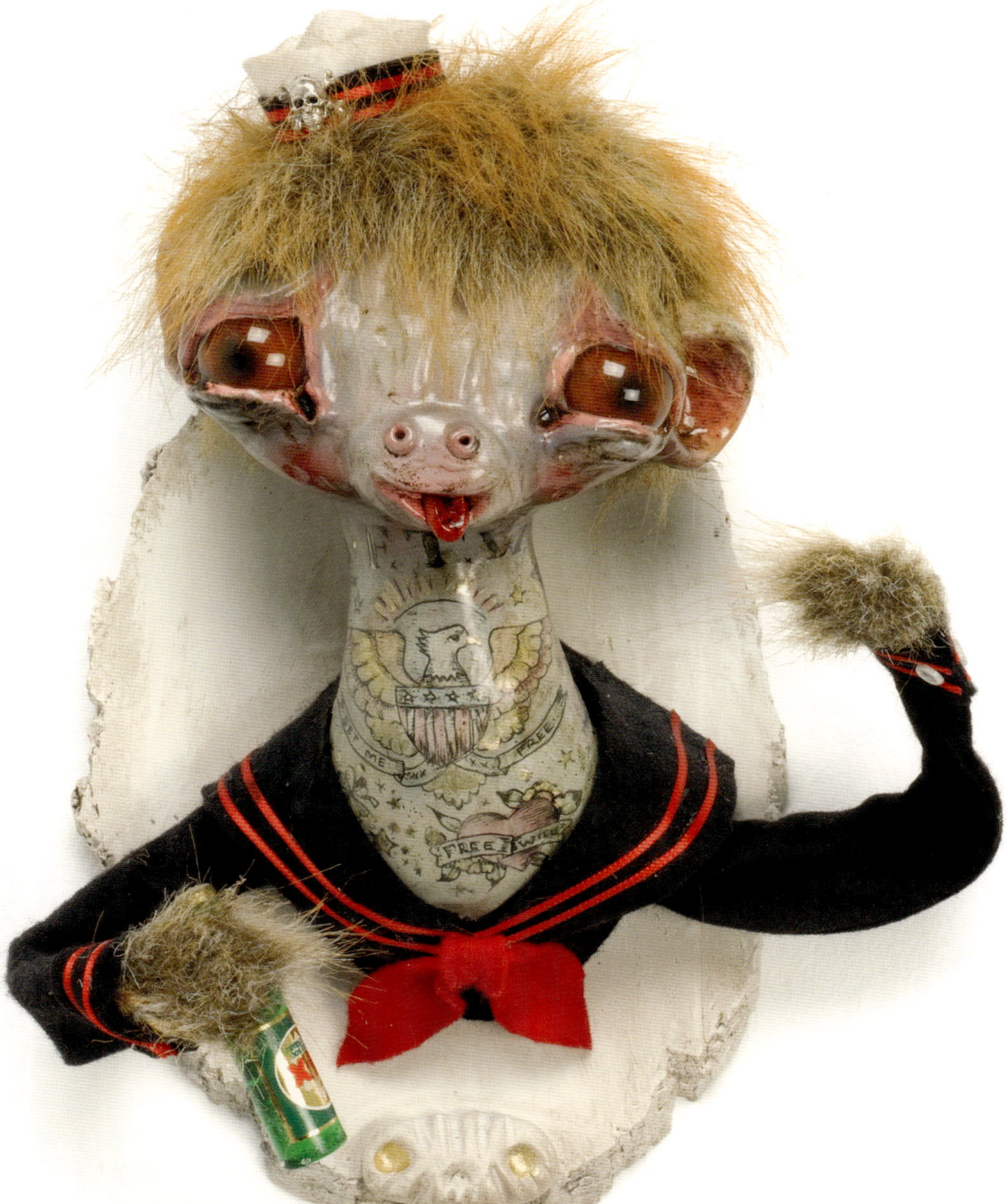

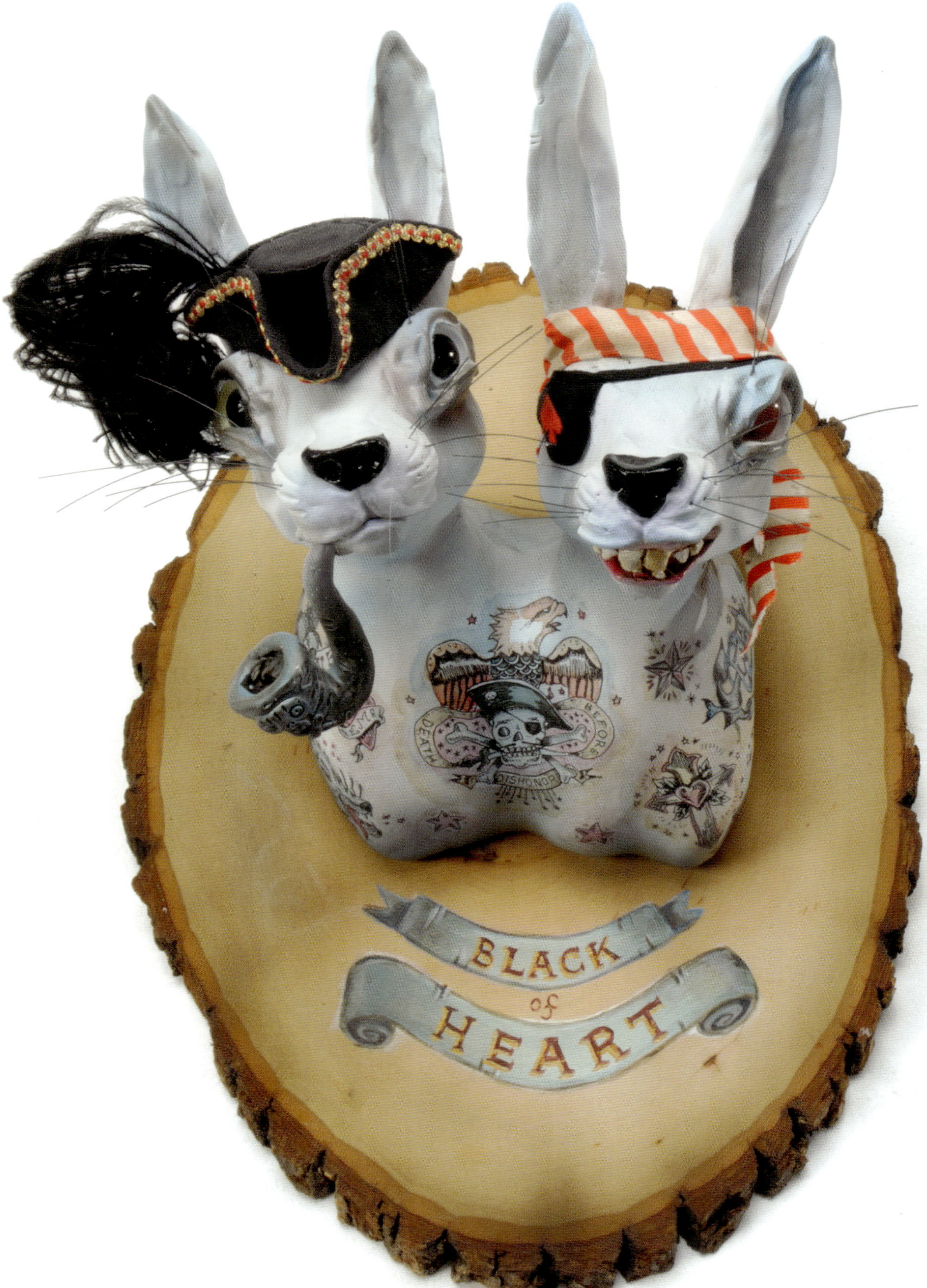
BLACK
of
HEART
DEATH BEFORE DISHONOR

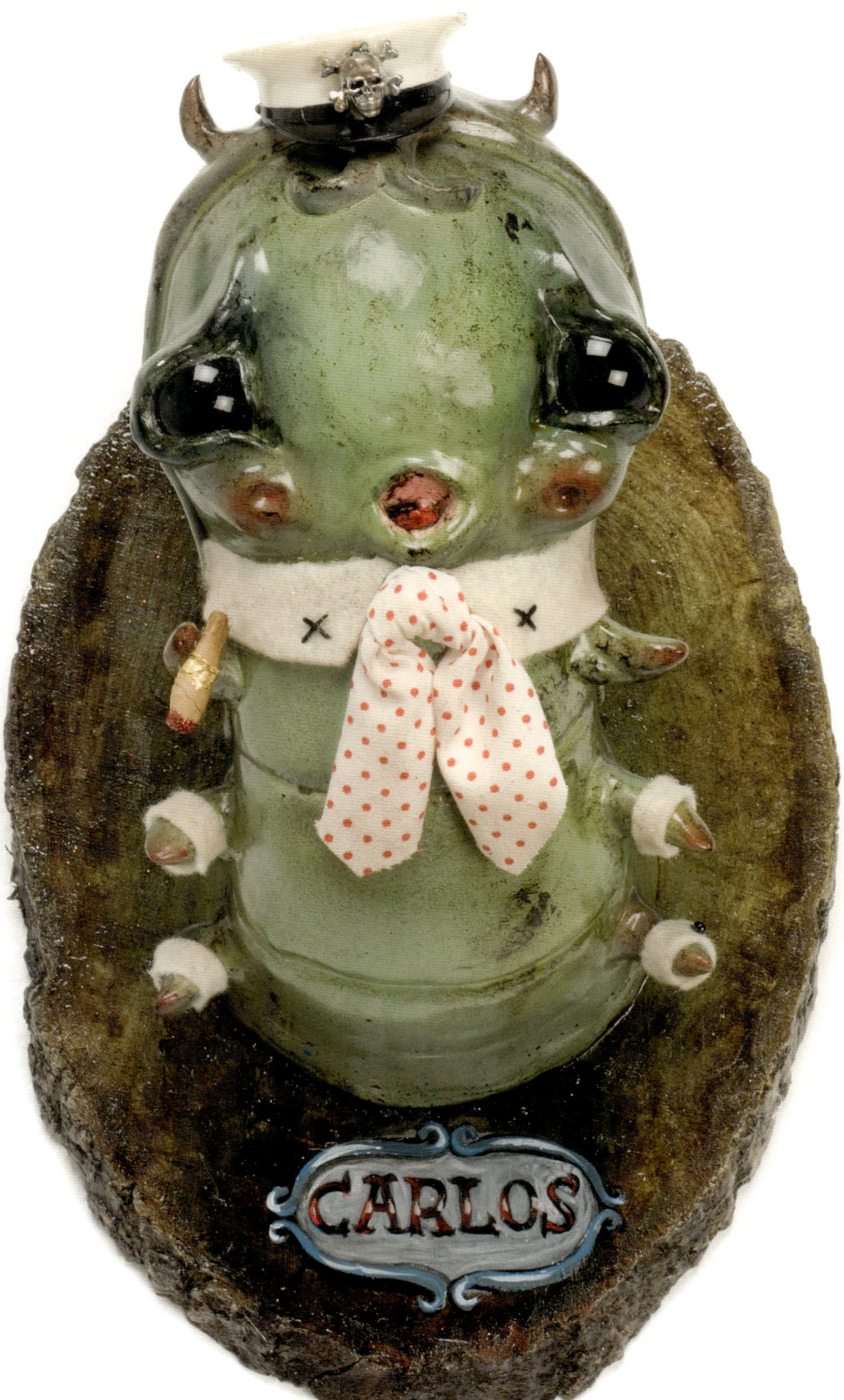
CARLOS

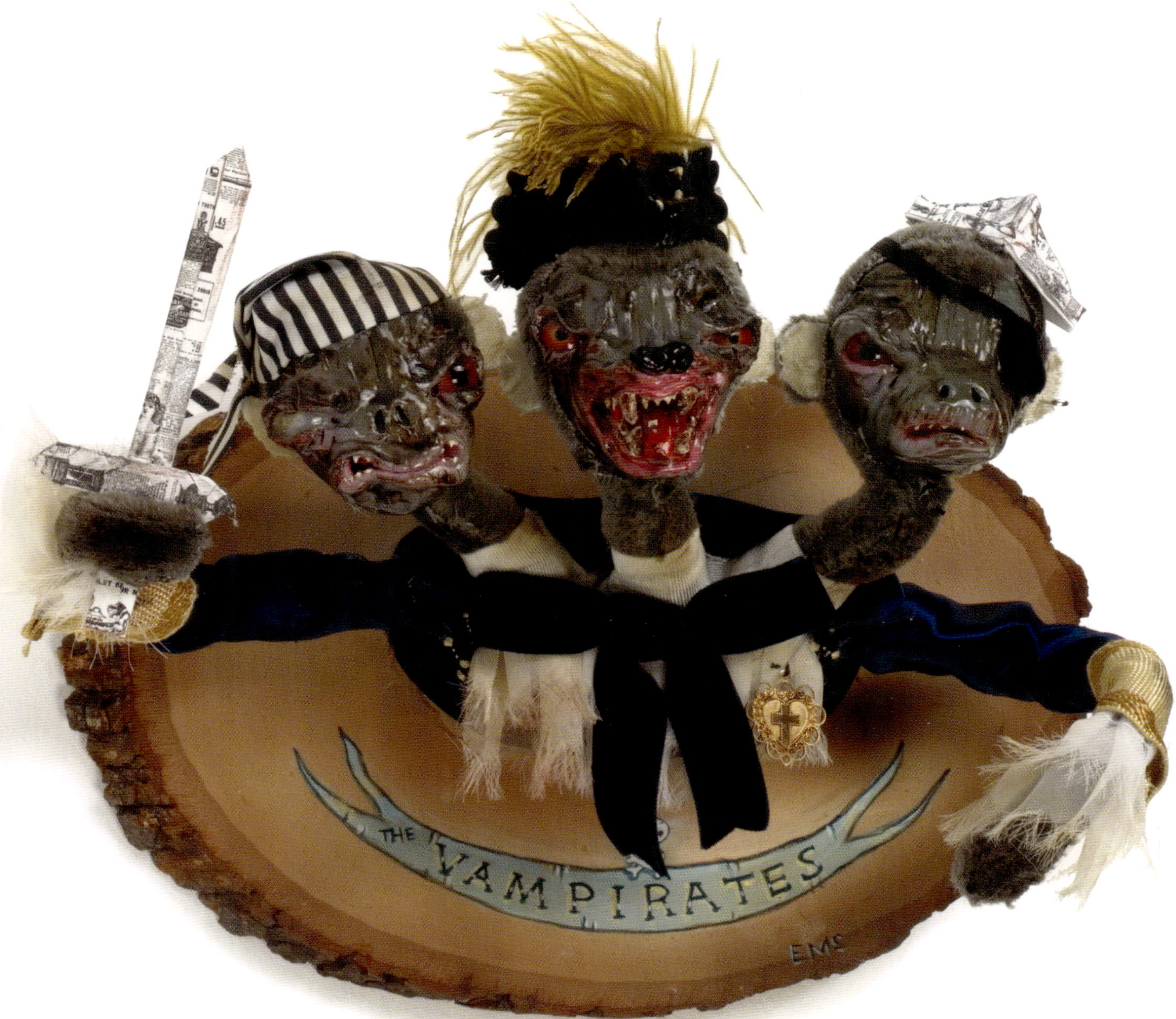
THE VAMPIRATES
EMc

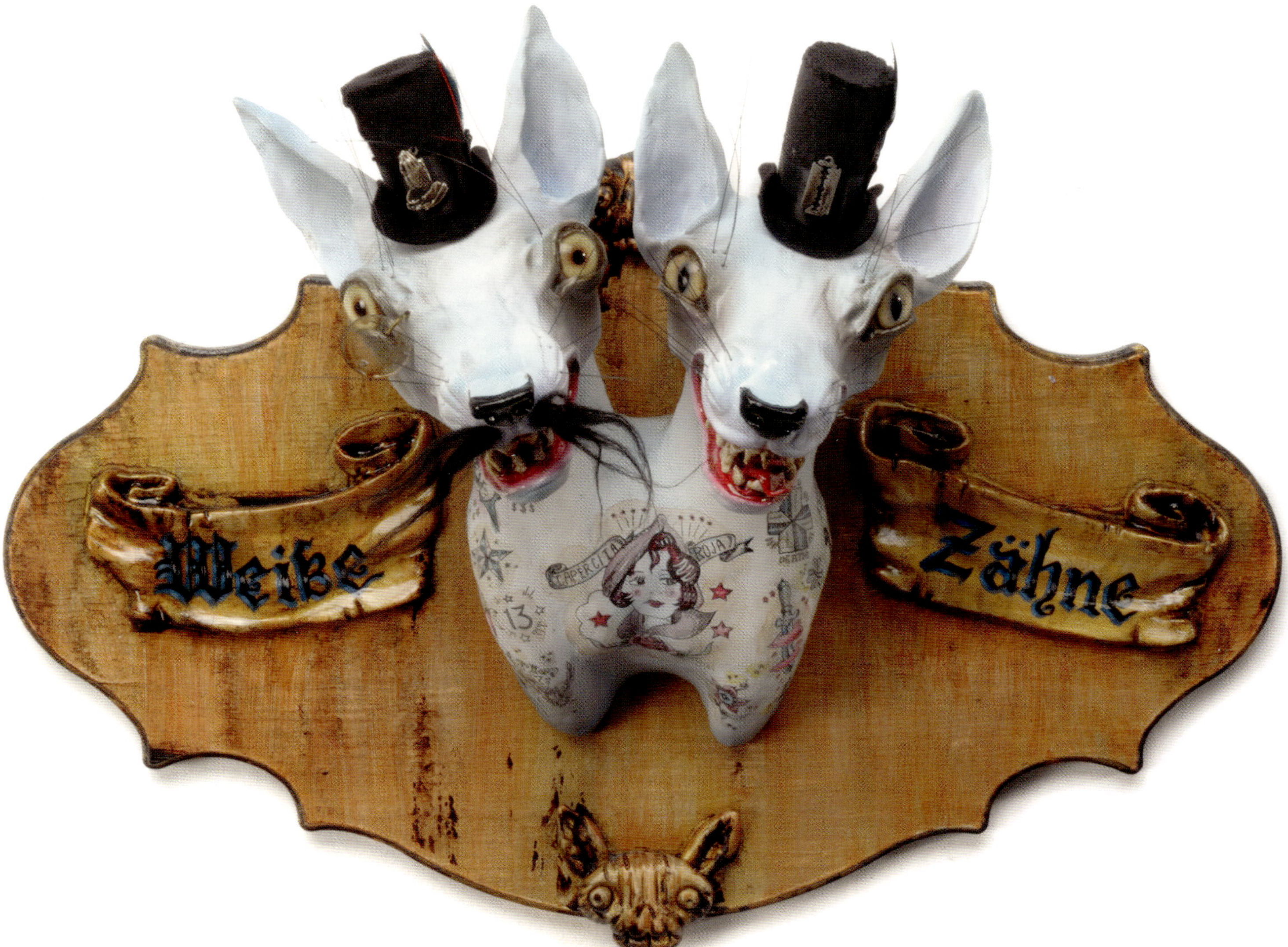
Weiße
Zähne

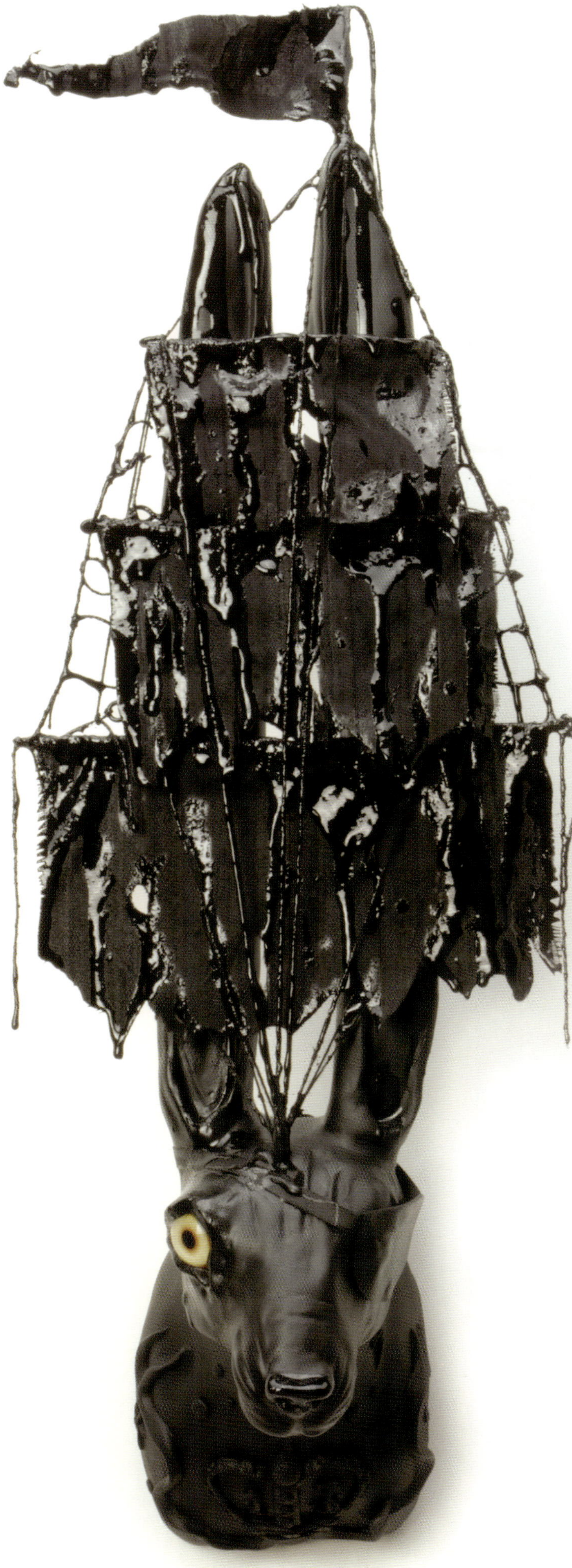

Shadowless Summer

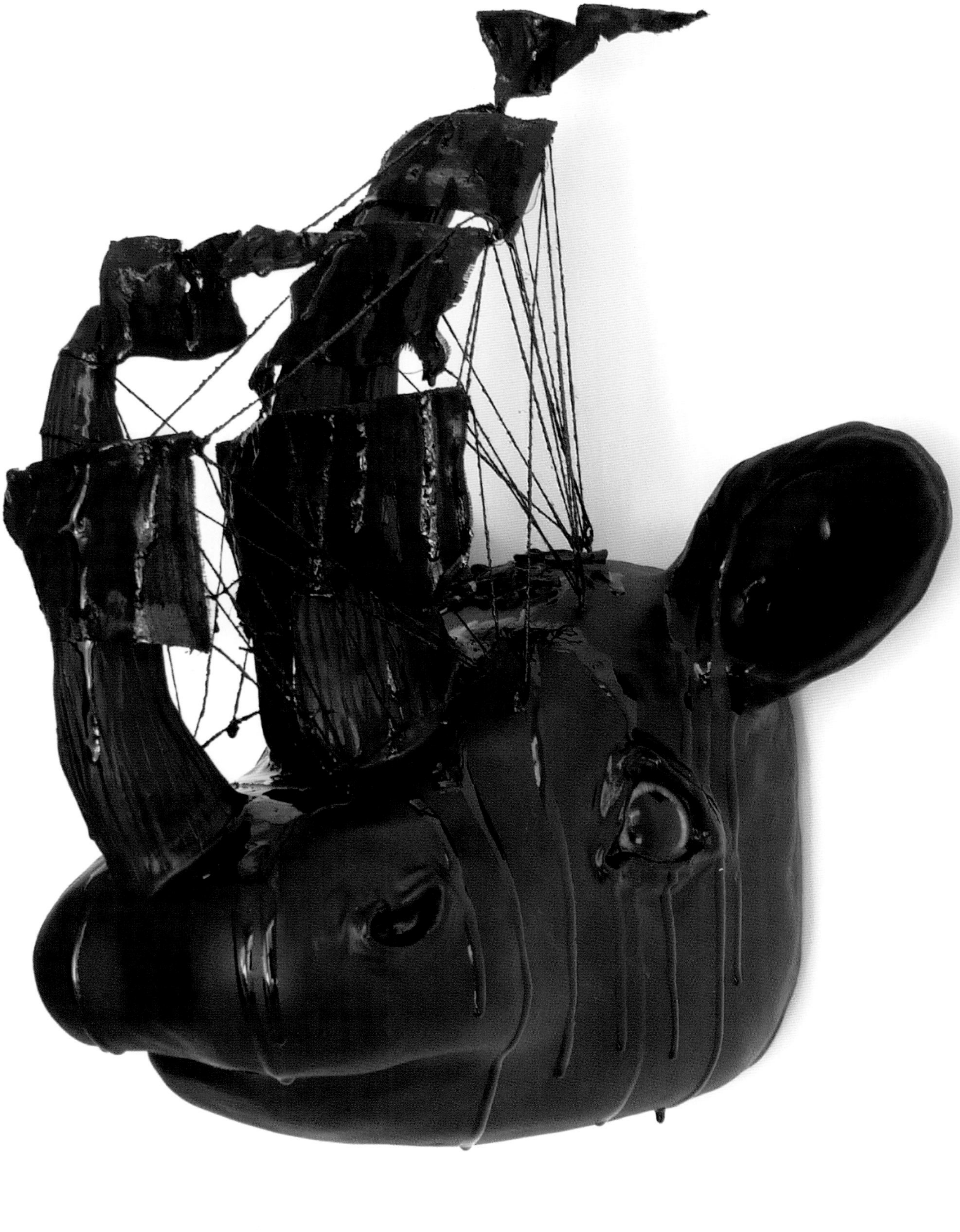

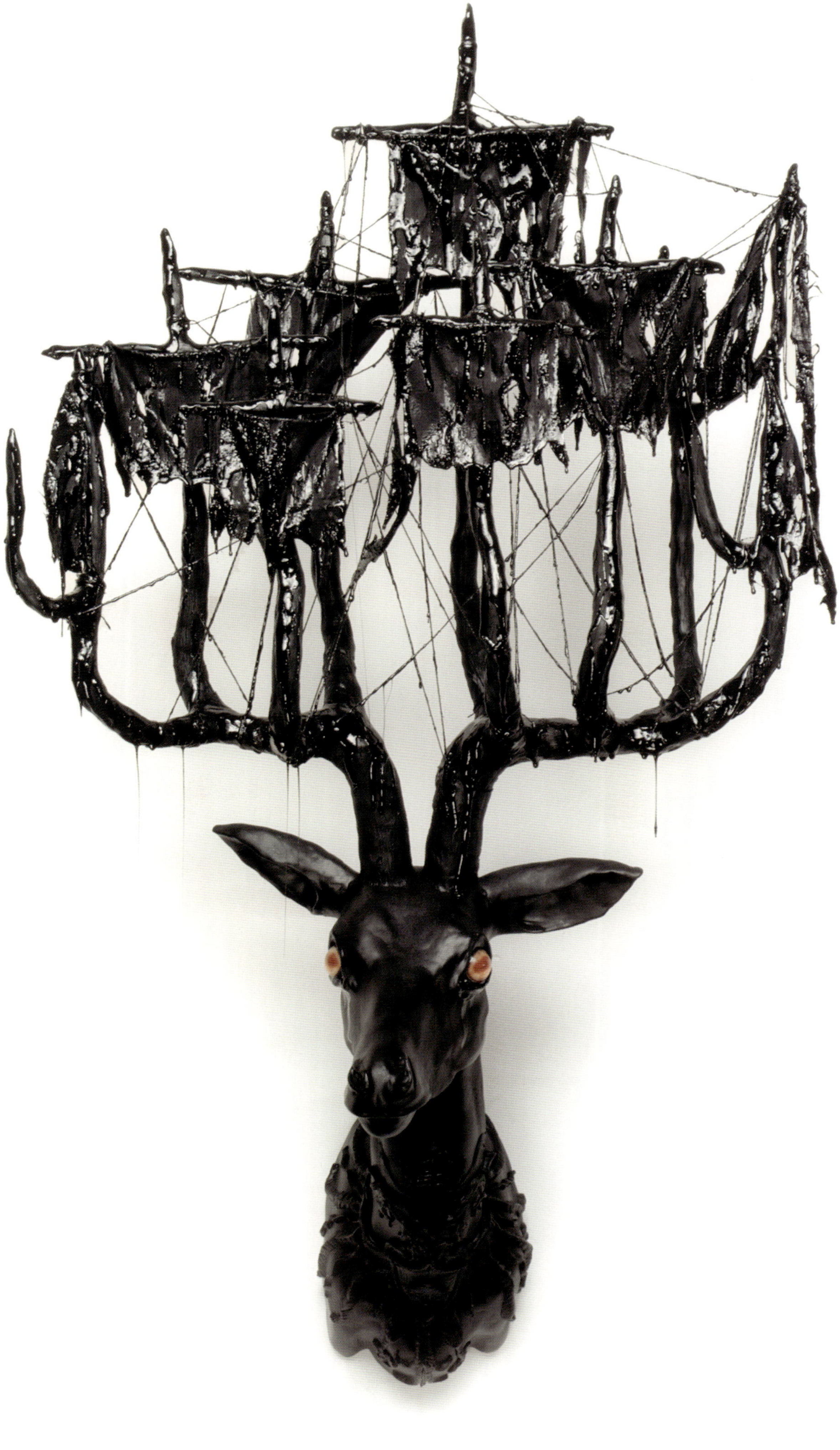

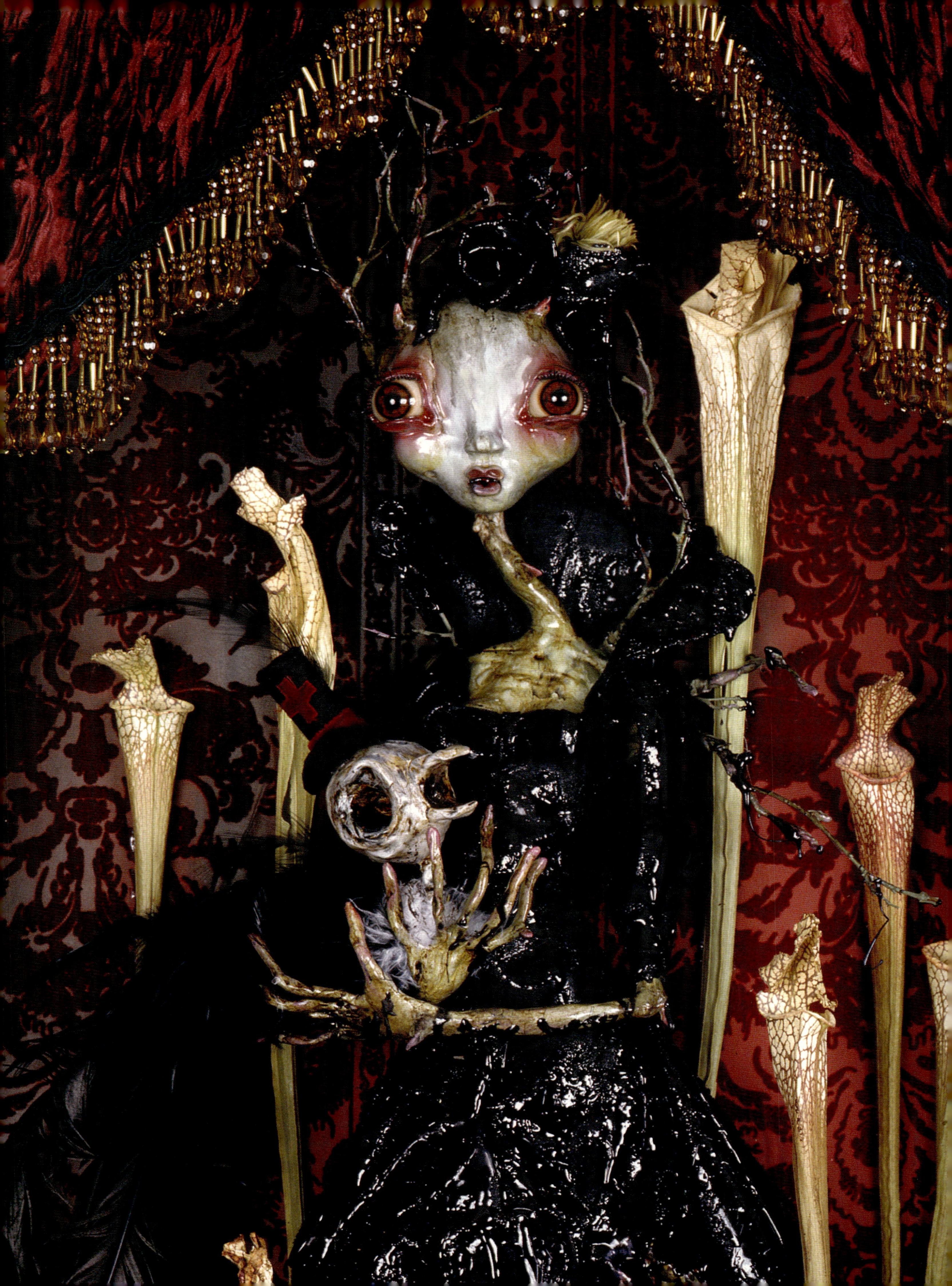

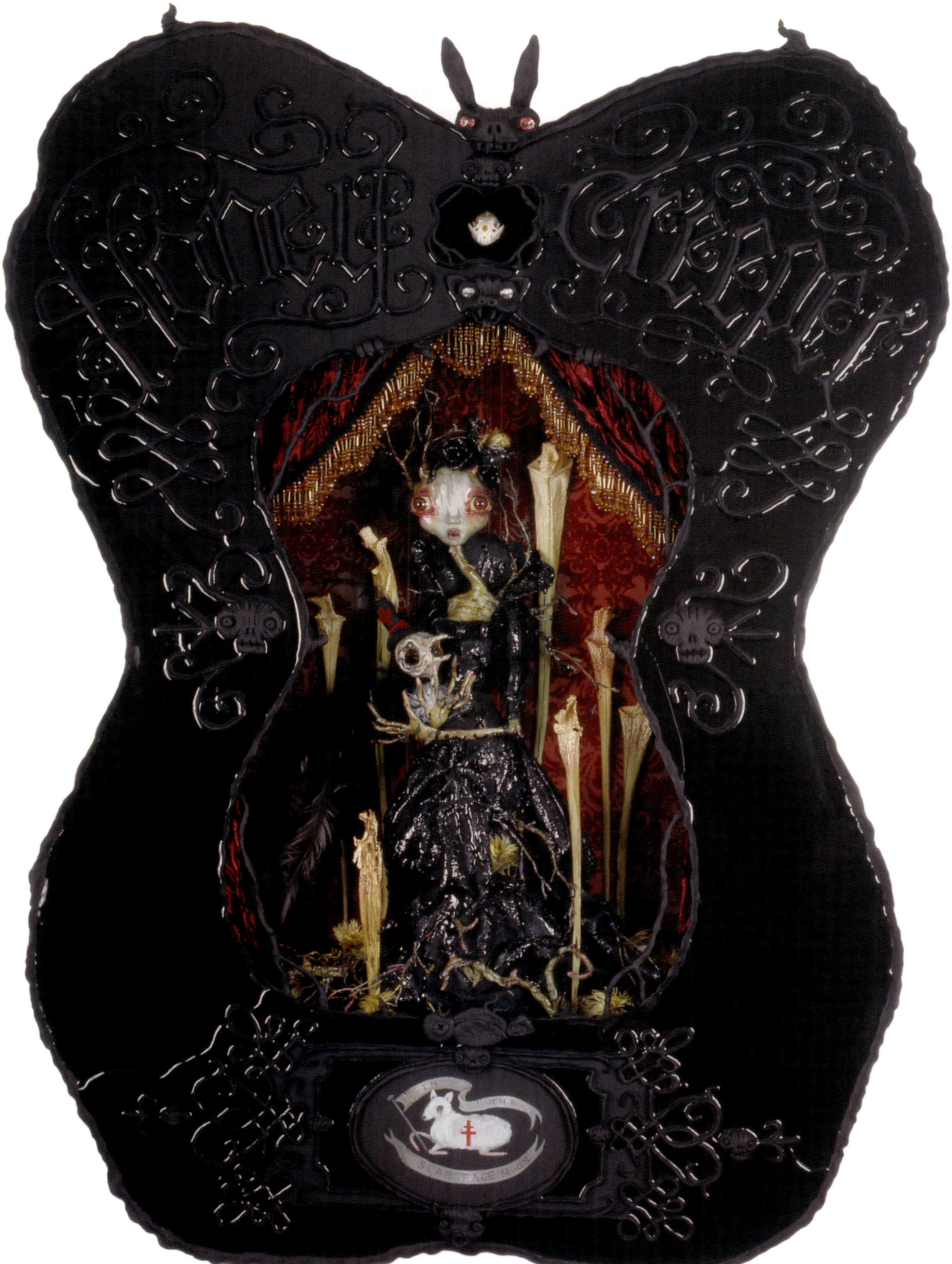

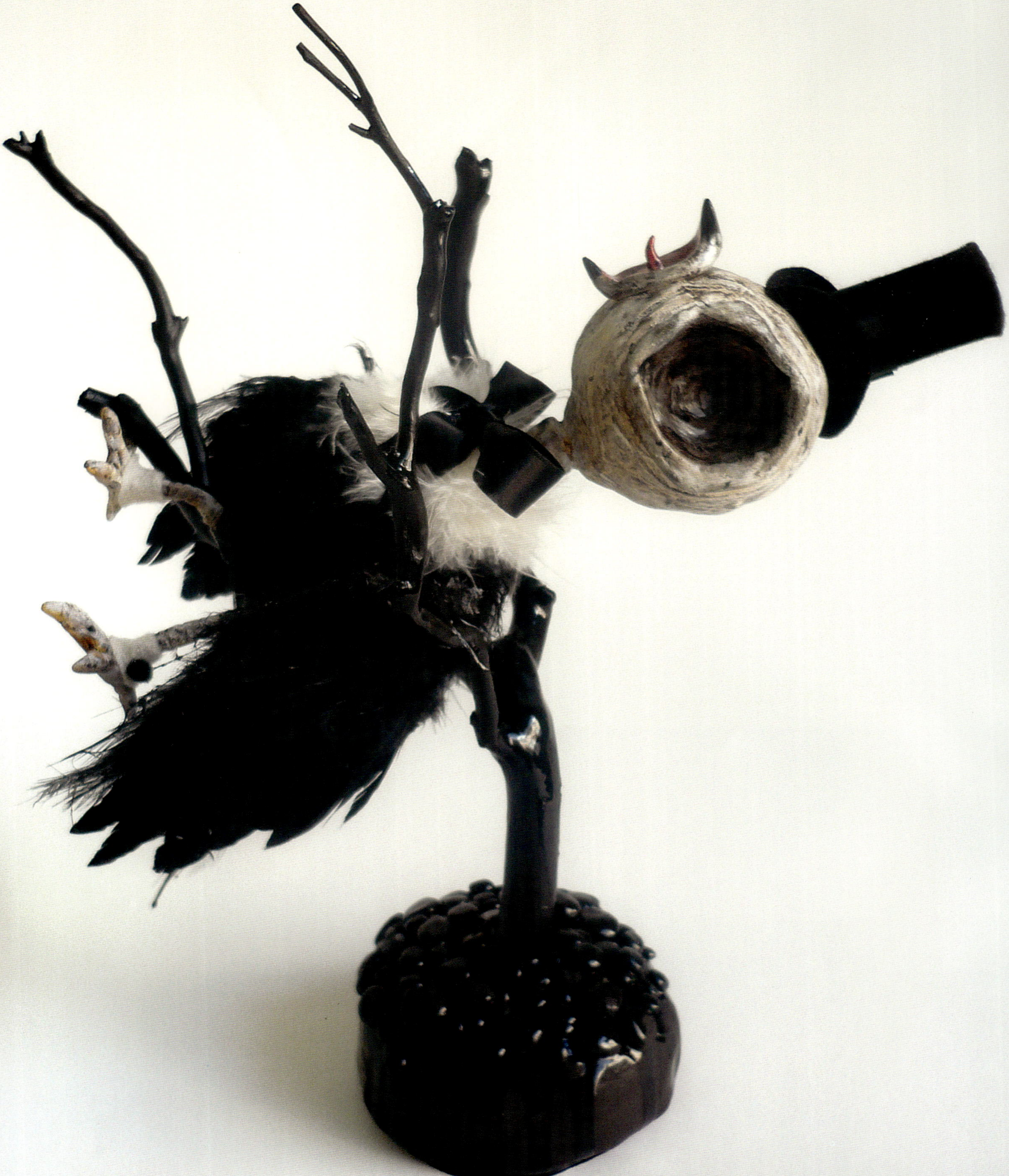

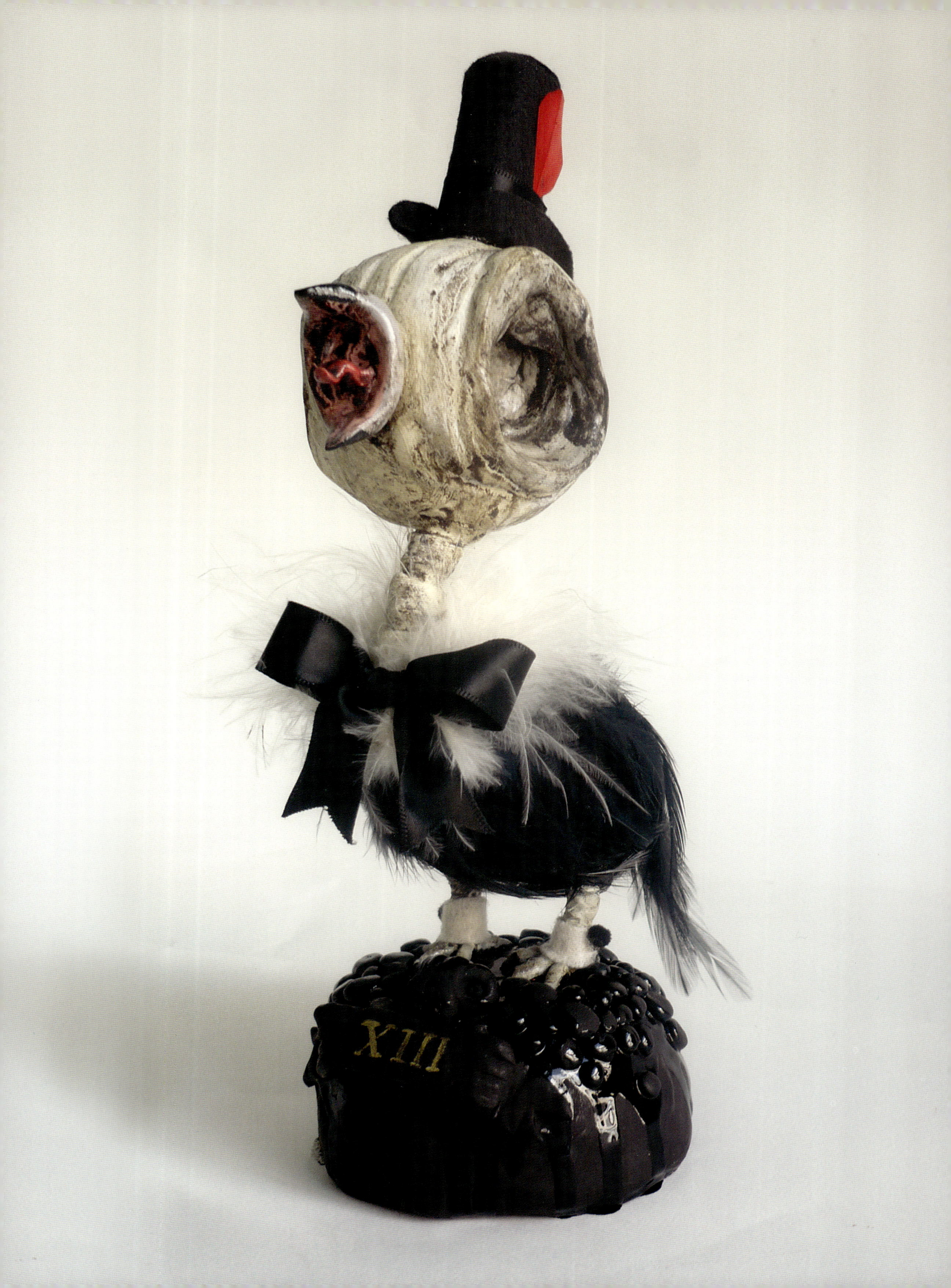
XIII

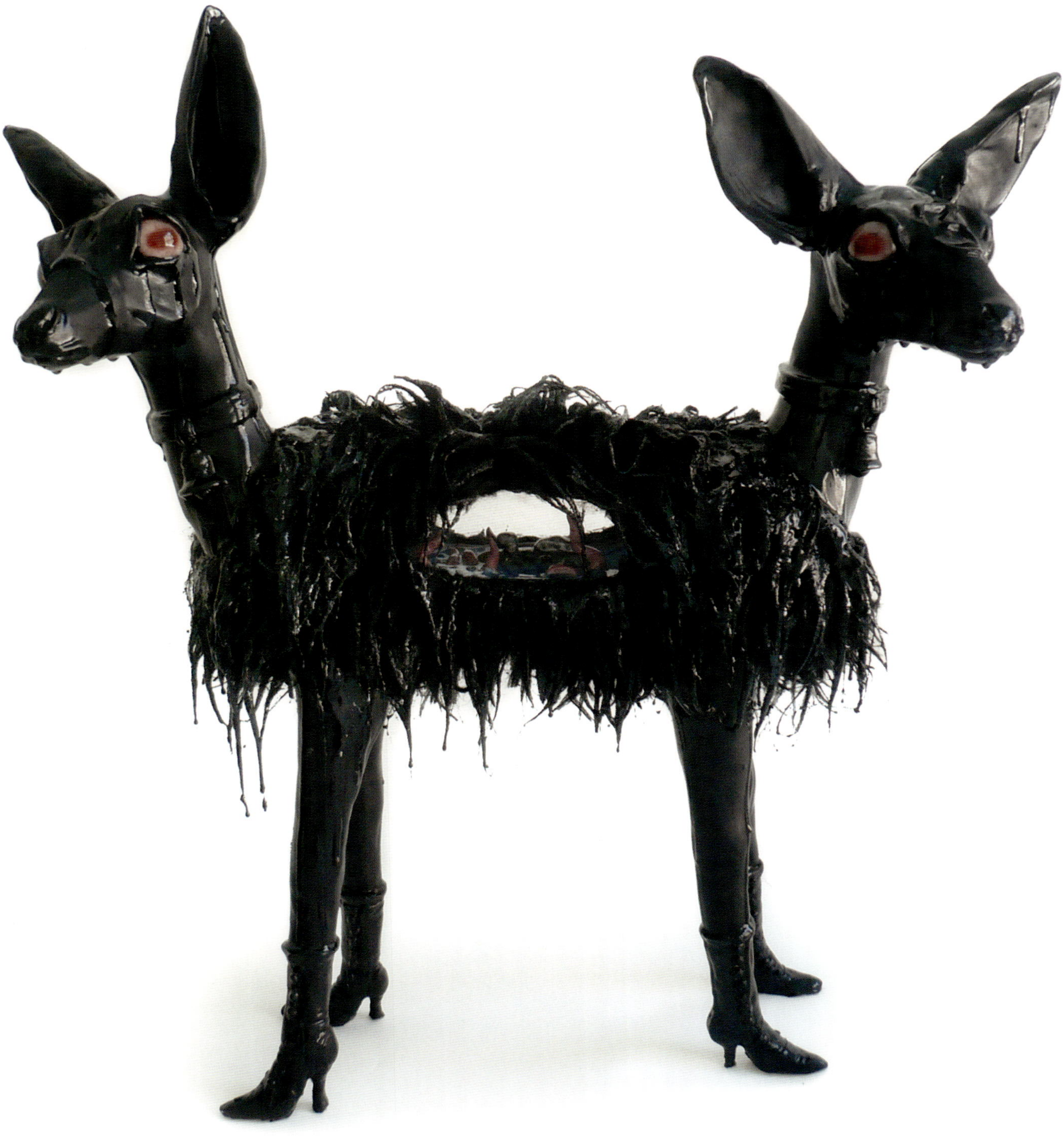

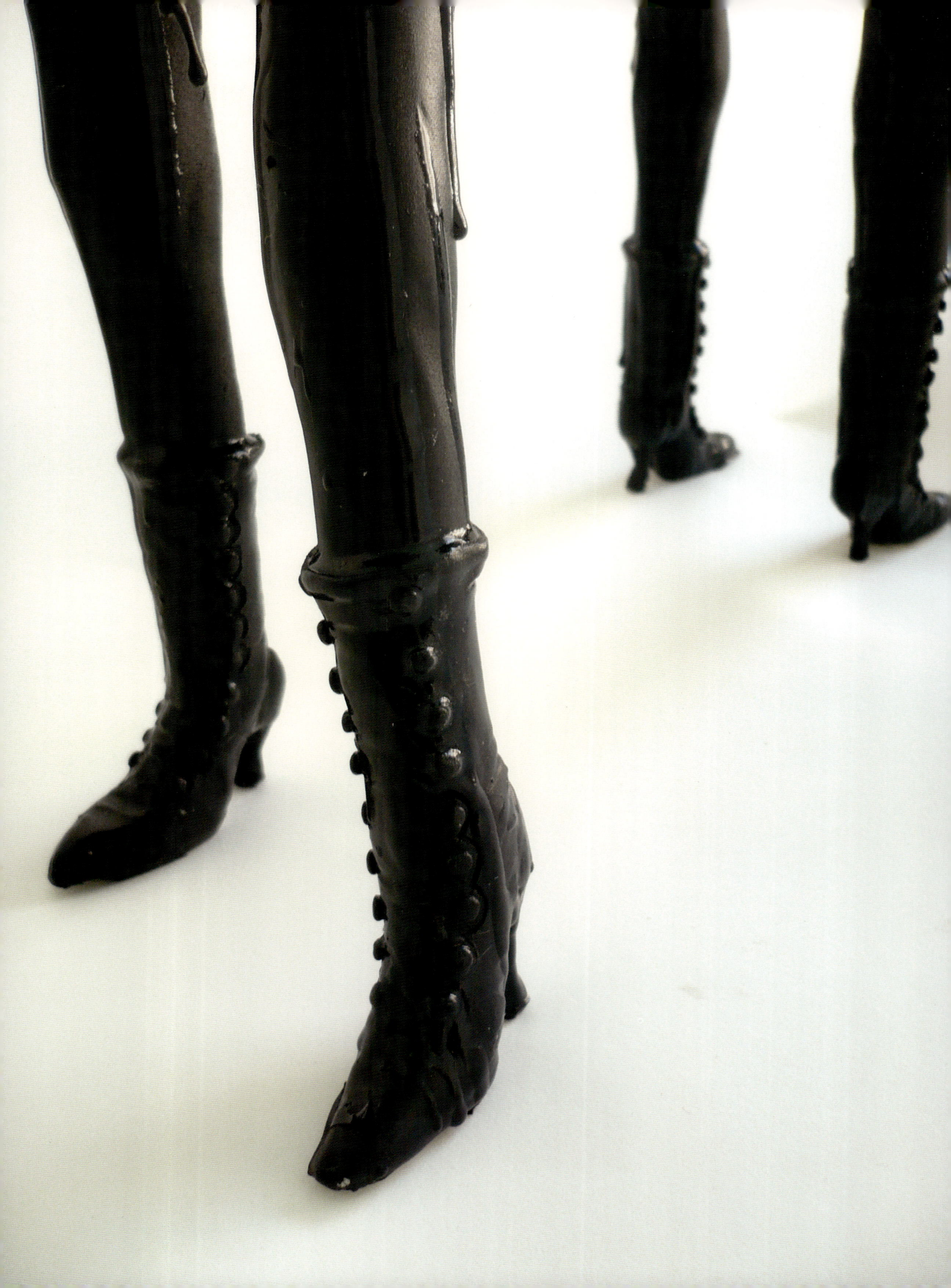

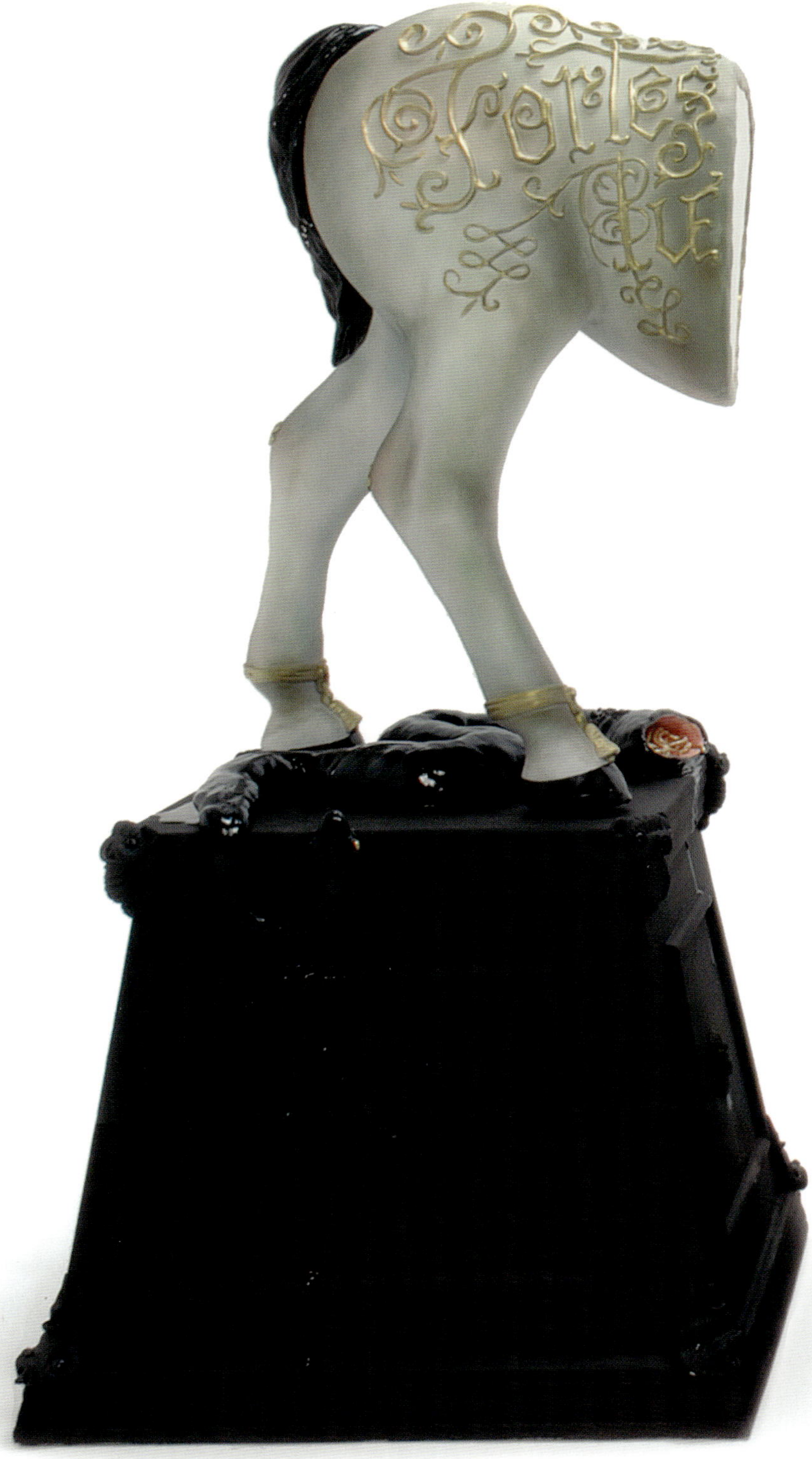

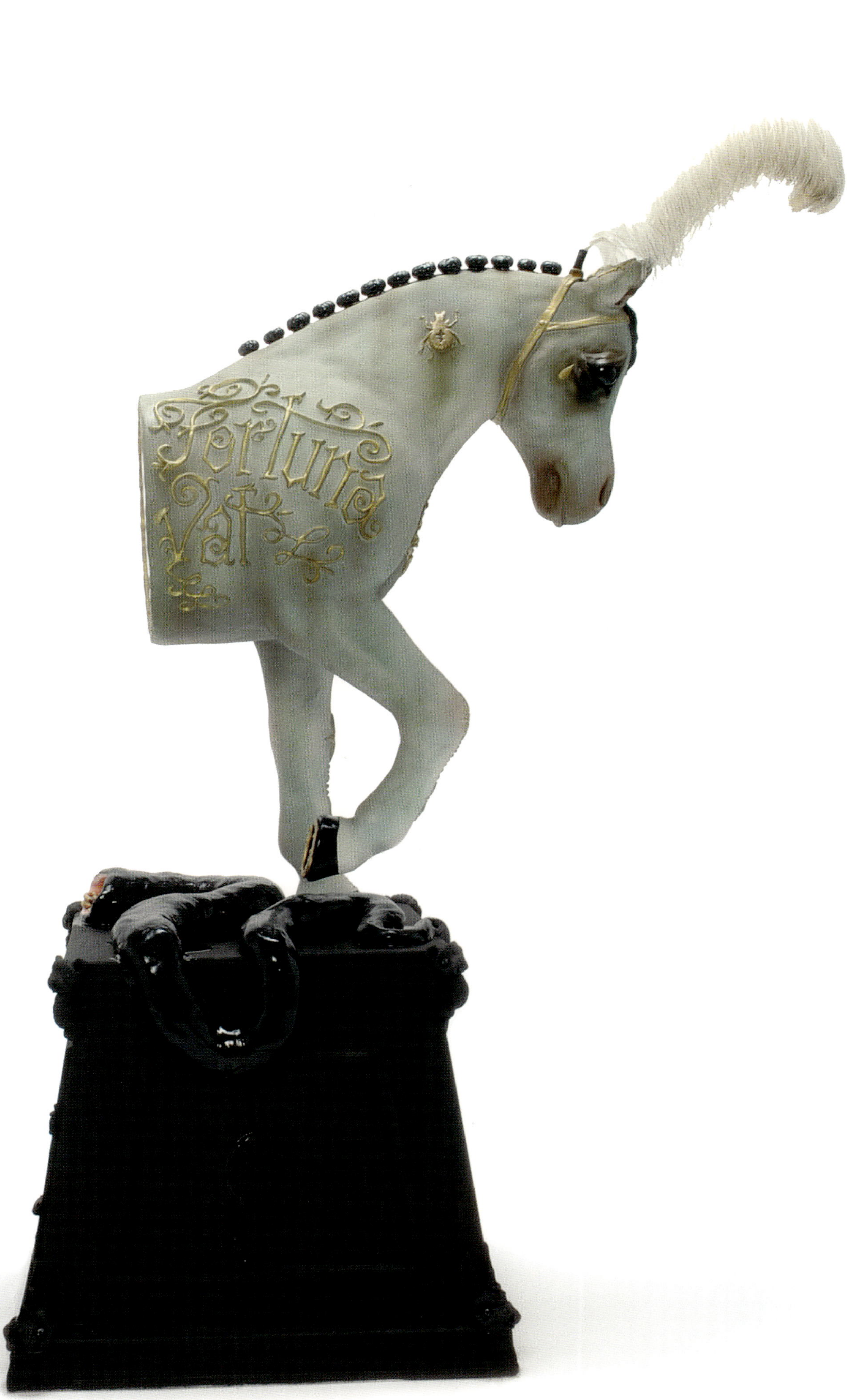
Fortuna
Vat

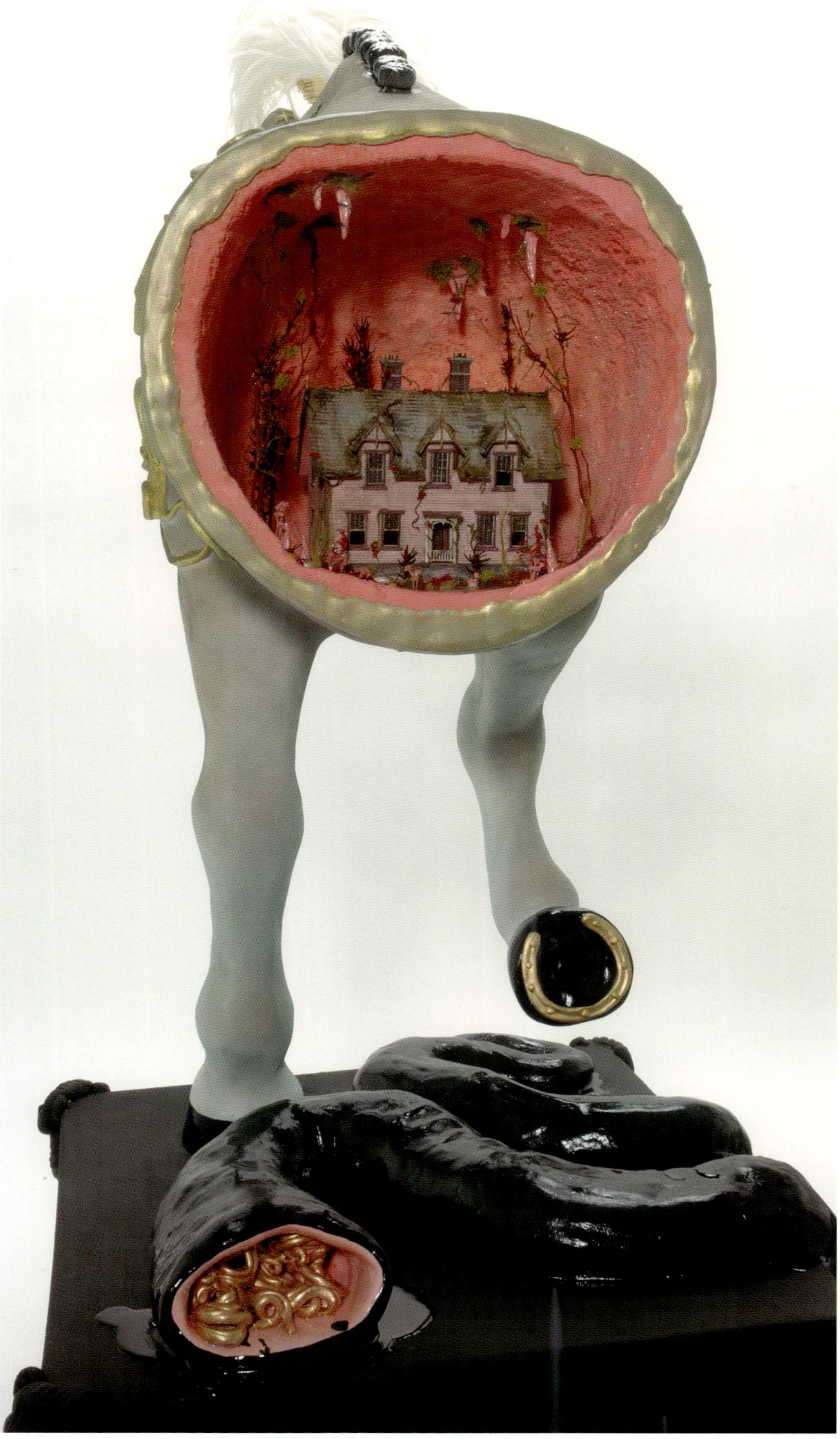

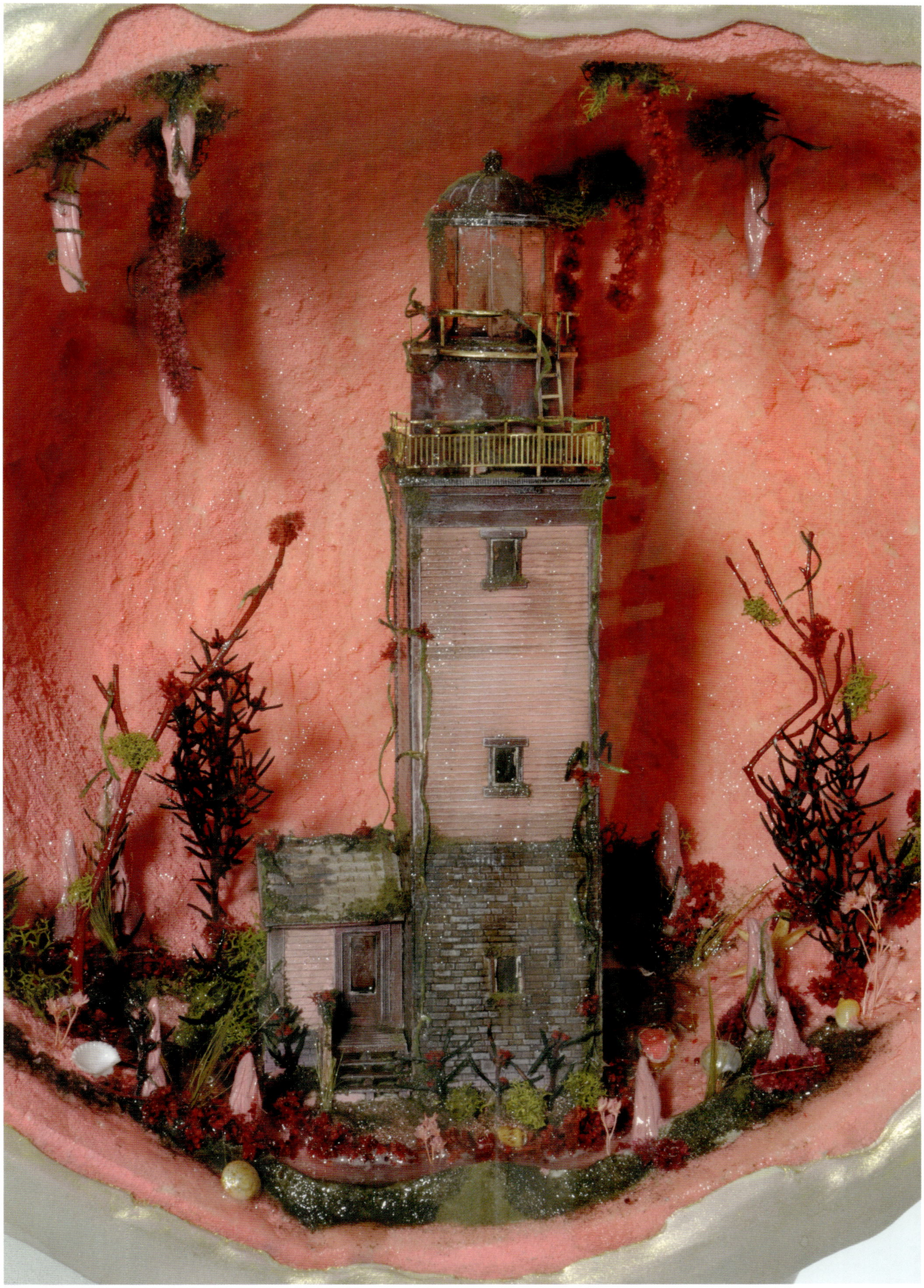

"Death glided by, shadowless,
among the empties on the grass."

Excerpt from
"The Crying of Lot 49"
Thomas Pynchon
1966

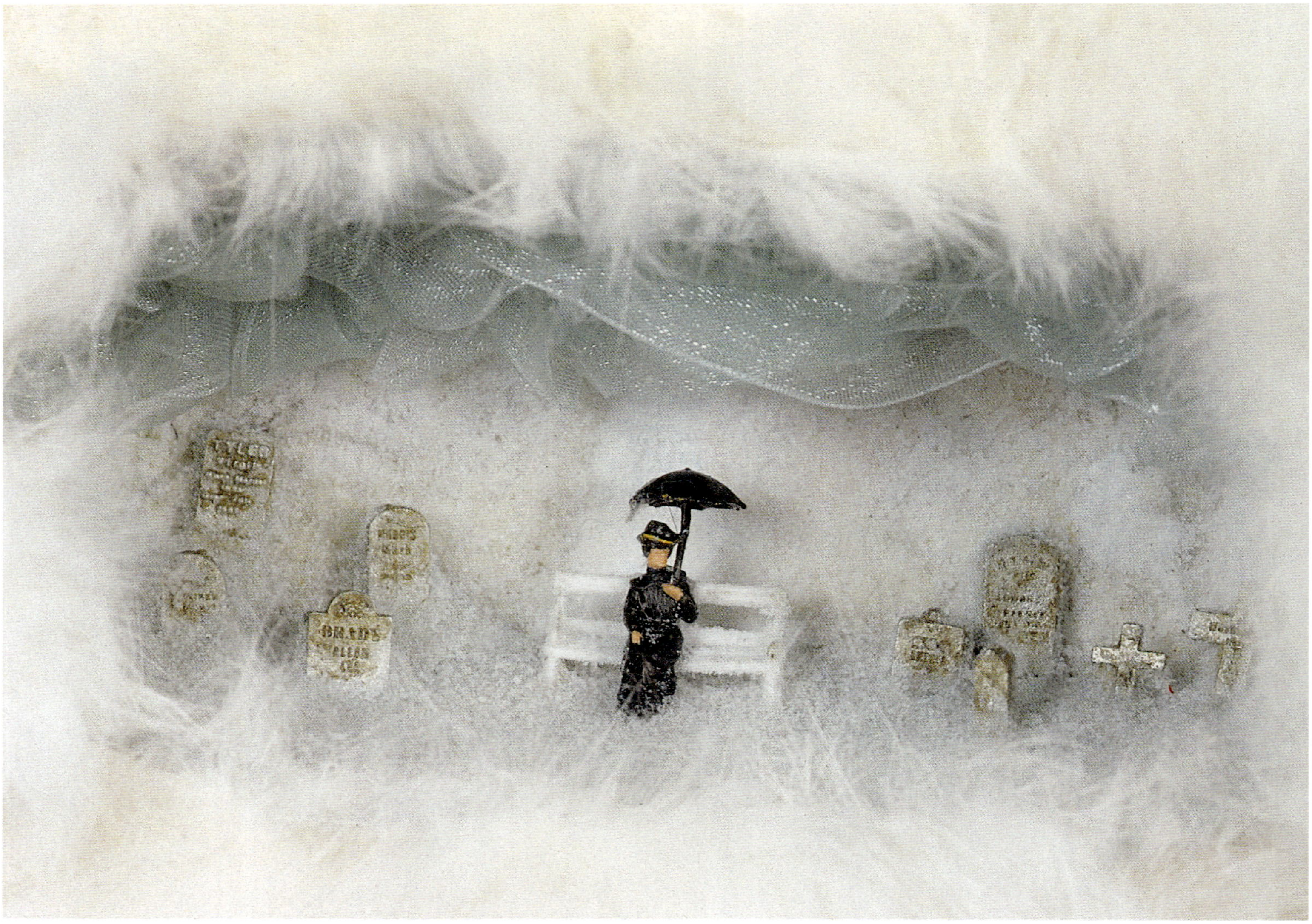

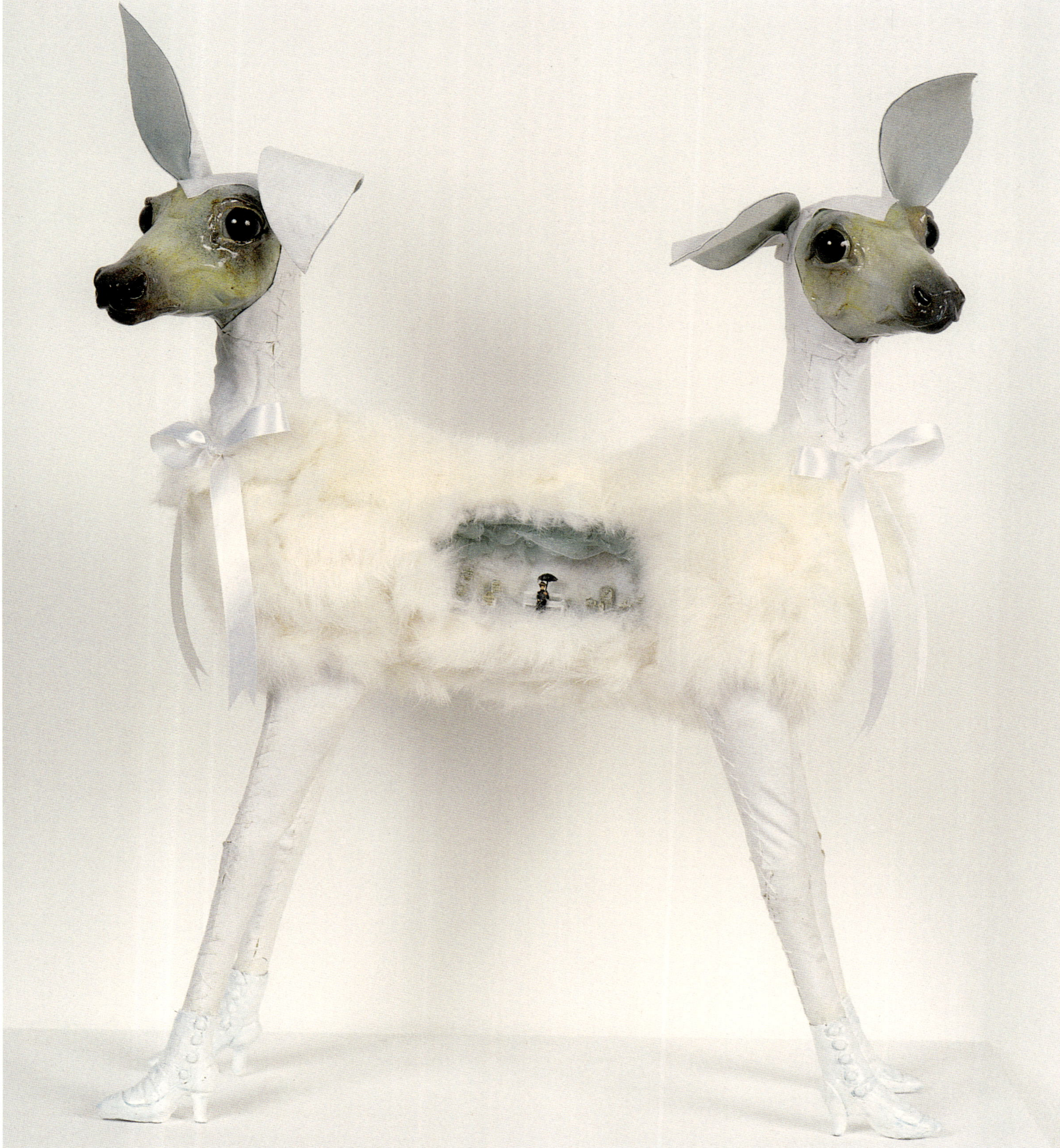

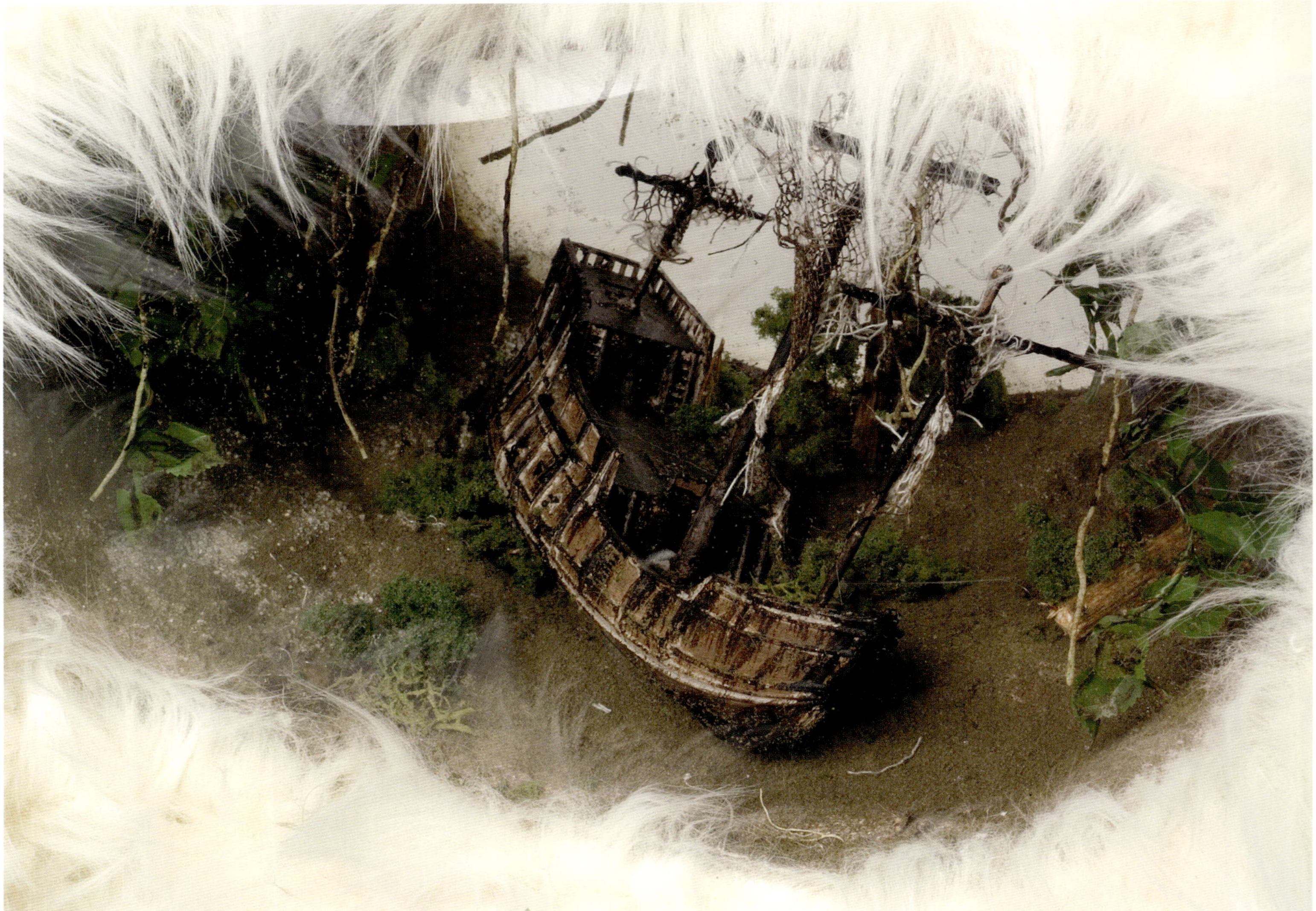

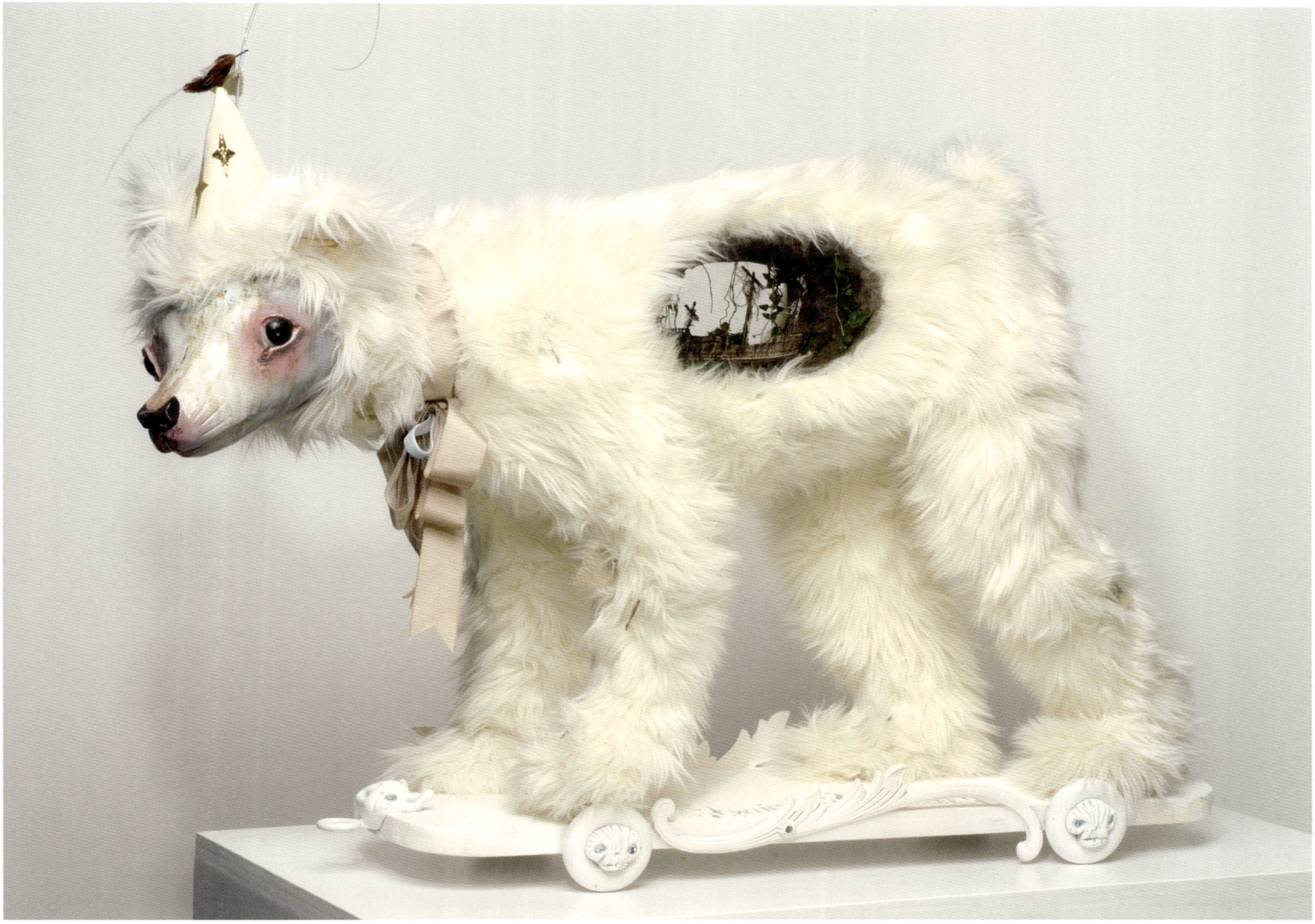

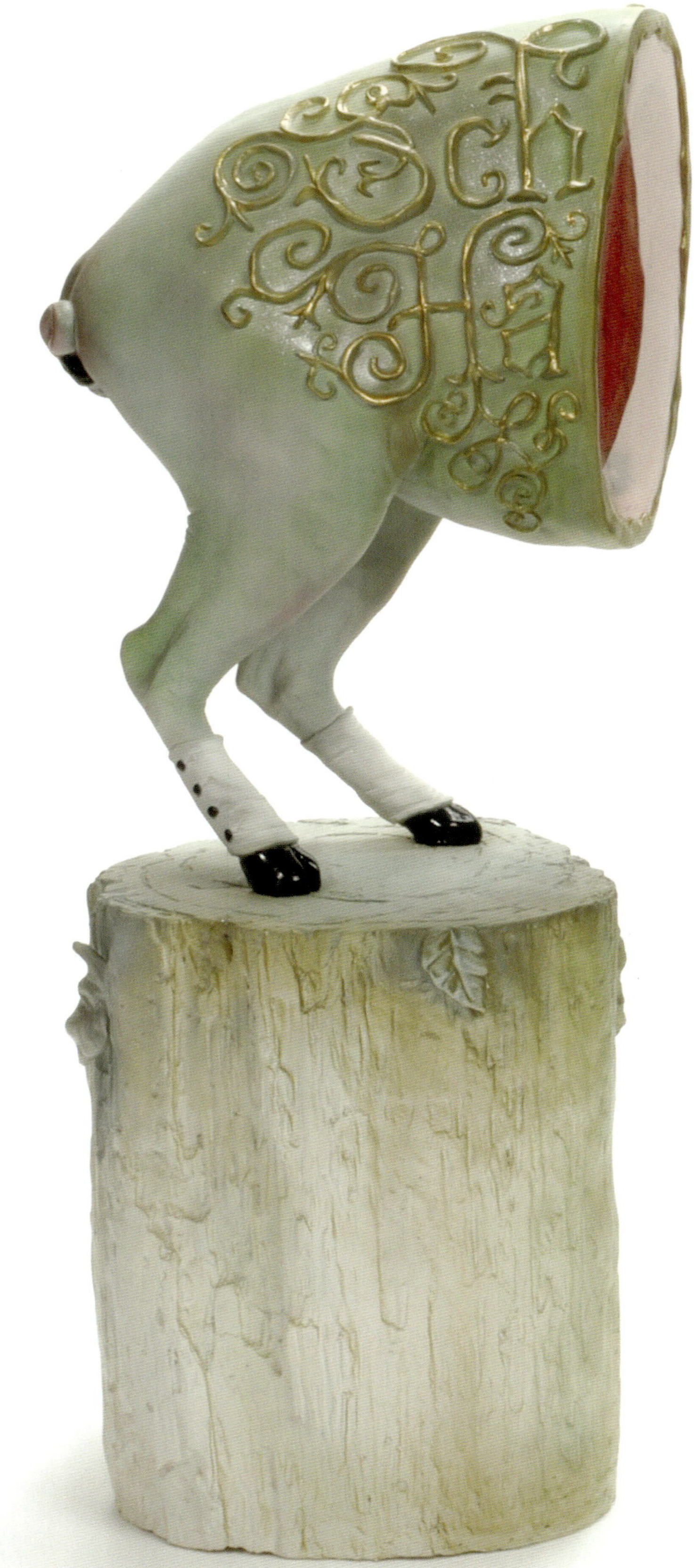

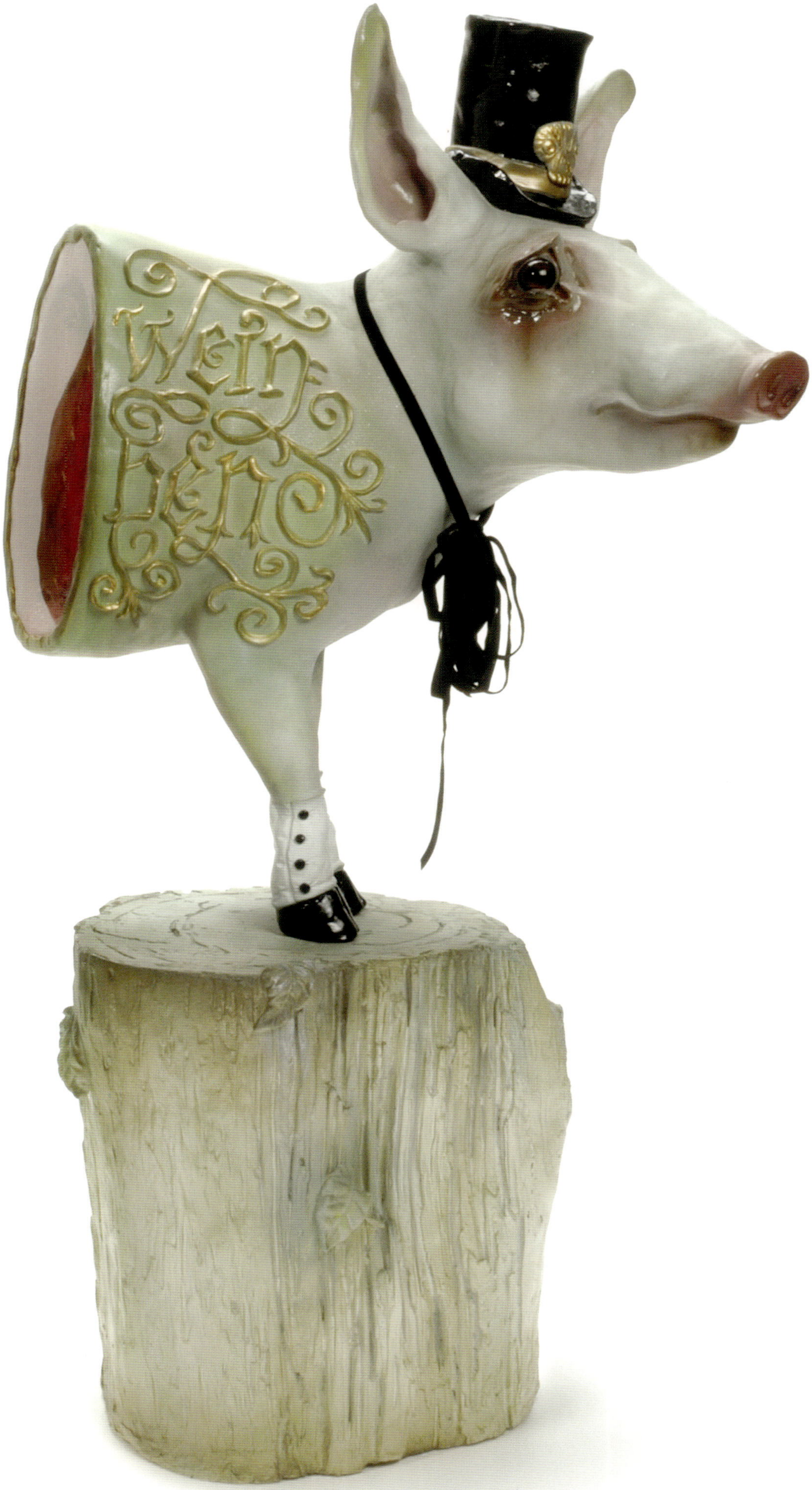

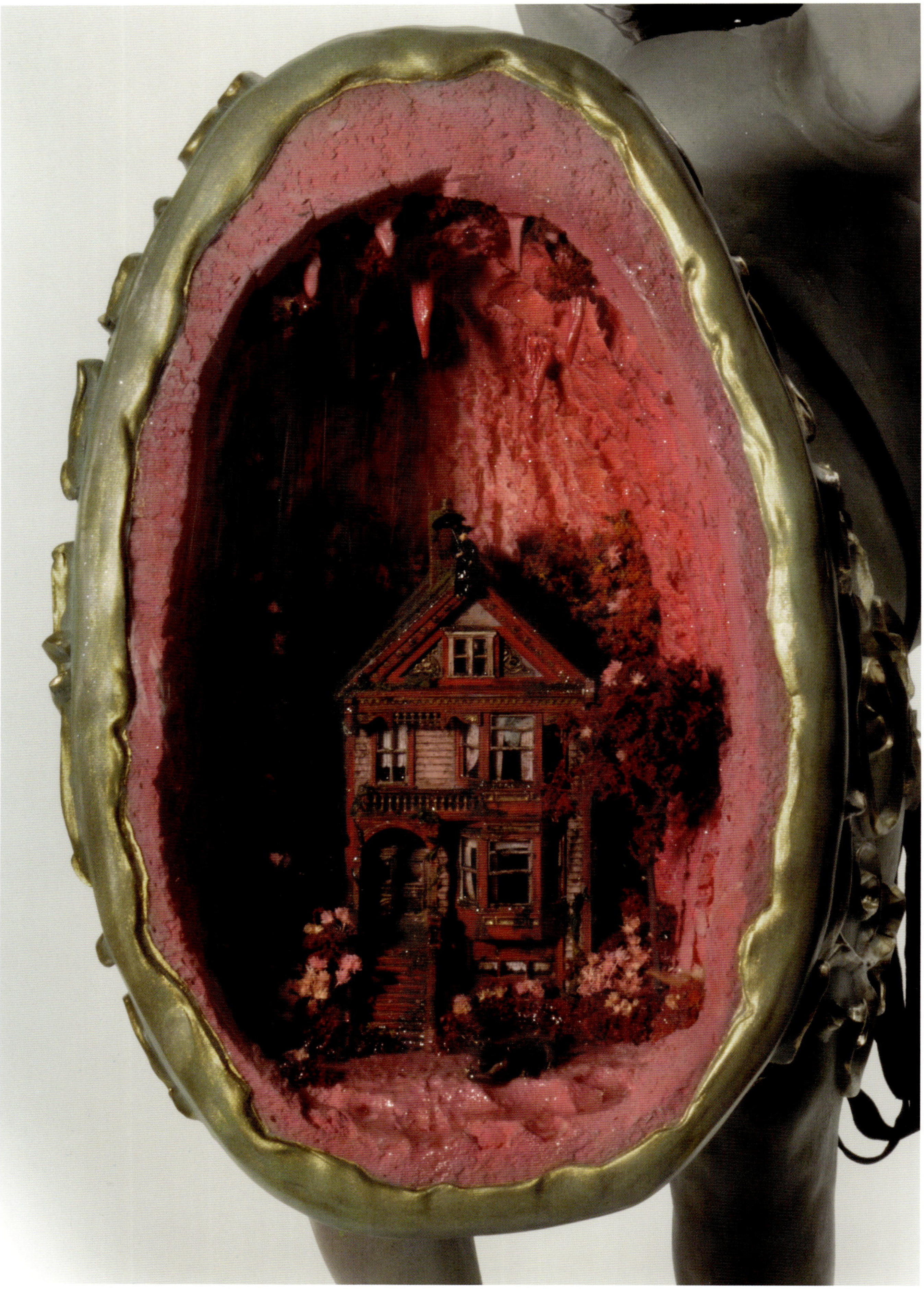

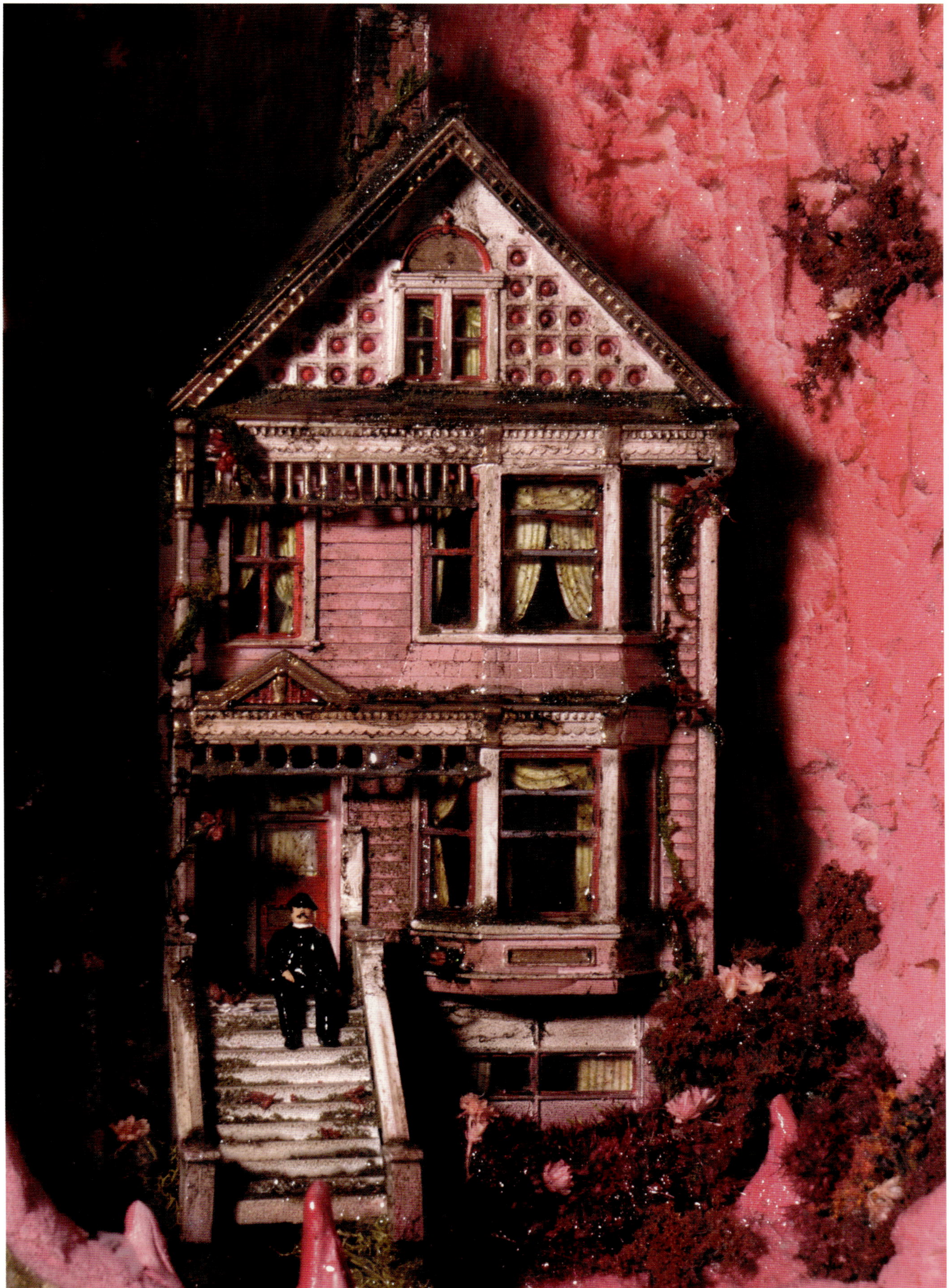

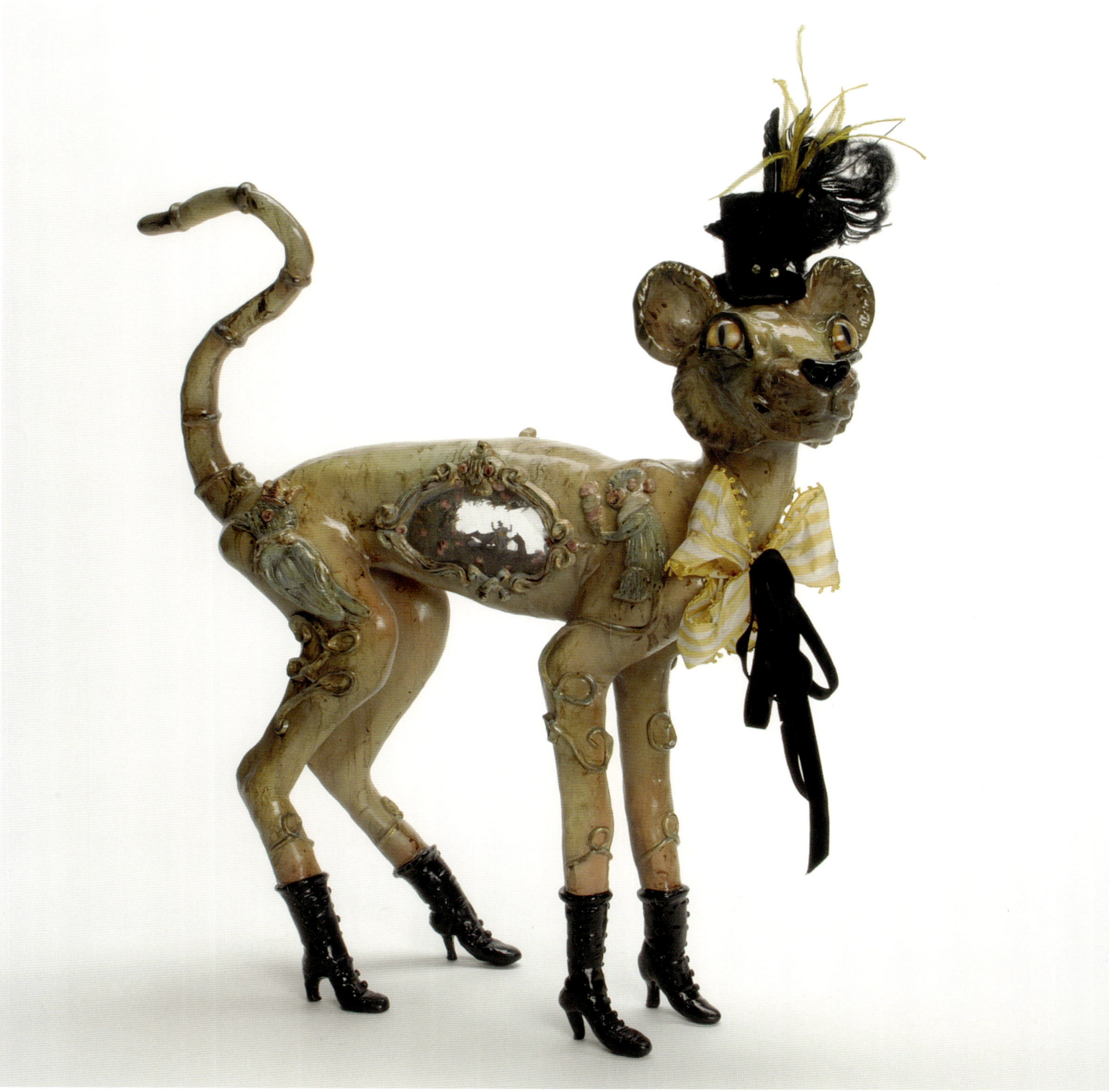

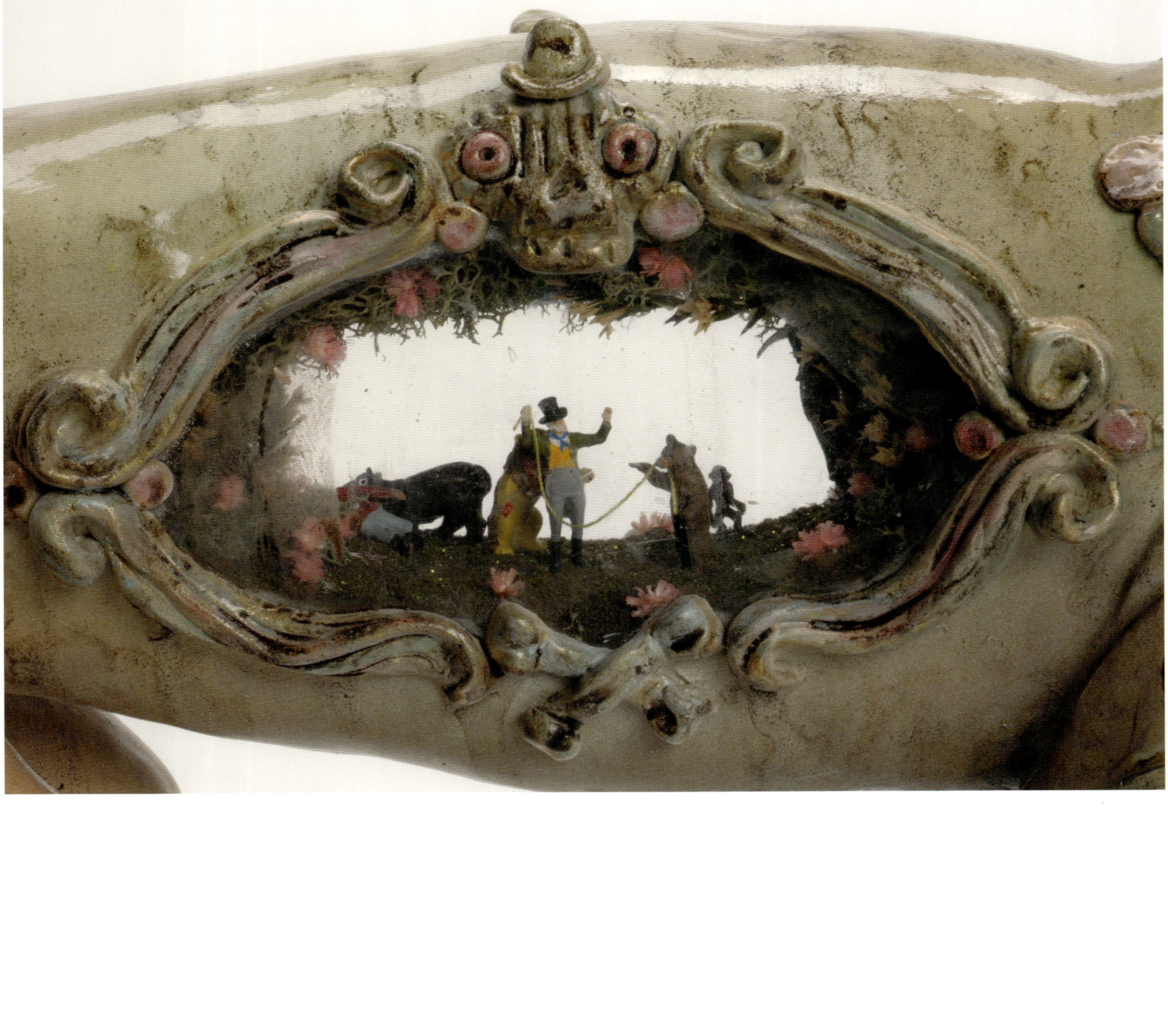

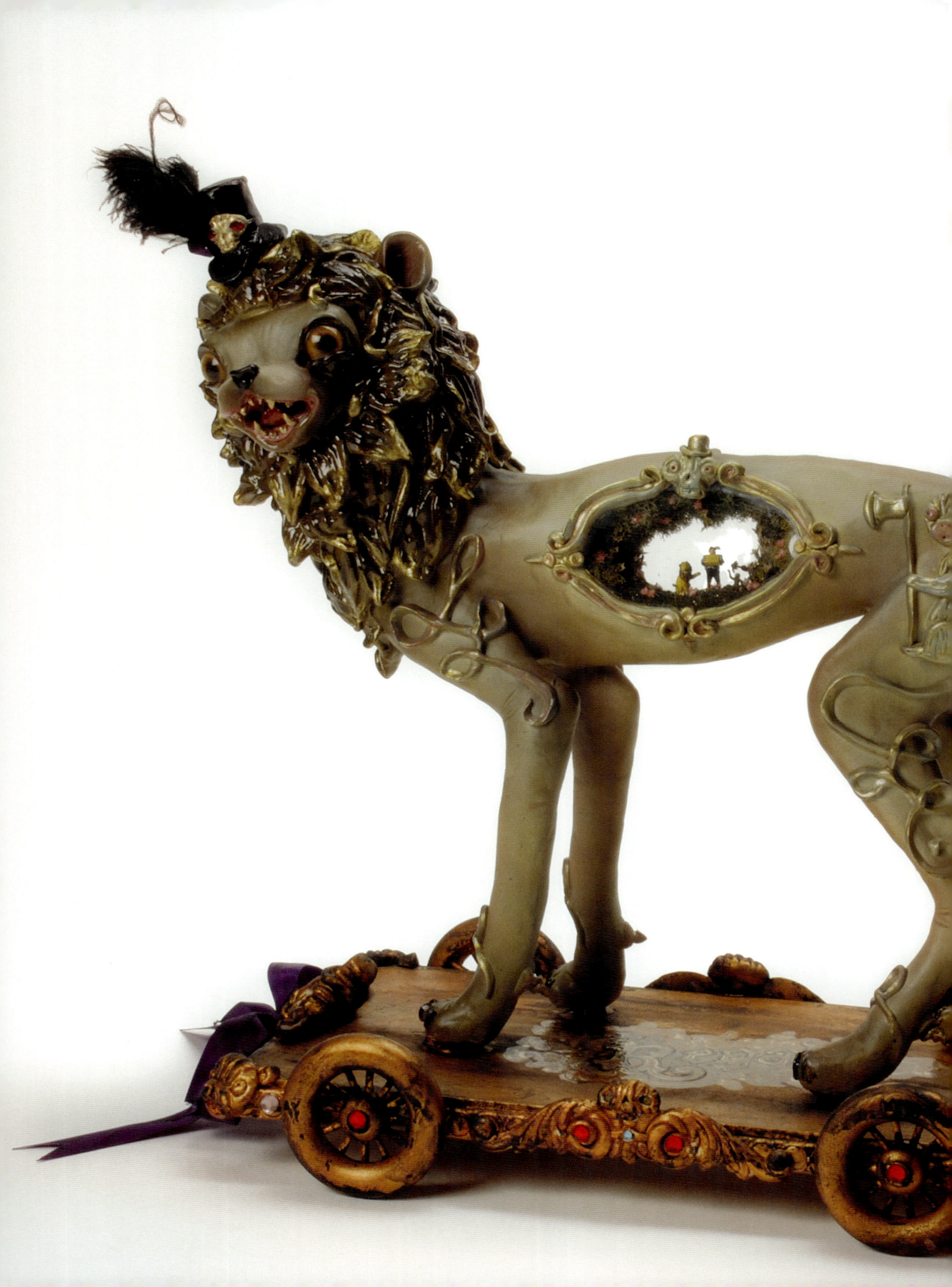

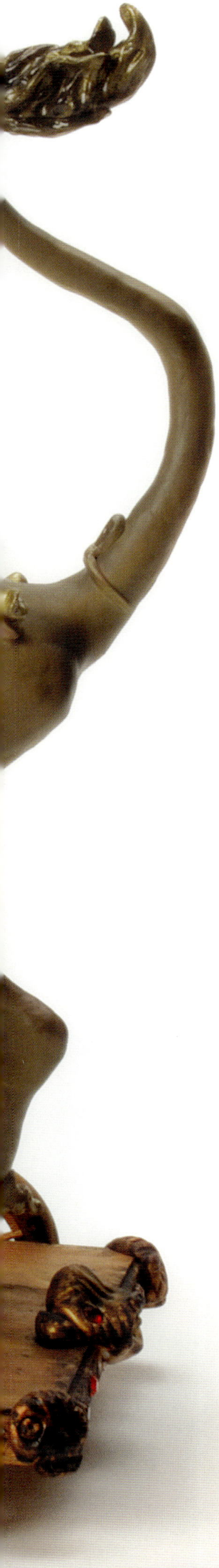

There are some days when gravity seems to pull a little more than usual and clouds sit low in the sky. These are bad days. Days when you can read minds and predict the future. The best thing to do is sit very still and dream... dream with reckless abandon. Dream about supernovae, murder, monks on mountaintops, and wild feral women. Dangerous like straight razors but when they smile... trees scream green, thieves replace hubcaps, the sun blushes, and lemmings hesitate at the cliff. This is the symbiosis of cloud and dream.

Jeremy Sims '93

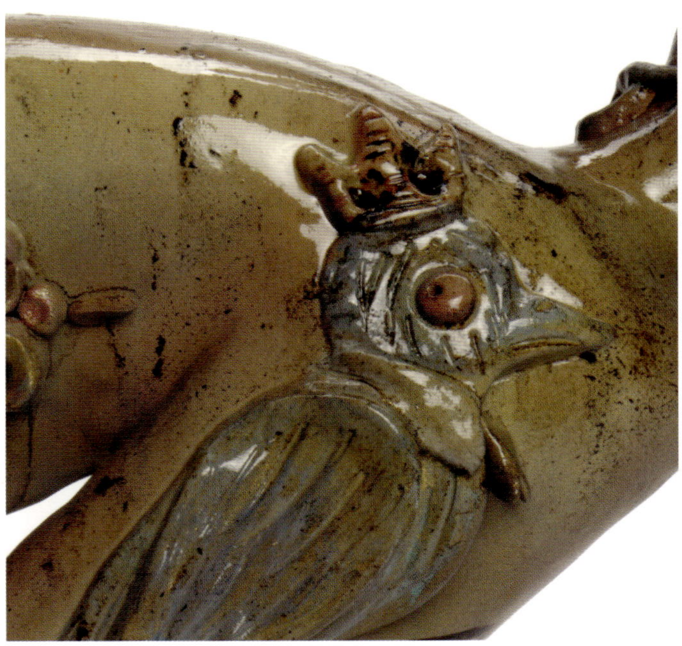

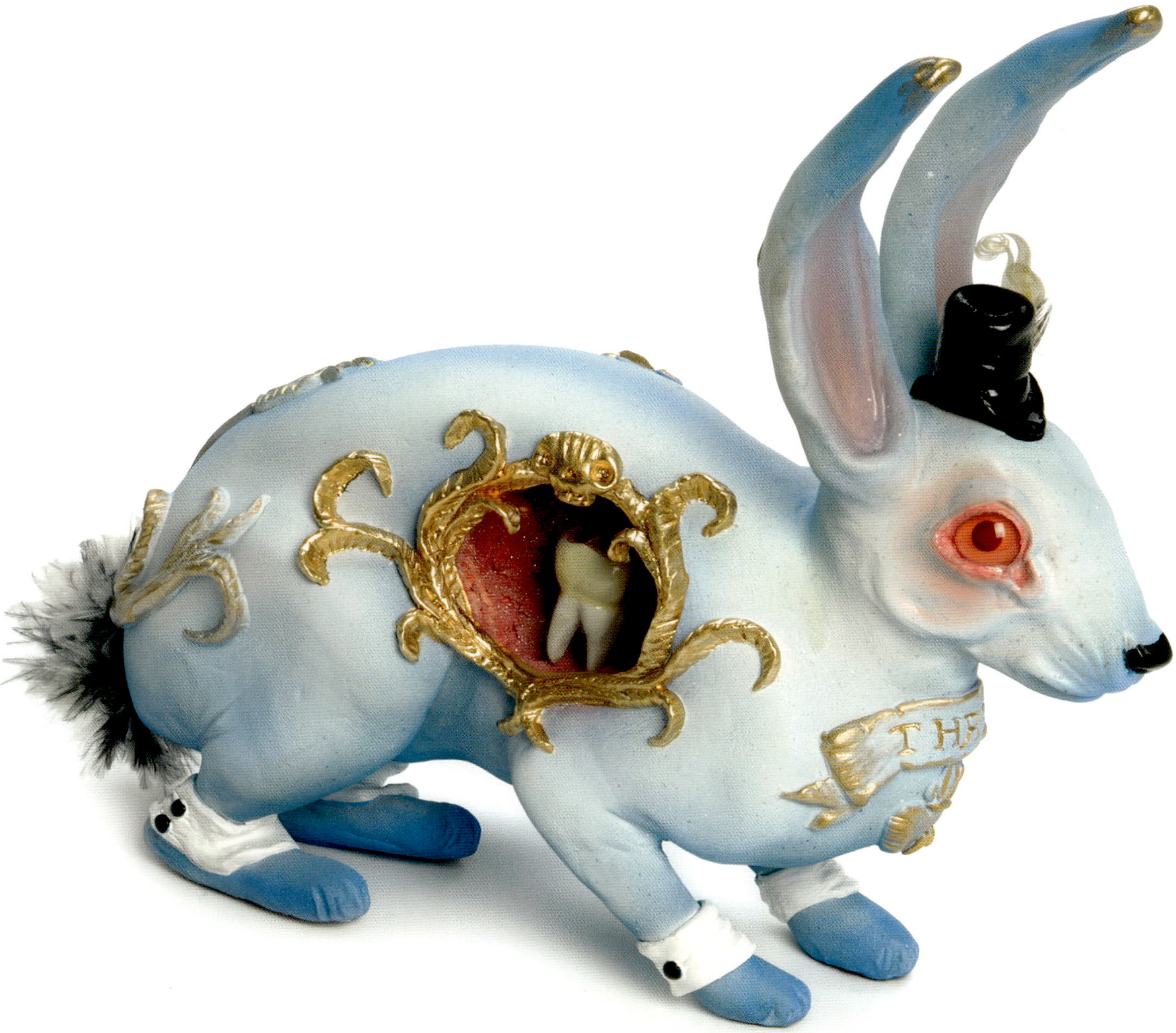

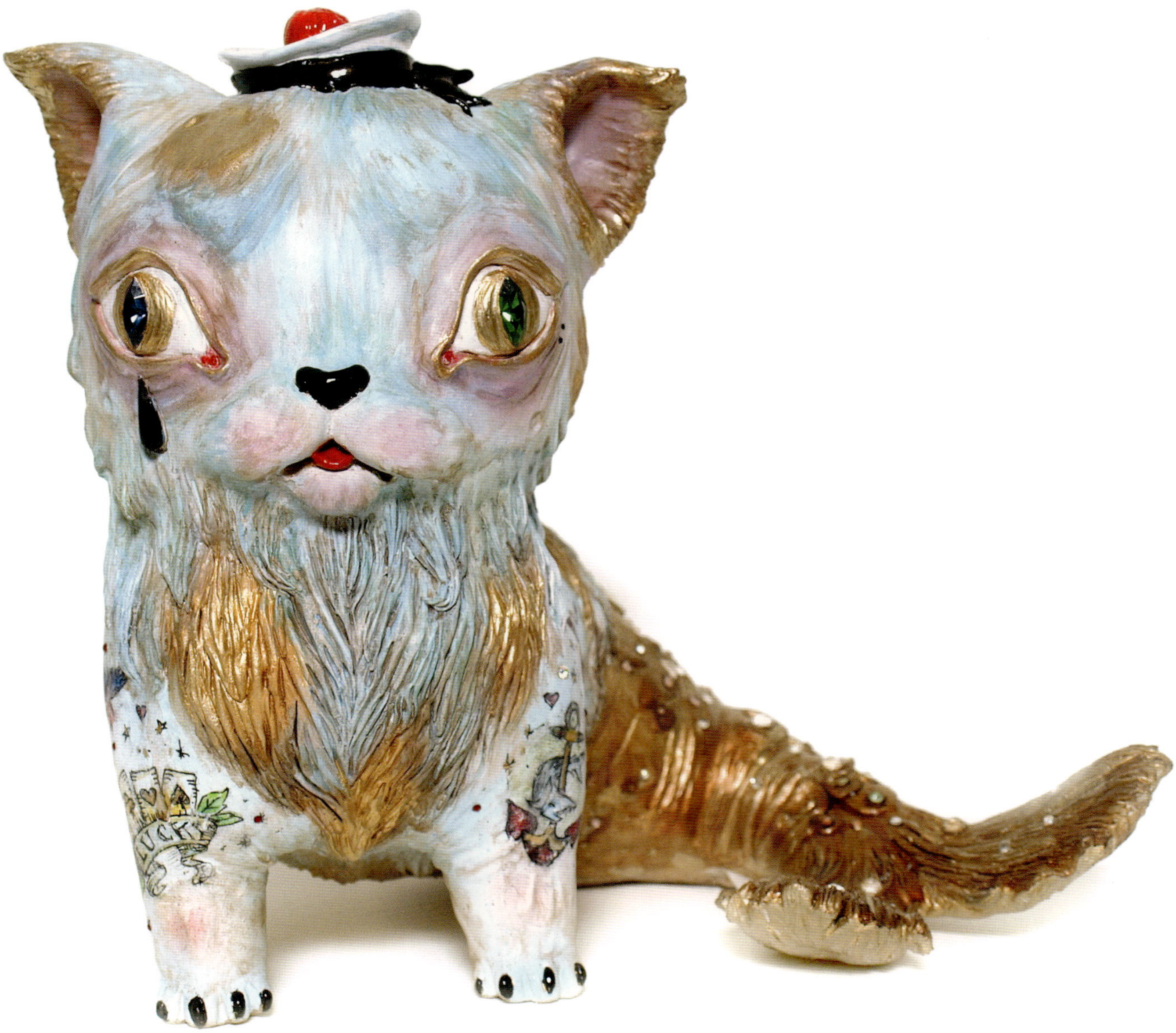

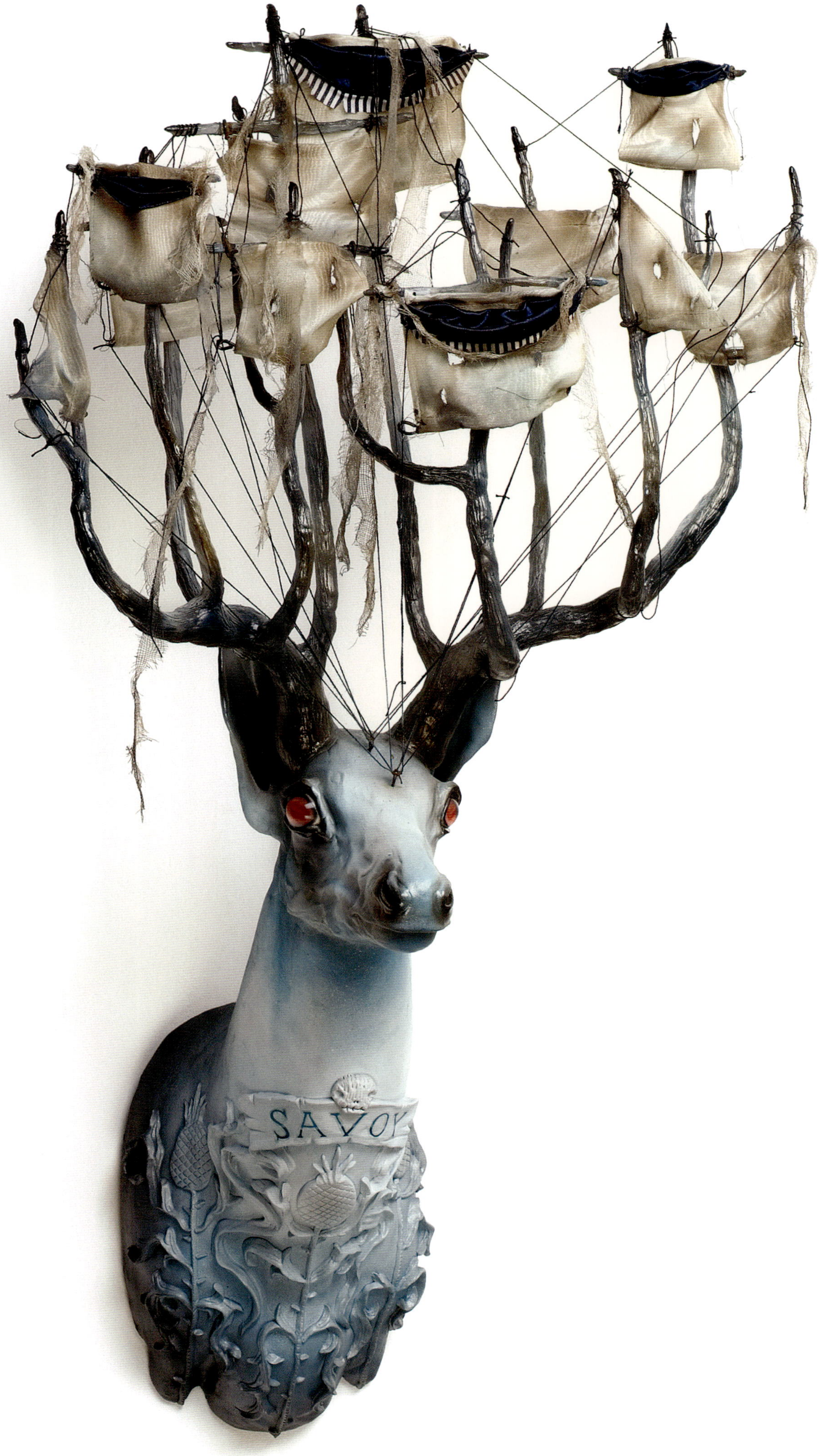
SAVOY

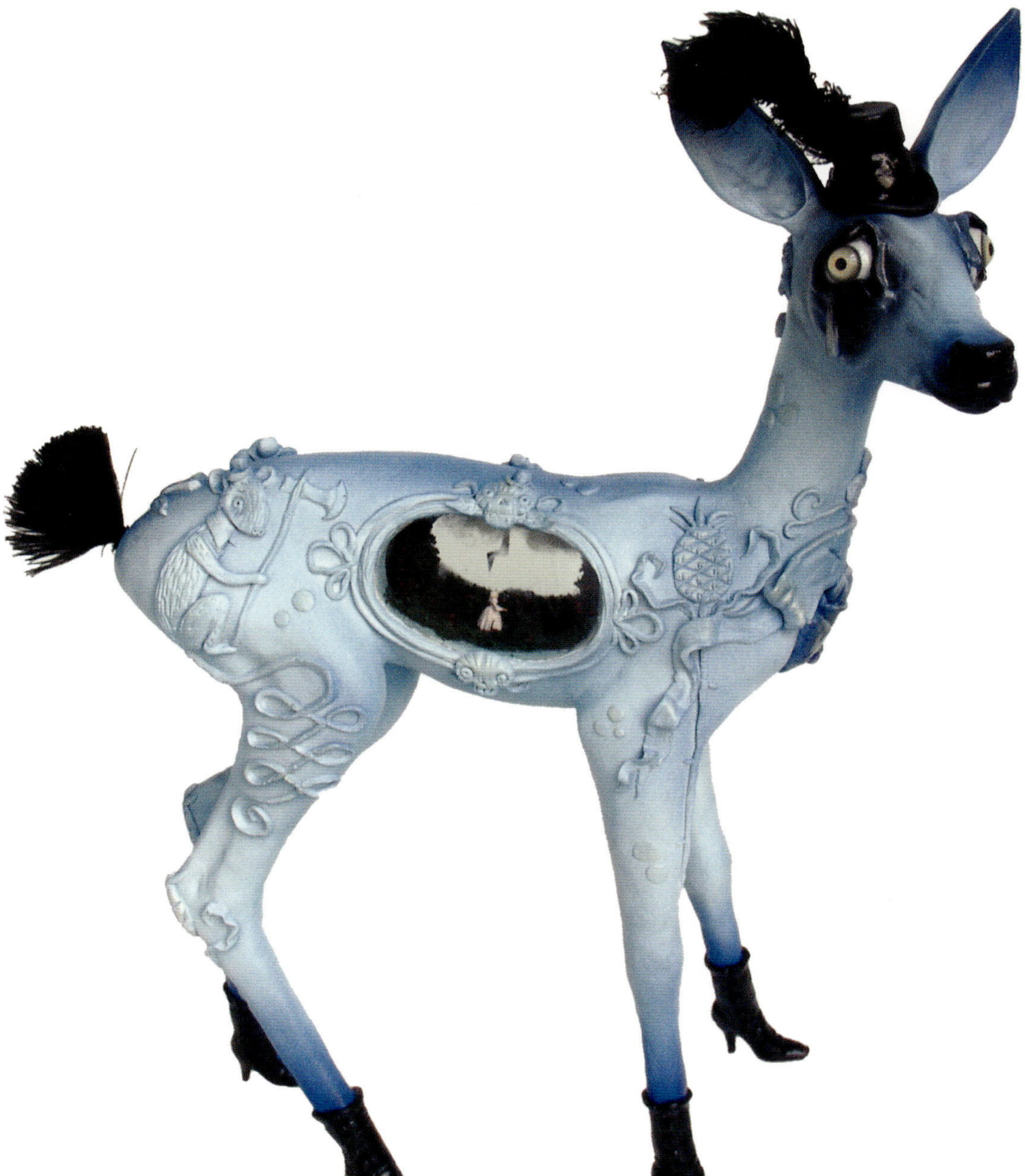

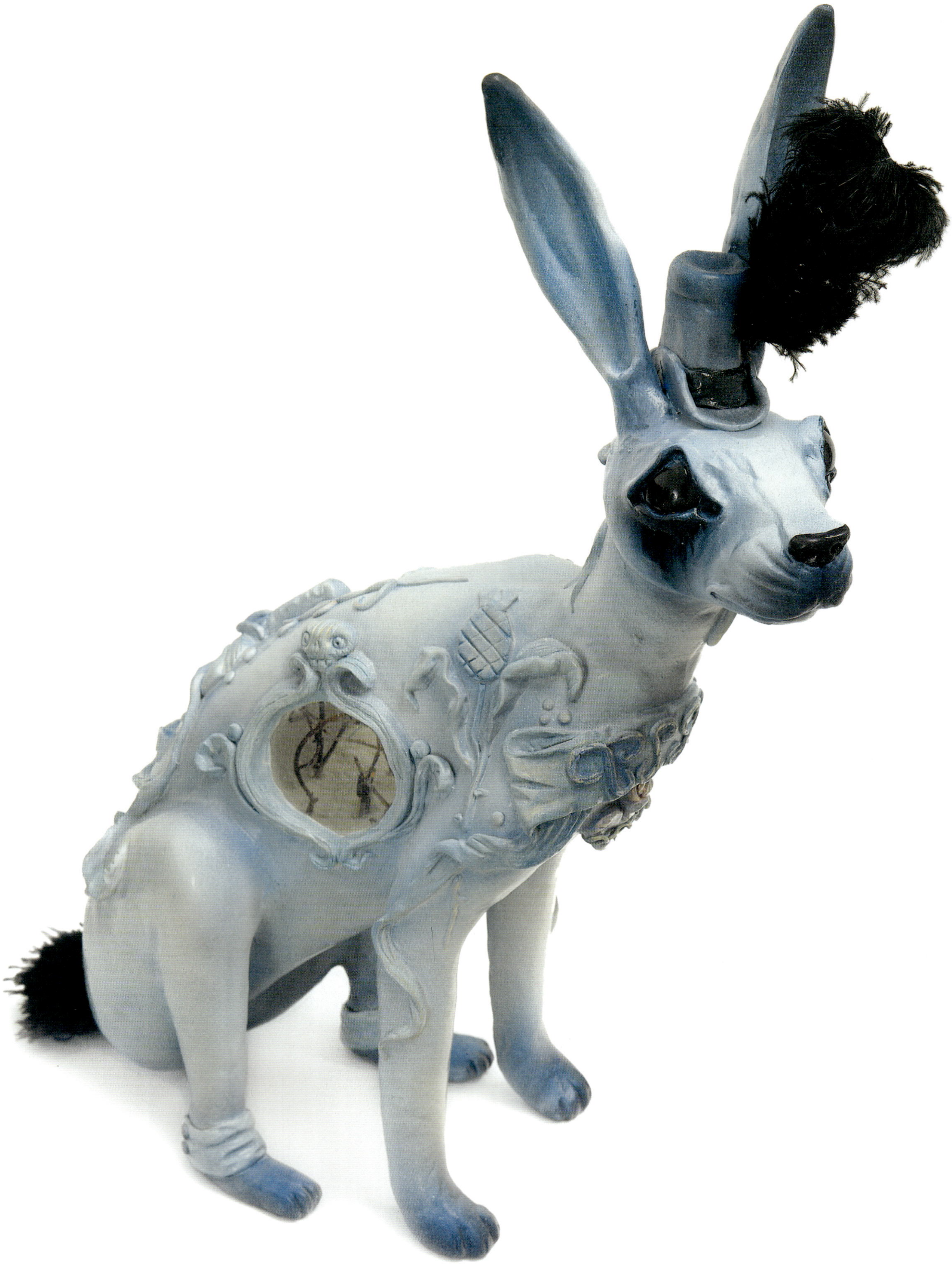

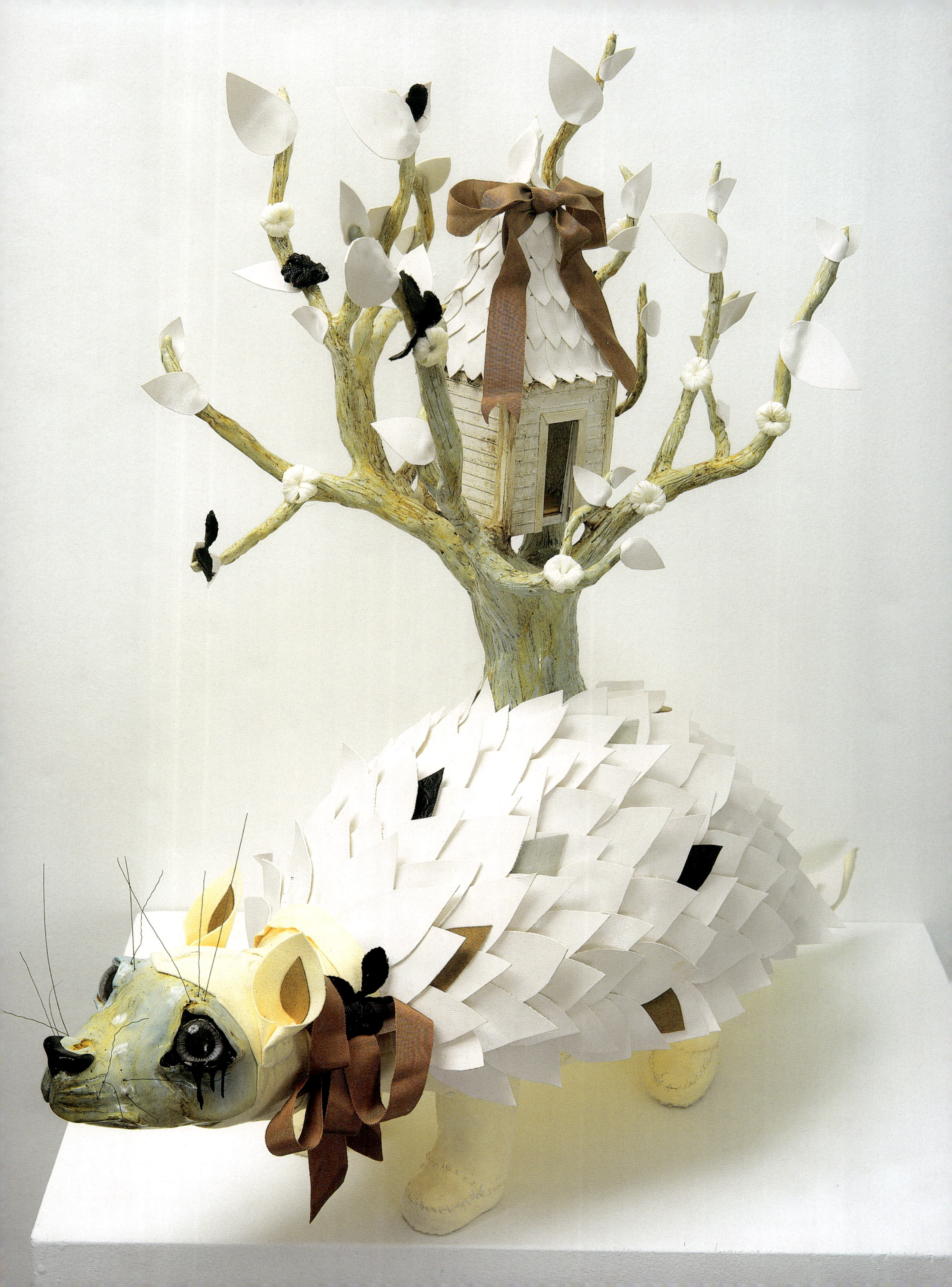

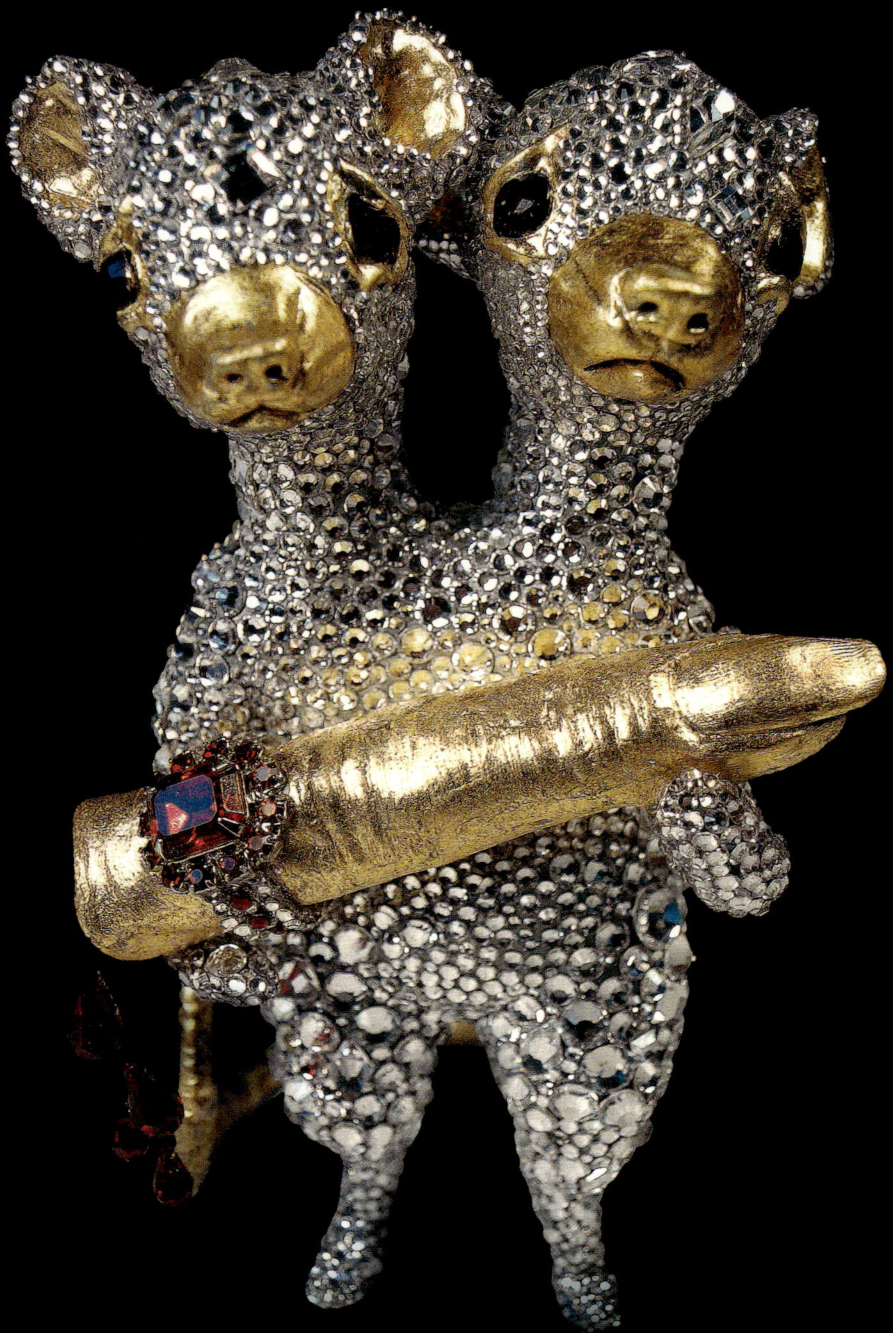

With Tomorrow's Scream

"In the end, all life I find is zeitgeist mixed with schadenfreude –and each and every future dream– is tempered with tomorrow's scream."

Quote from

Redmond King

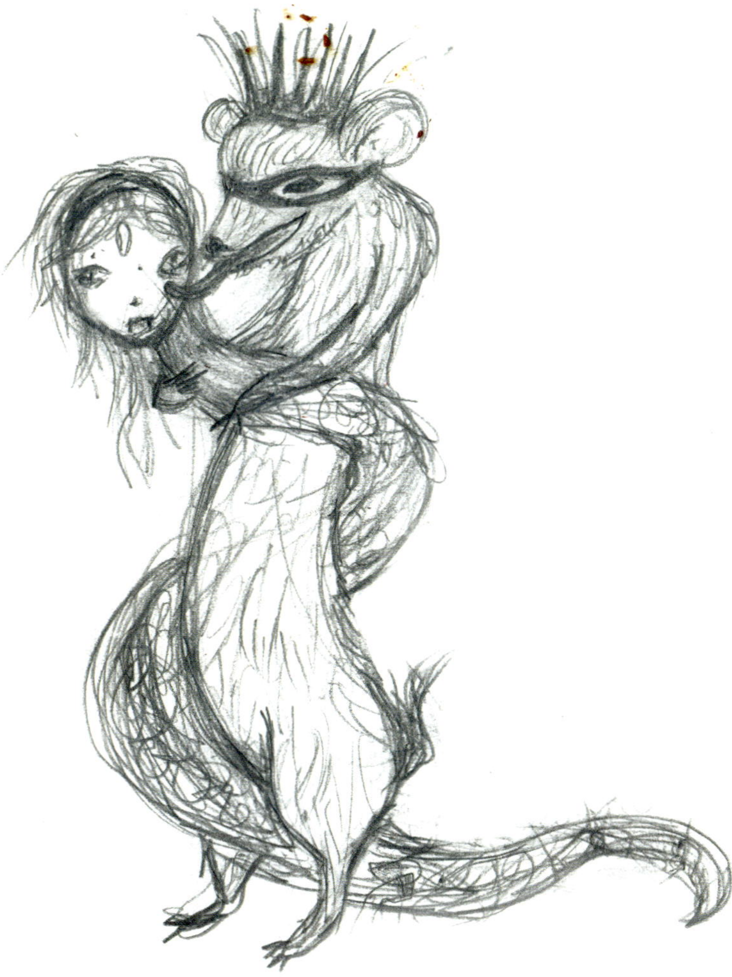

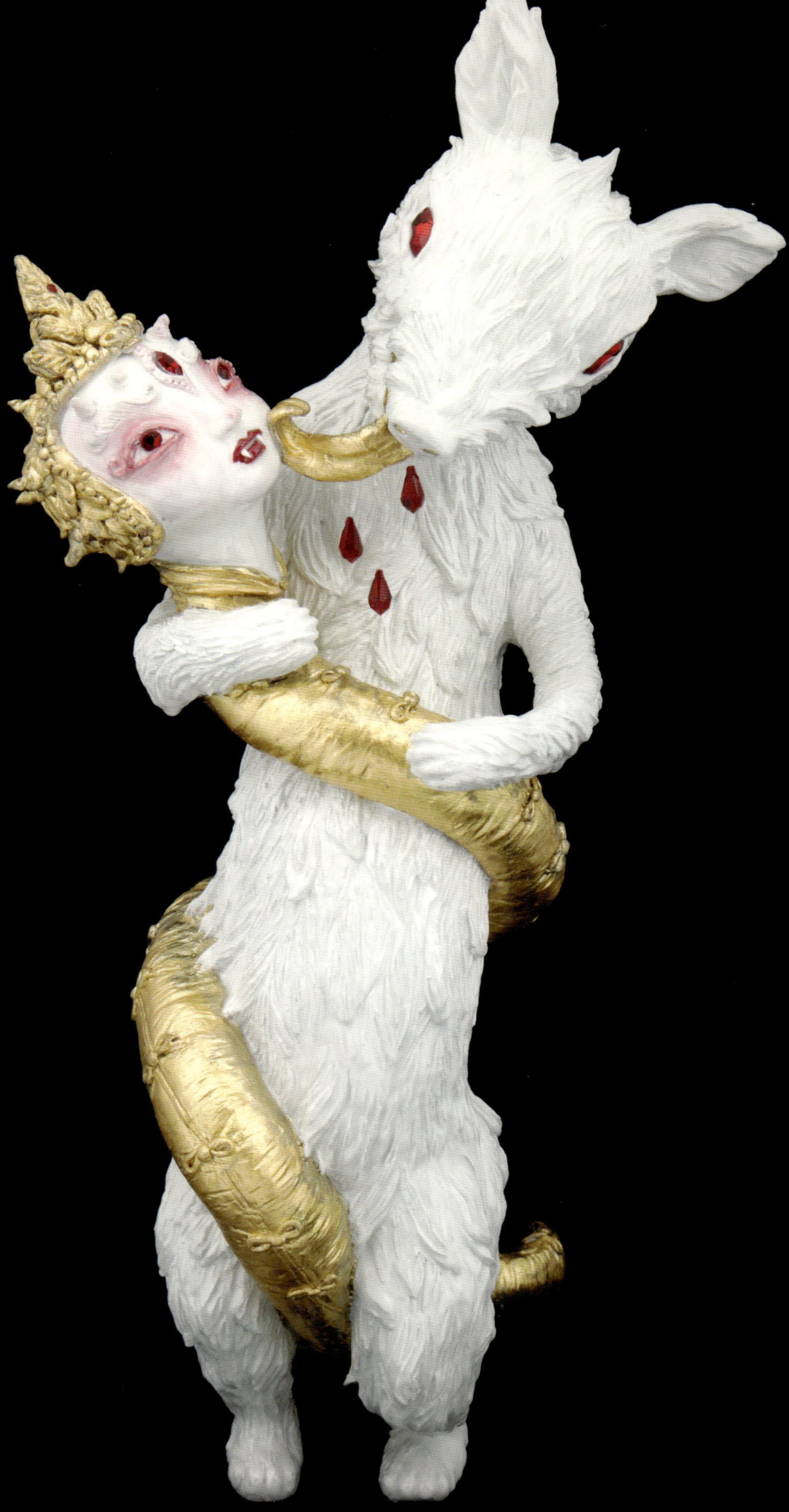

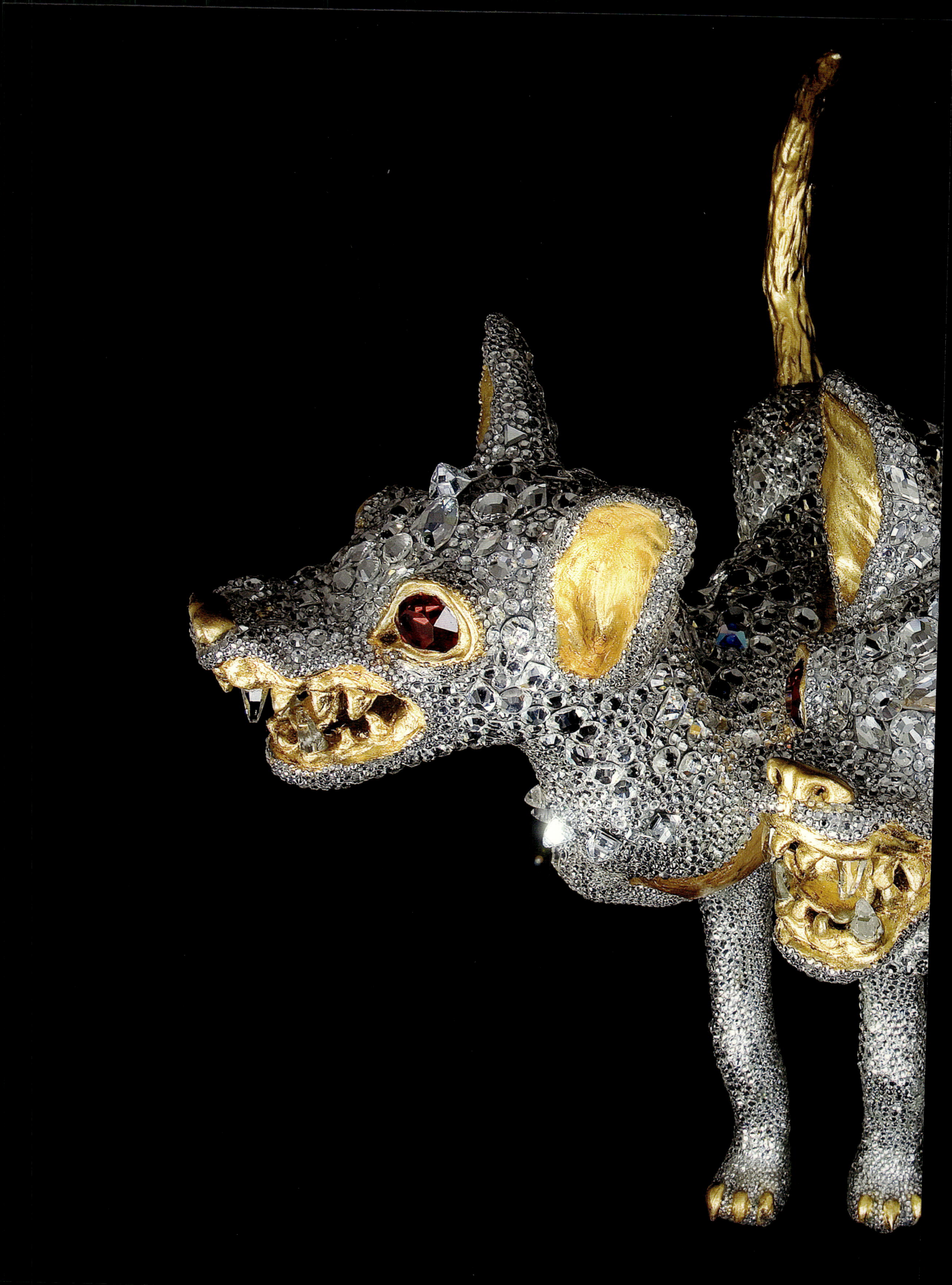

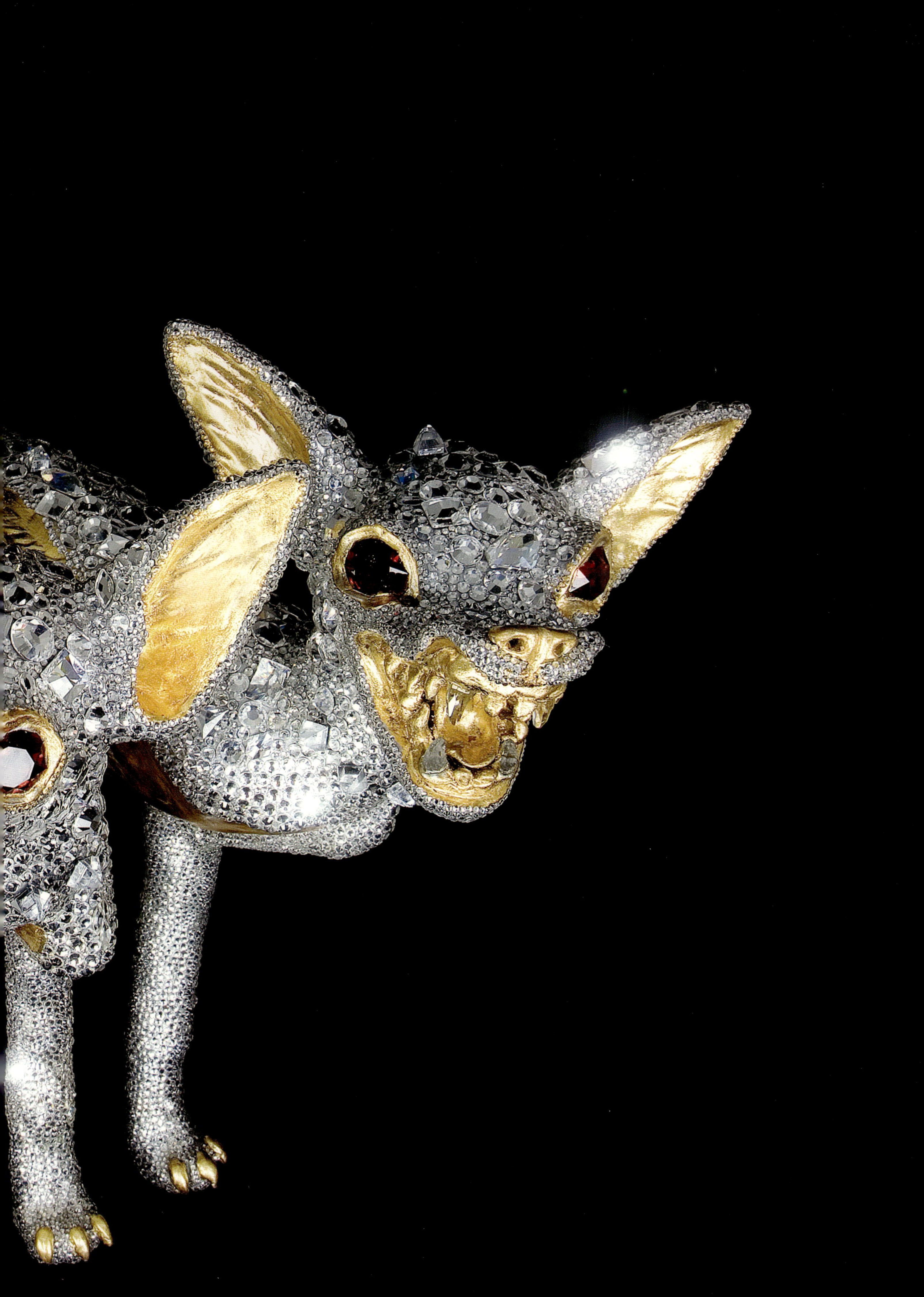

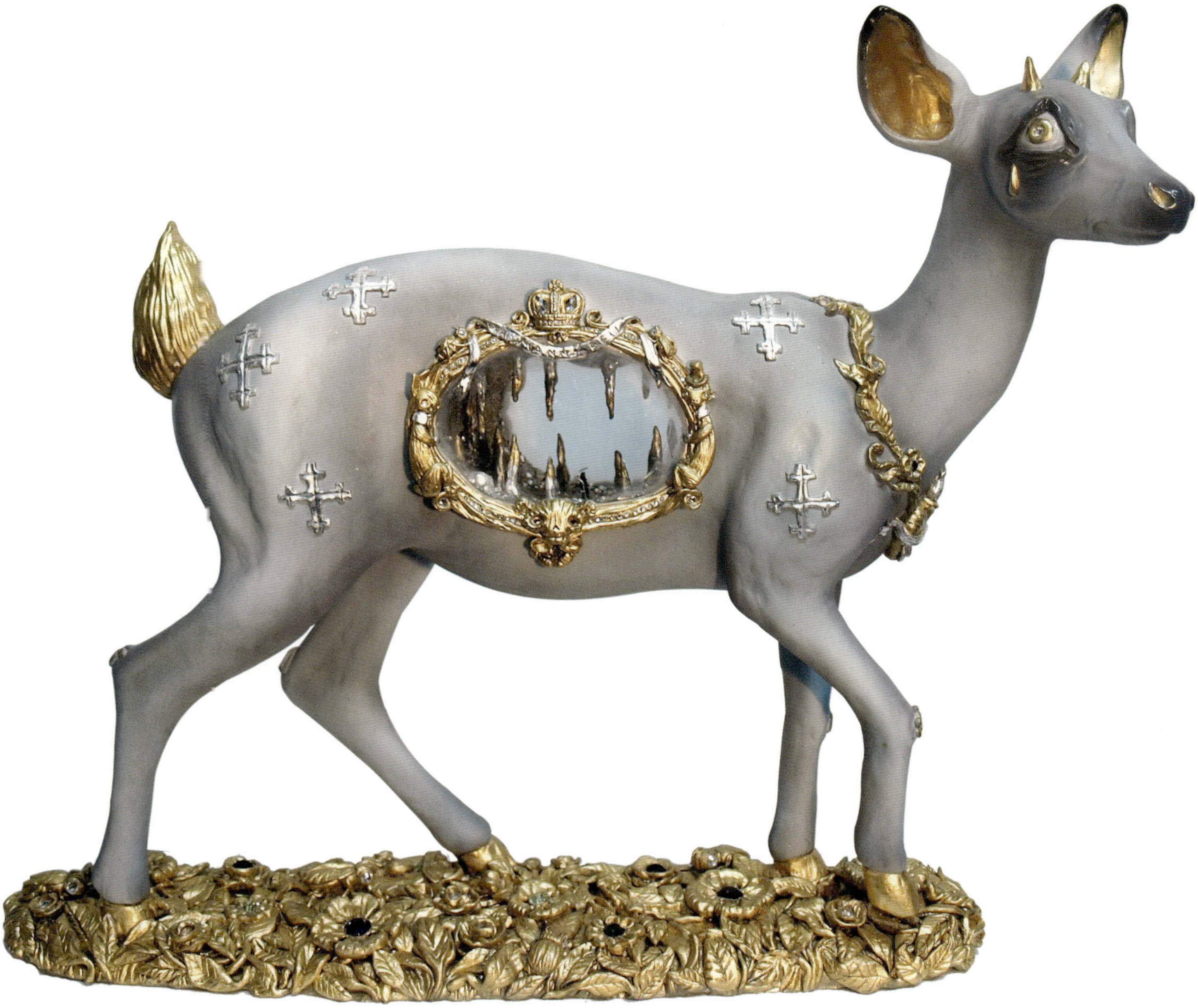

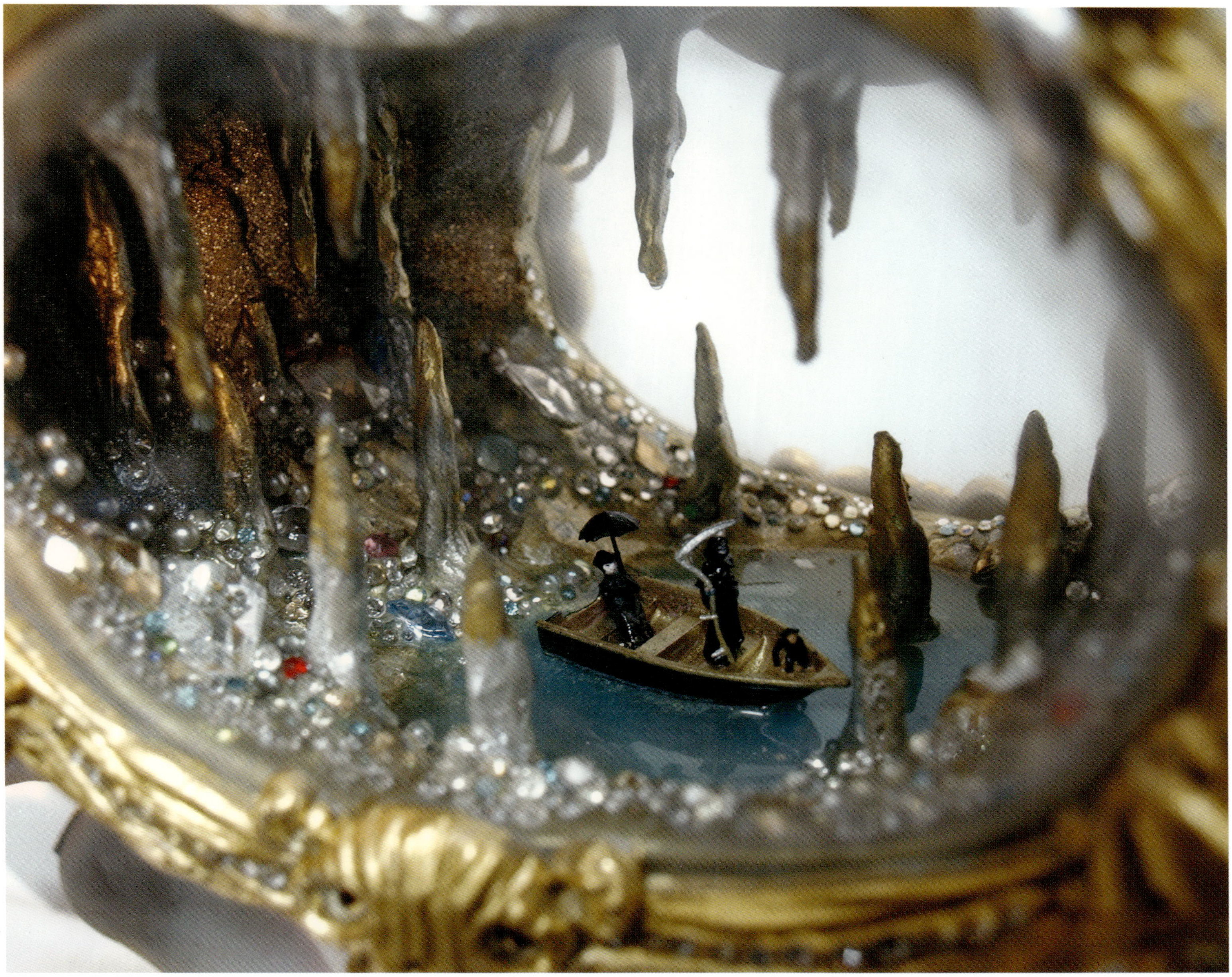

Born in the seventh century, Hubertus was an avid hunter and woodsman. According to legend, while hunting in the forest Hubertus encountered the awe-inspiring image of a shimmering albino stag carrying a glorious cross between its antlers. Through this vision, Hubertus was moved to transform his life. He resigned his high ranks of office, distributed his riches among the poor and church and dedicated his life to protecting animals from needless suffering.

Today, Hubertus is the patron saint of hunters and animal protectionists in northern Europe. His followers honor him in a variety of ways including organizing fundraising festivals and caring for animals, both domestic and wild.

With "The Folly of St. Hubertus," McGrath re-imagines Hubertus' transformative vision in gold leaf and over 60,000 hand-placed Swarovski crystals. McGrath's fantasy eight-legged creature, glittering with bands of reflective light and pierced by golden arrows, is simultaneously confrontational and ethereal. He at once entices with glorious beauty and shocks with profound sadness, leaving the viewer no choice but to consider one's own relationship with nature, the environment, those less fortunate, and those who cannot speak for themselves.

Alix Sloan

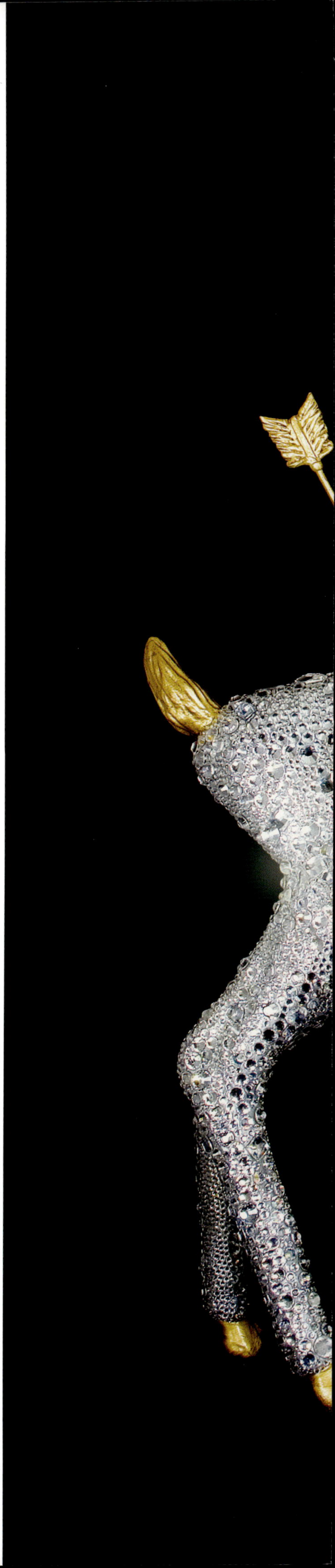

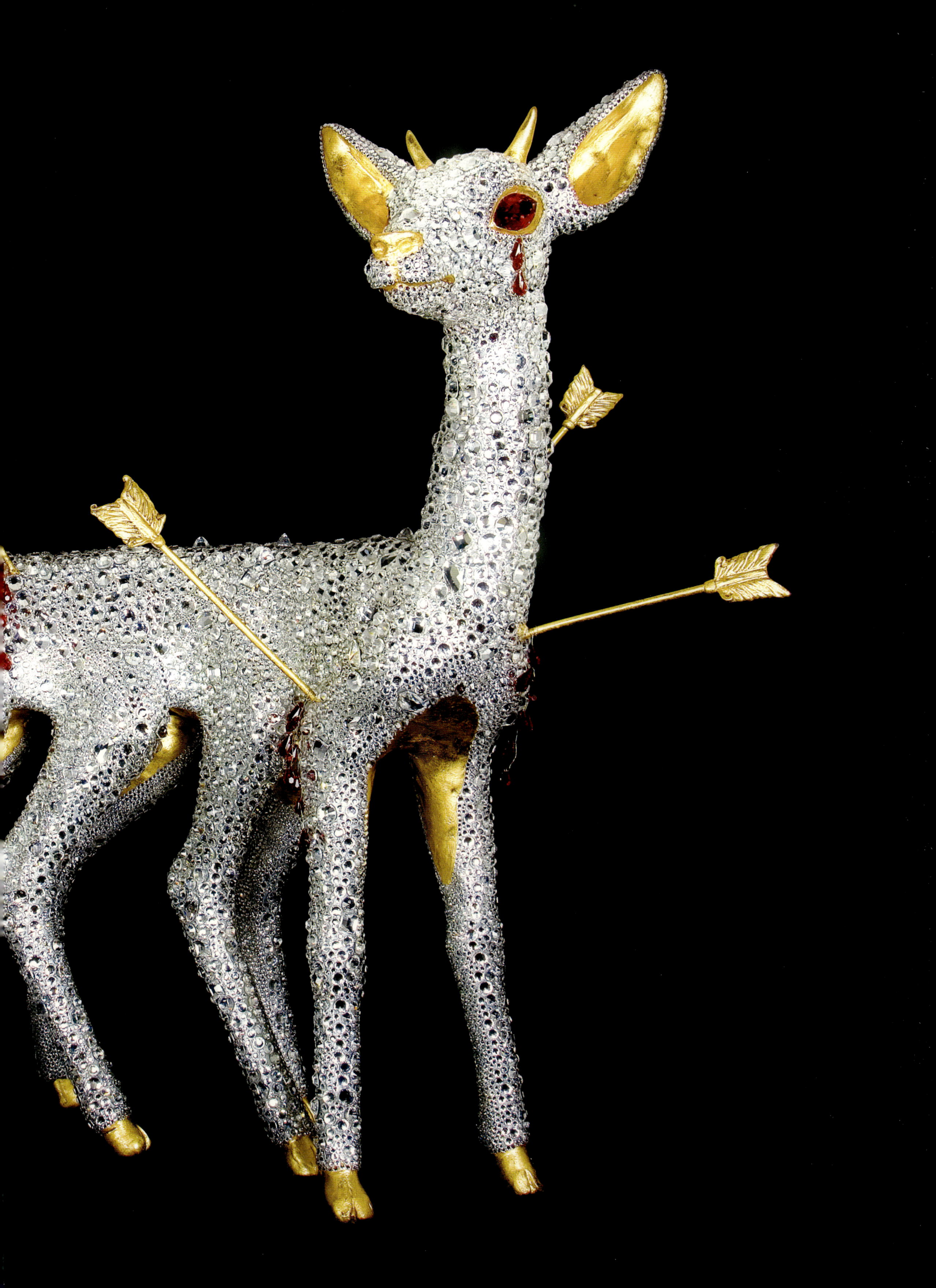

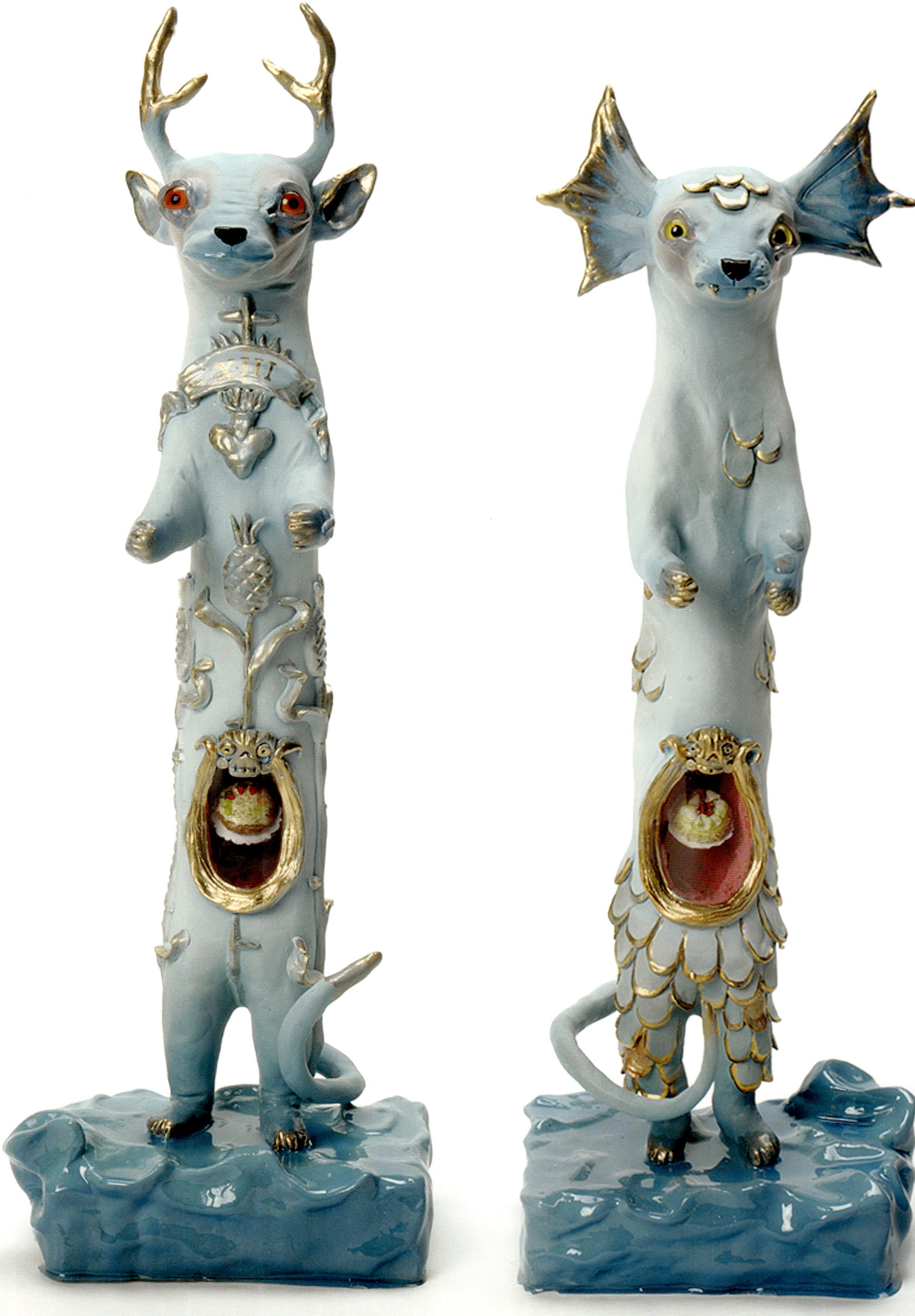
XIII

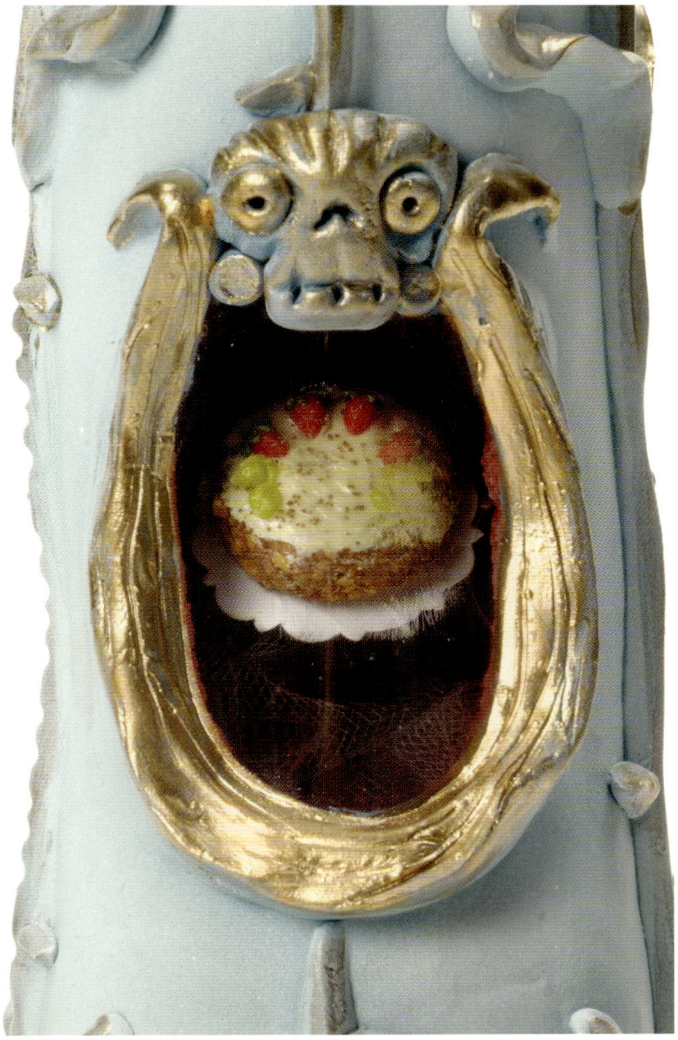

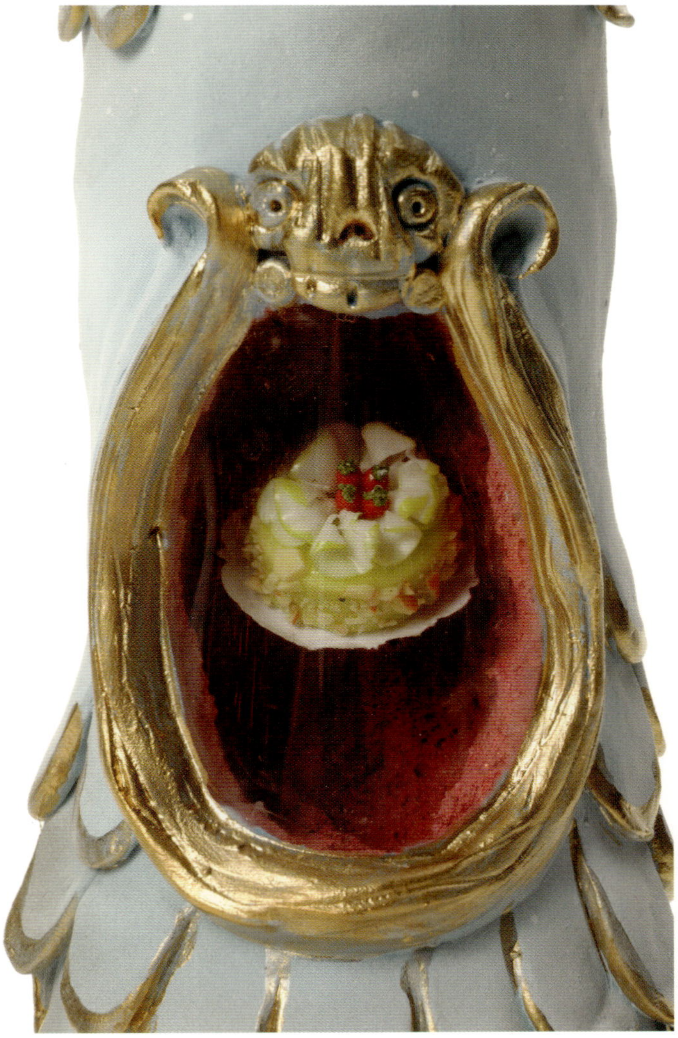

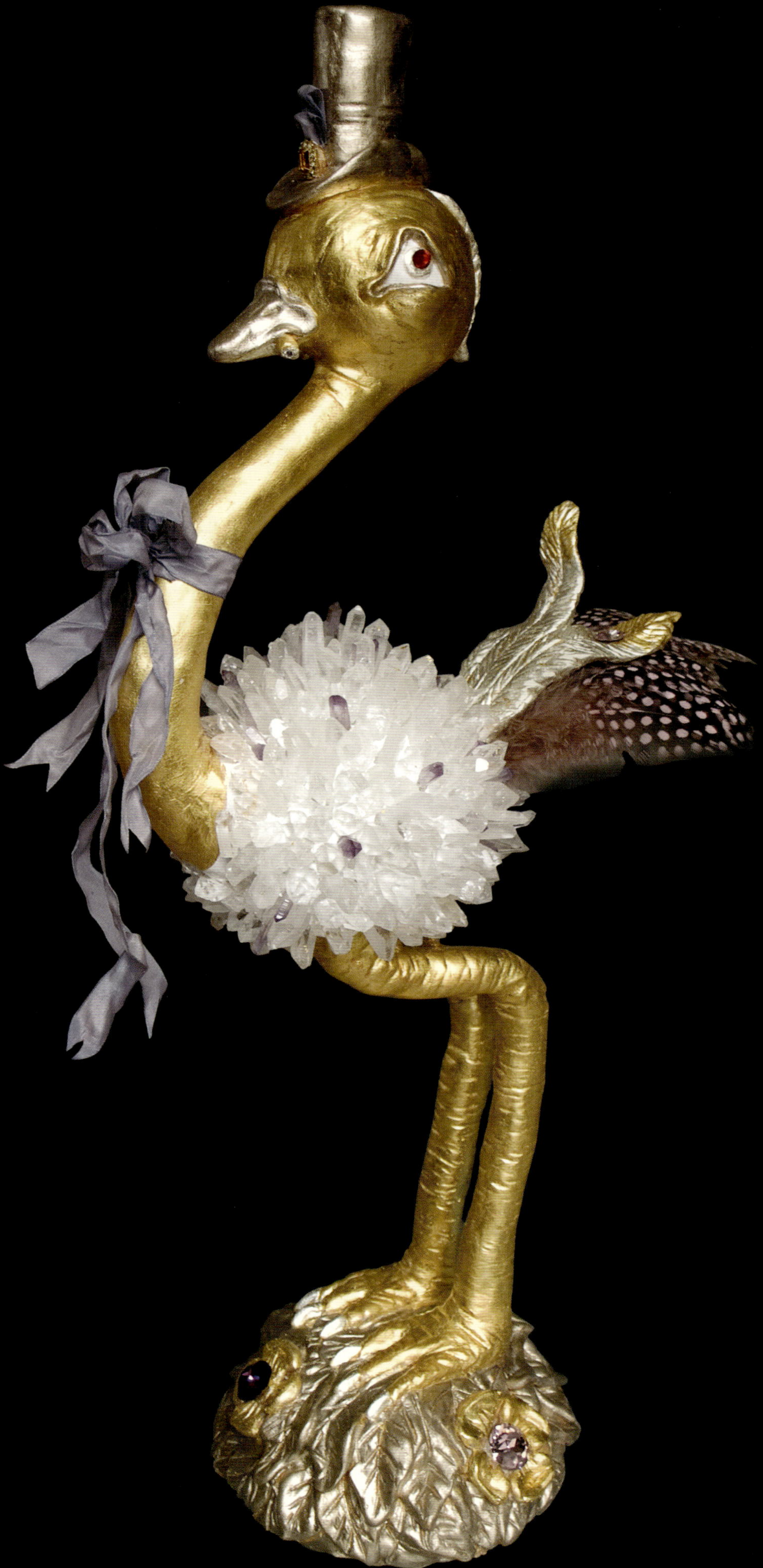

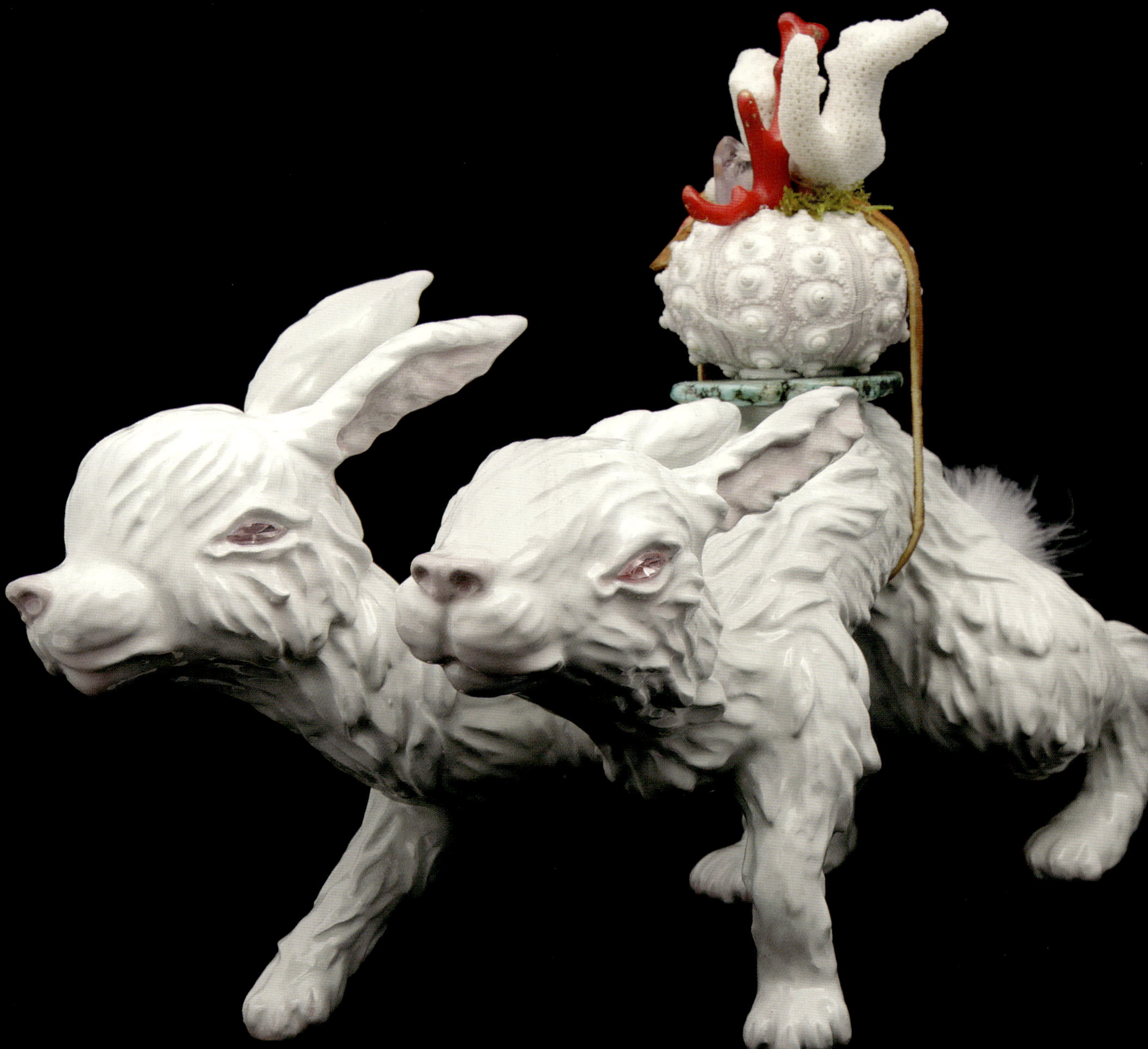

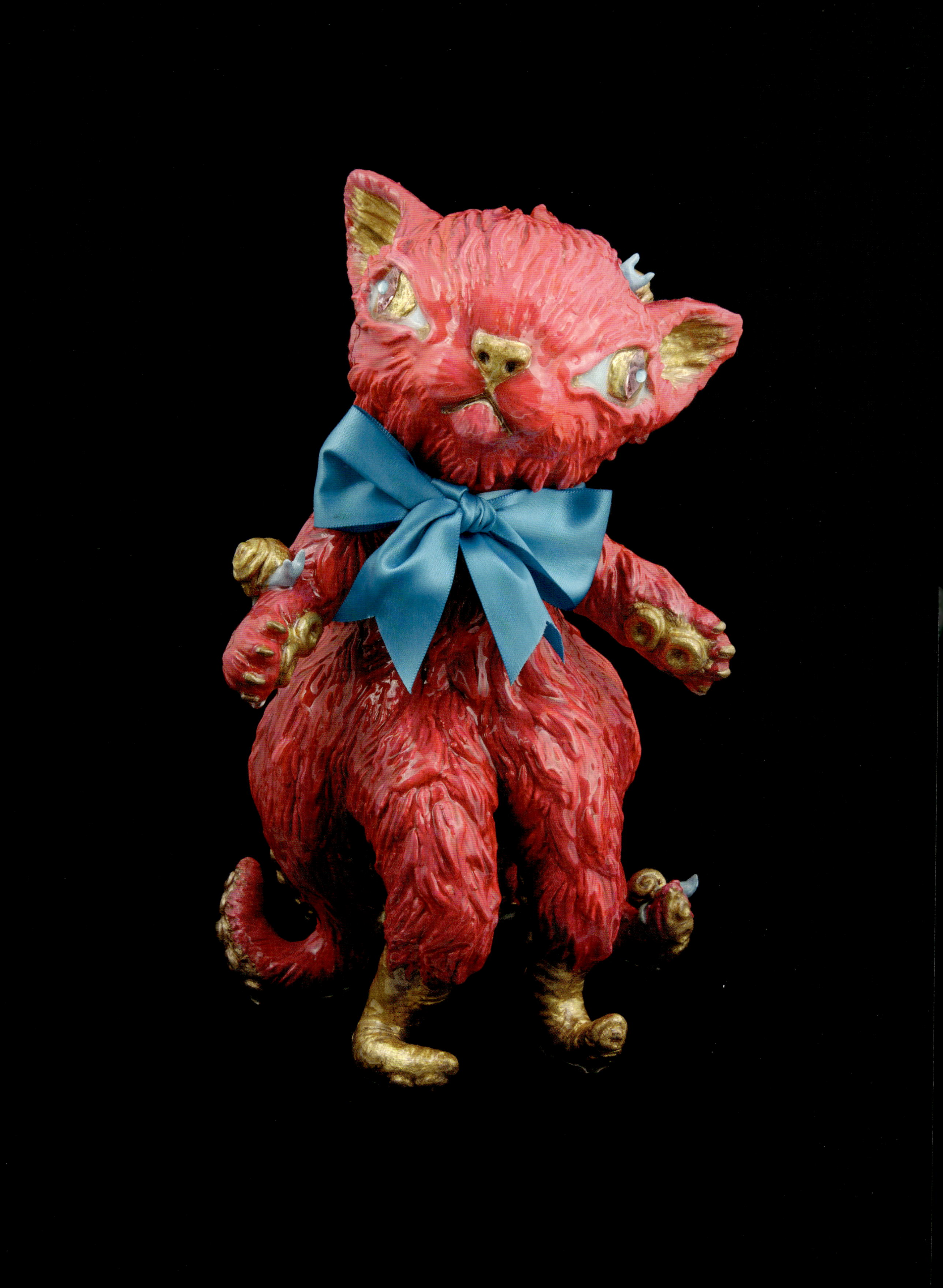

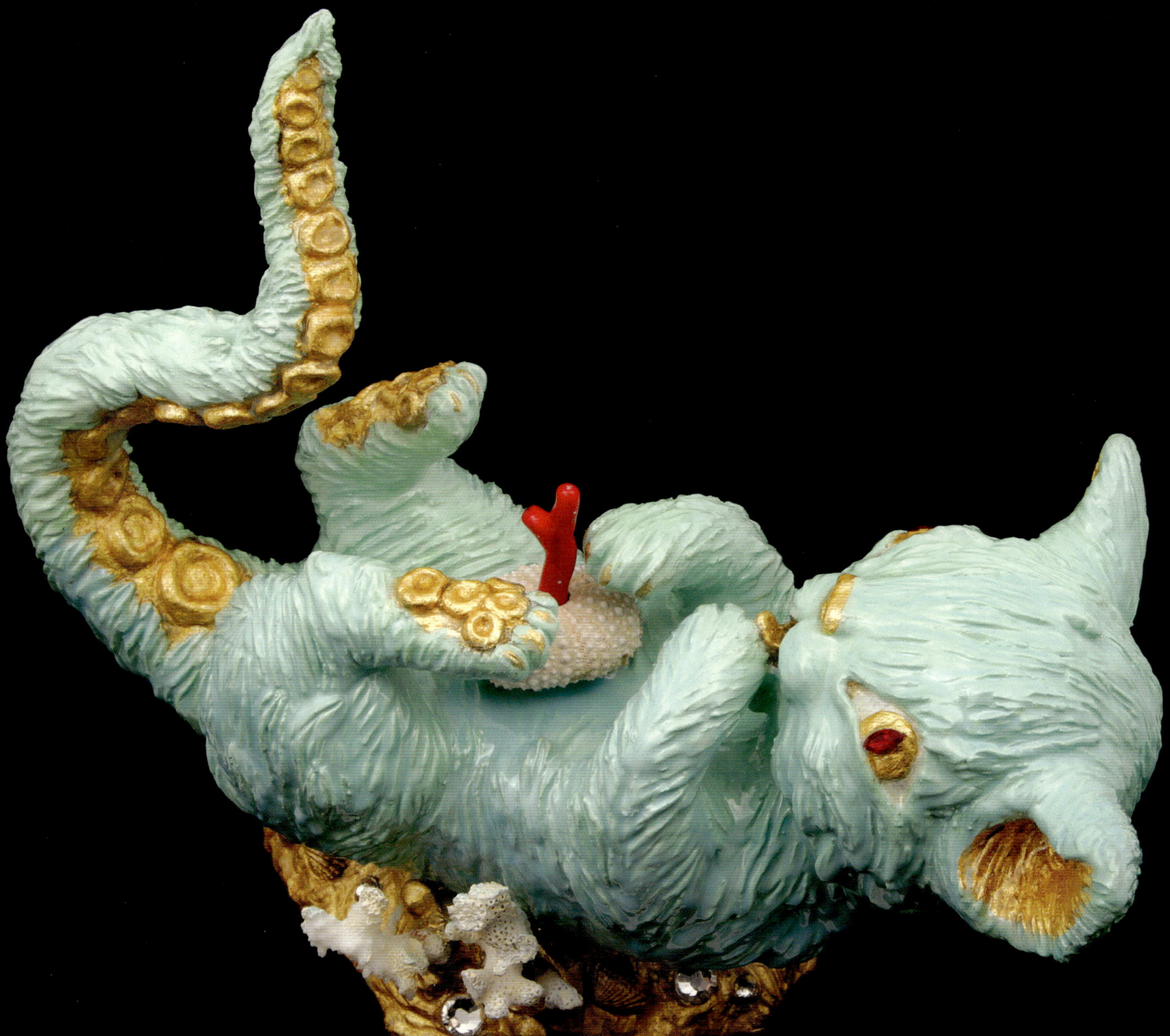

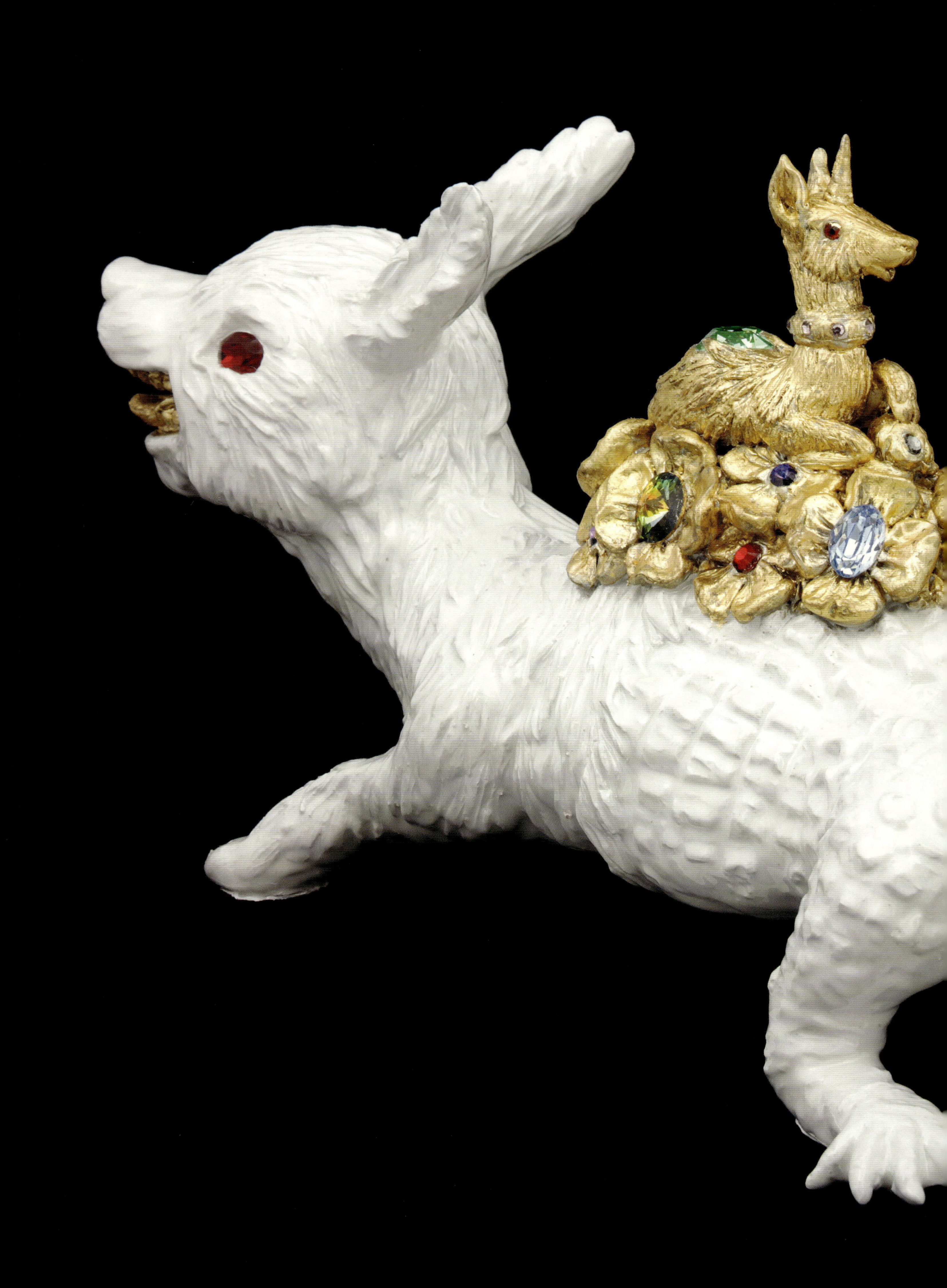

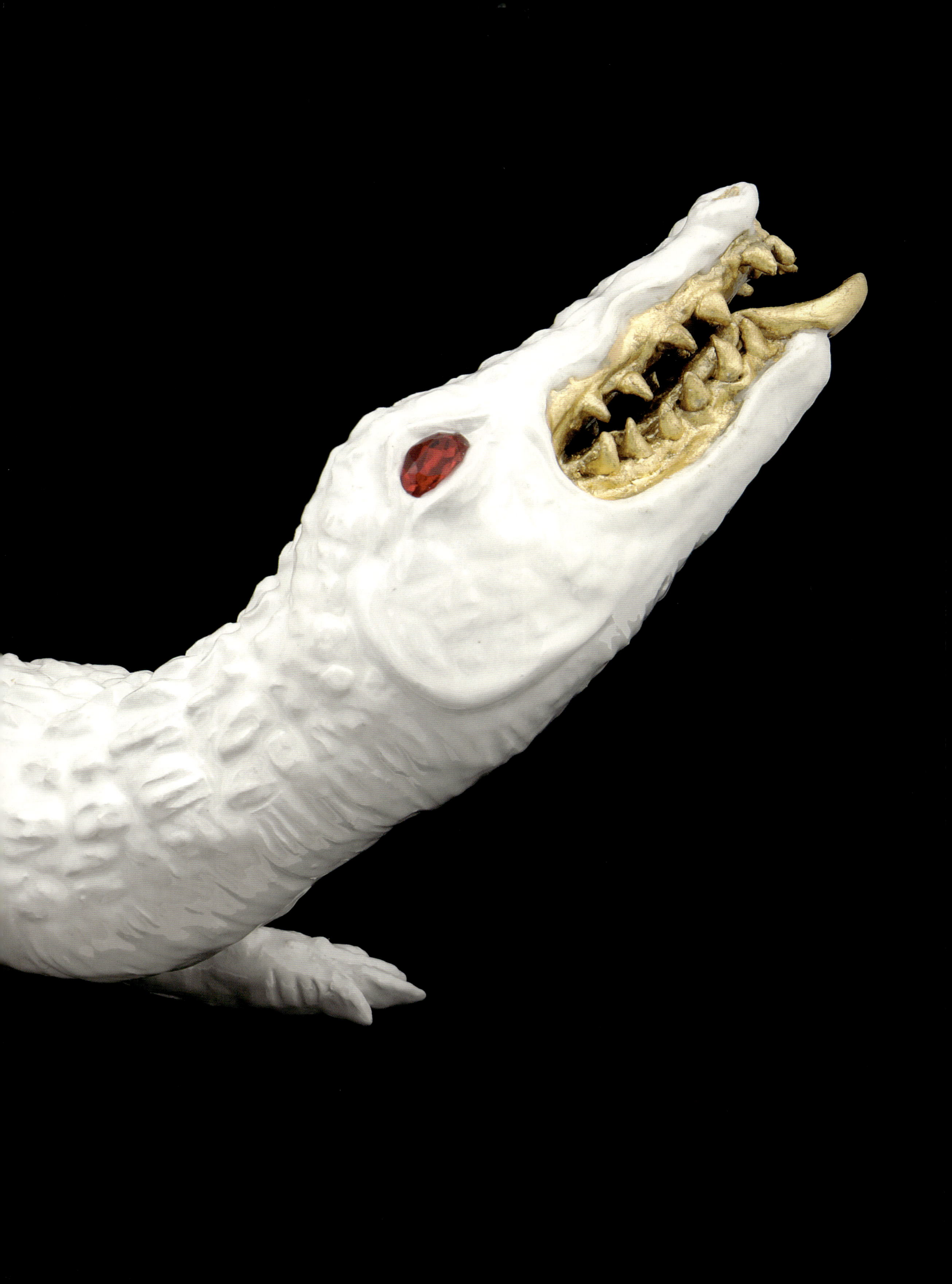

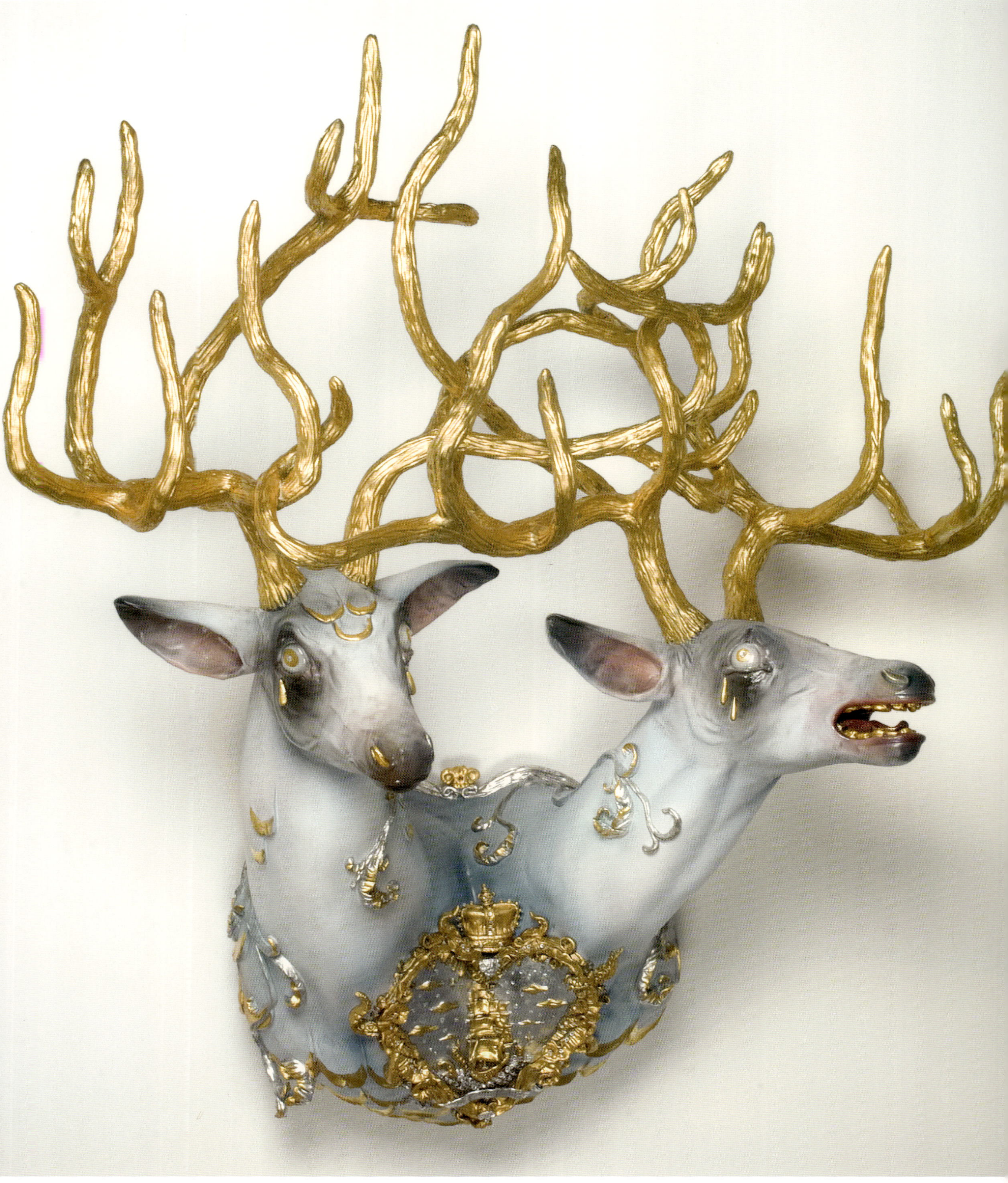

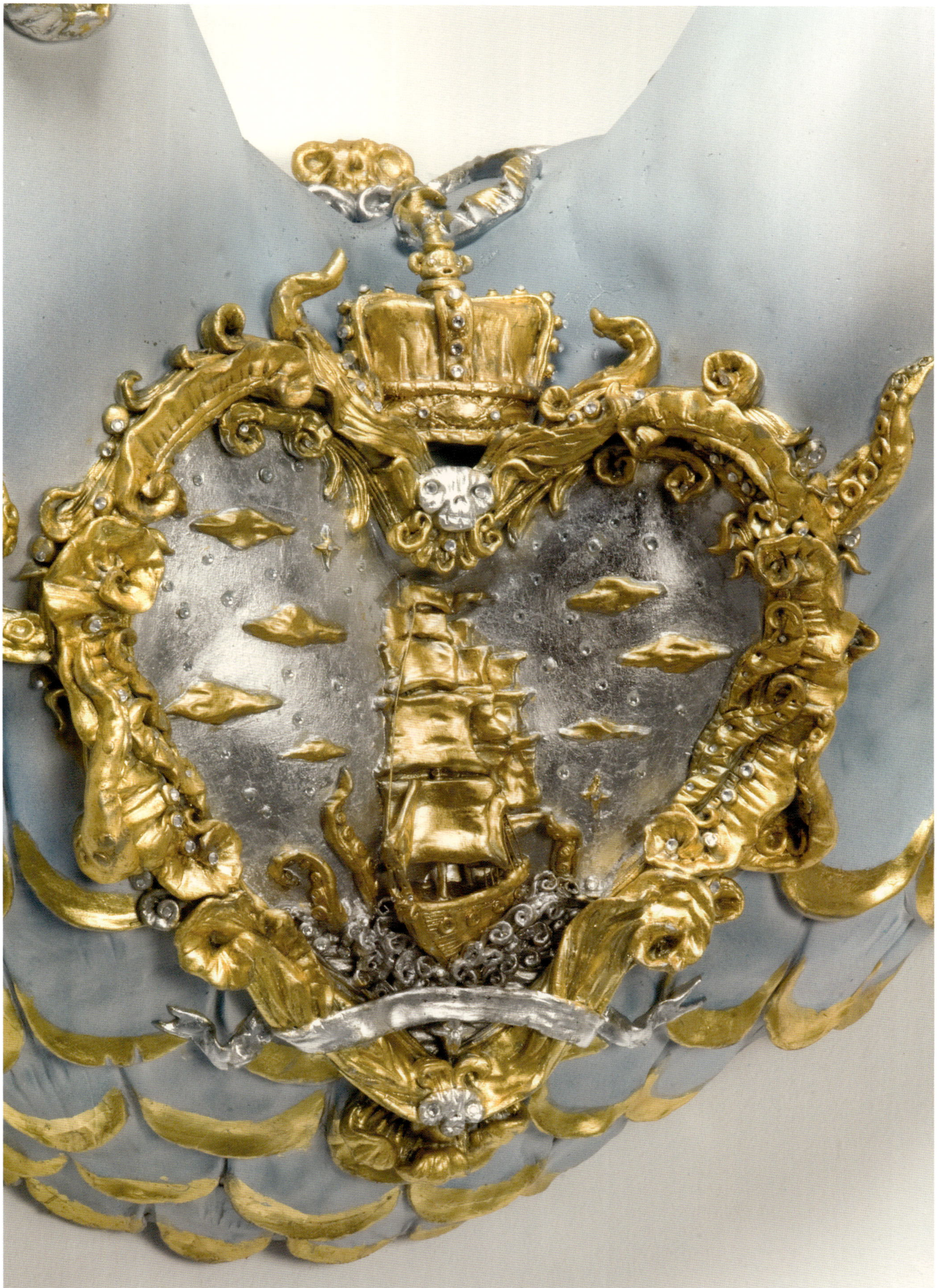

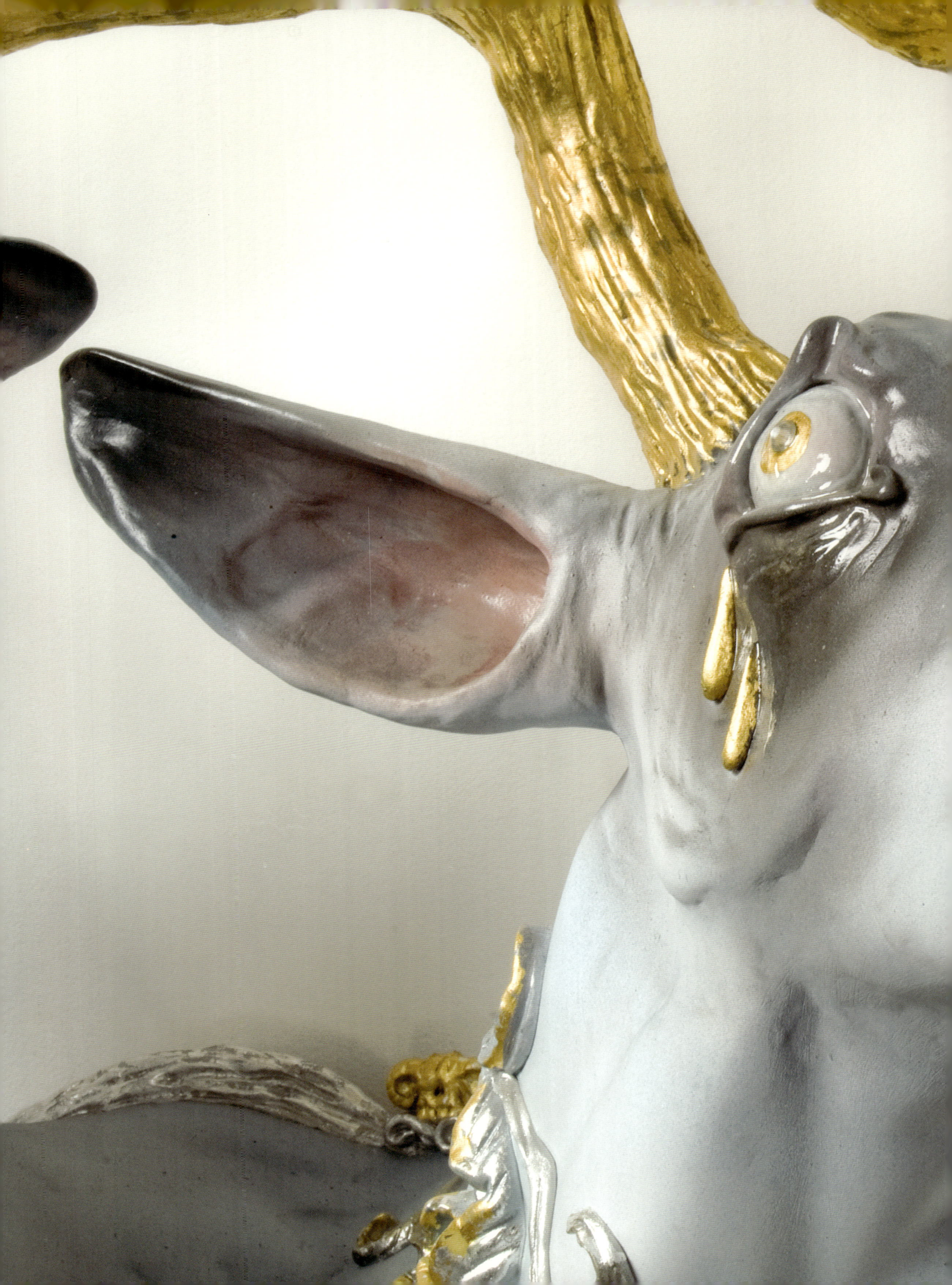

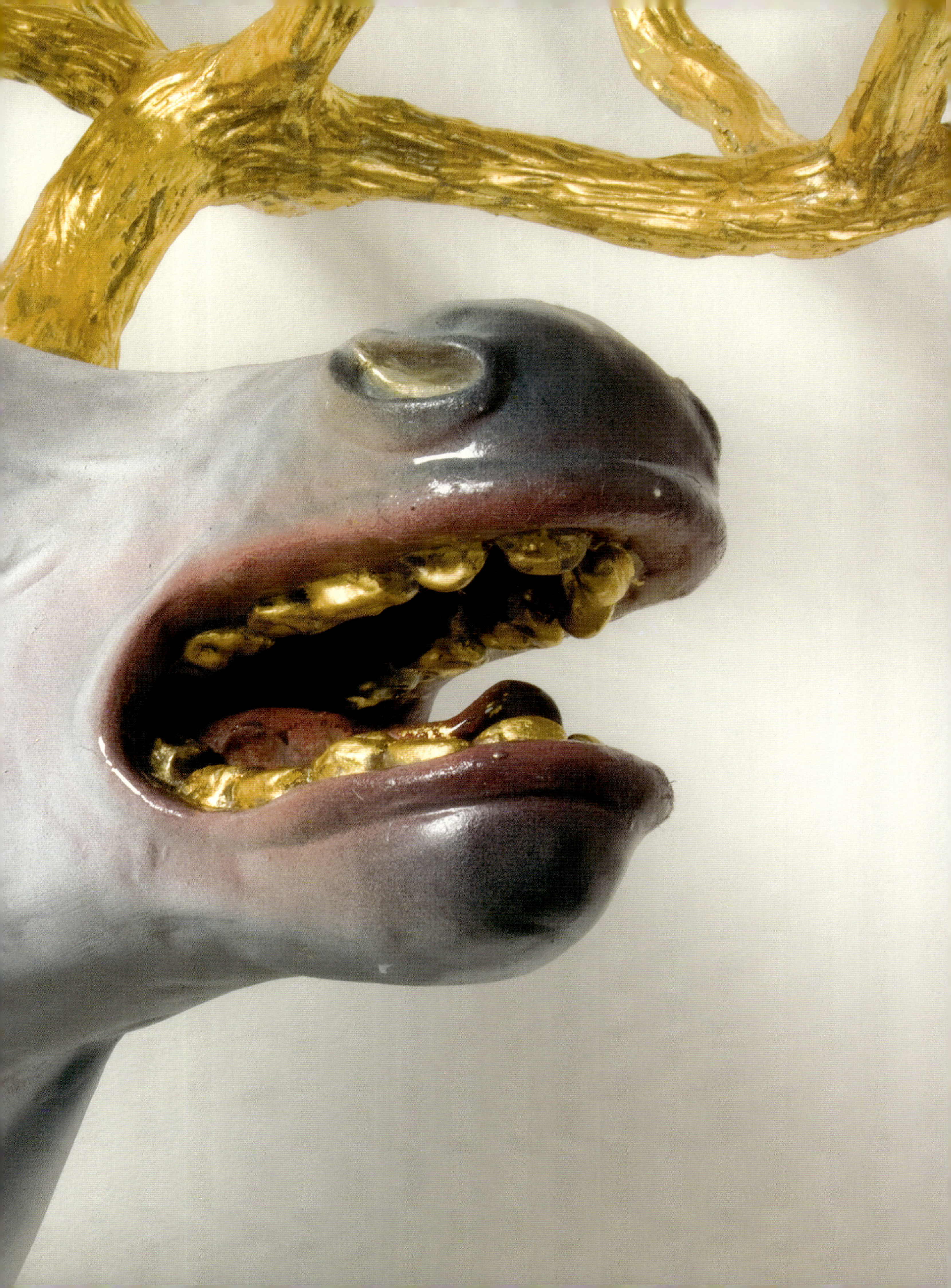

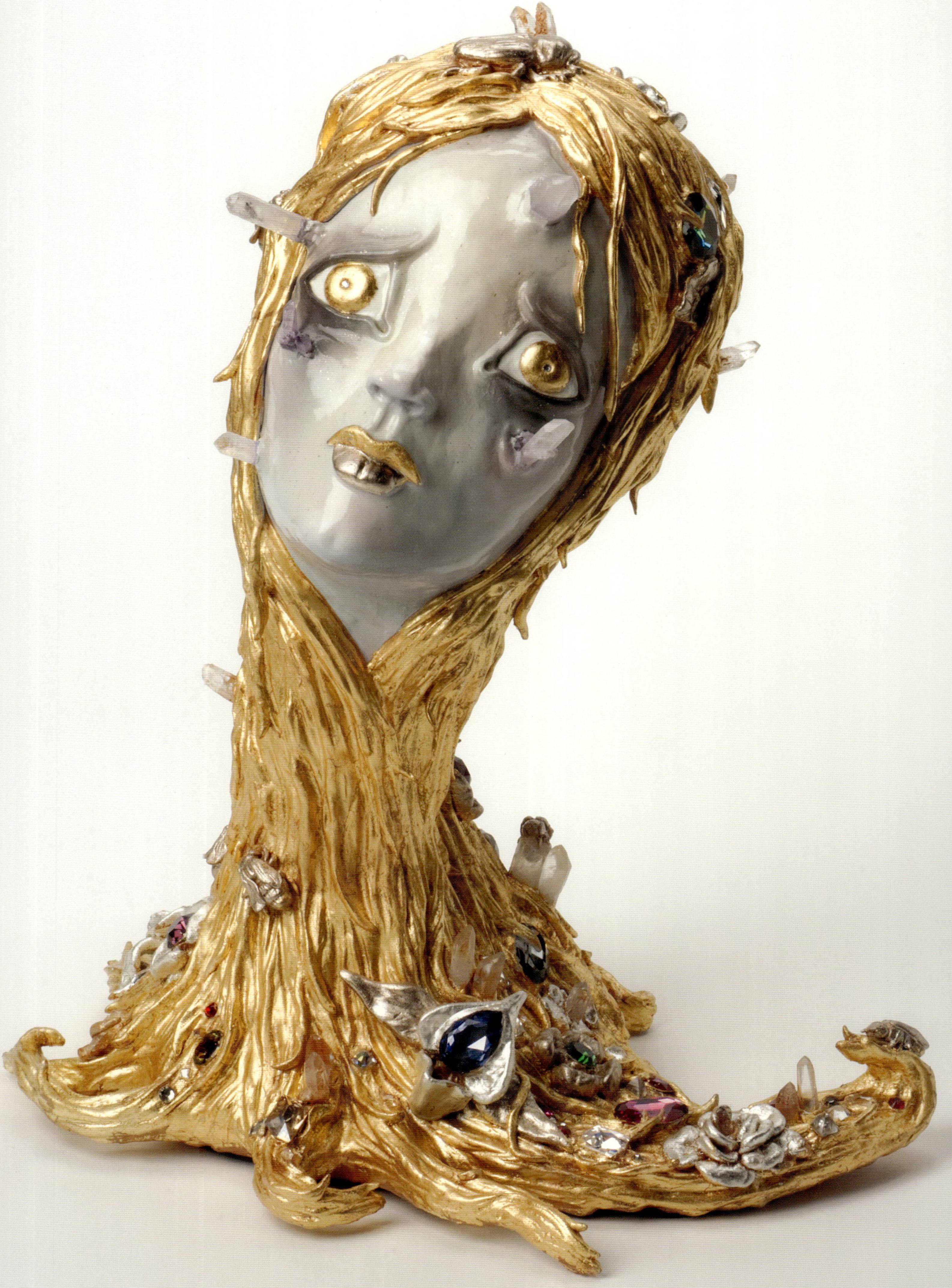

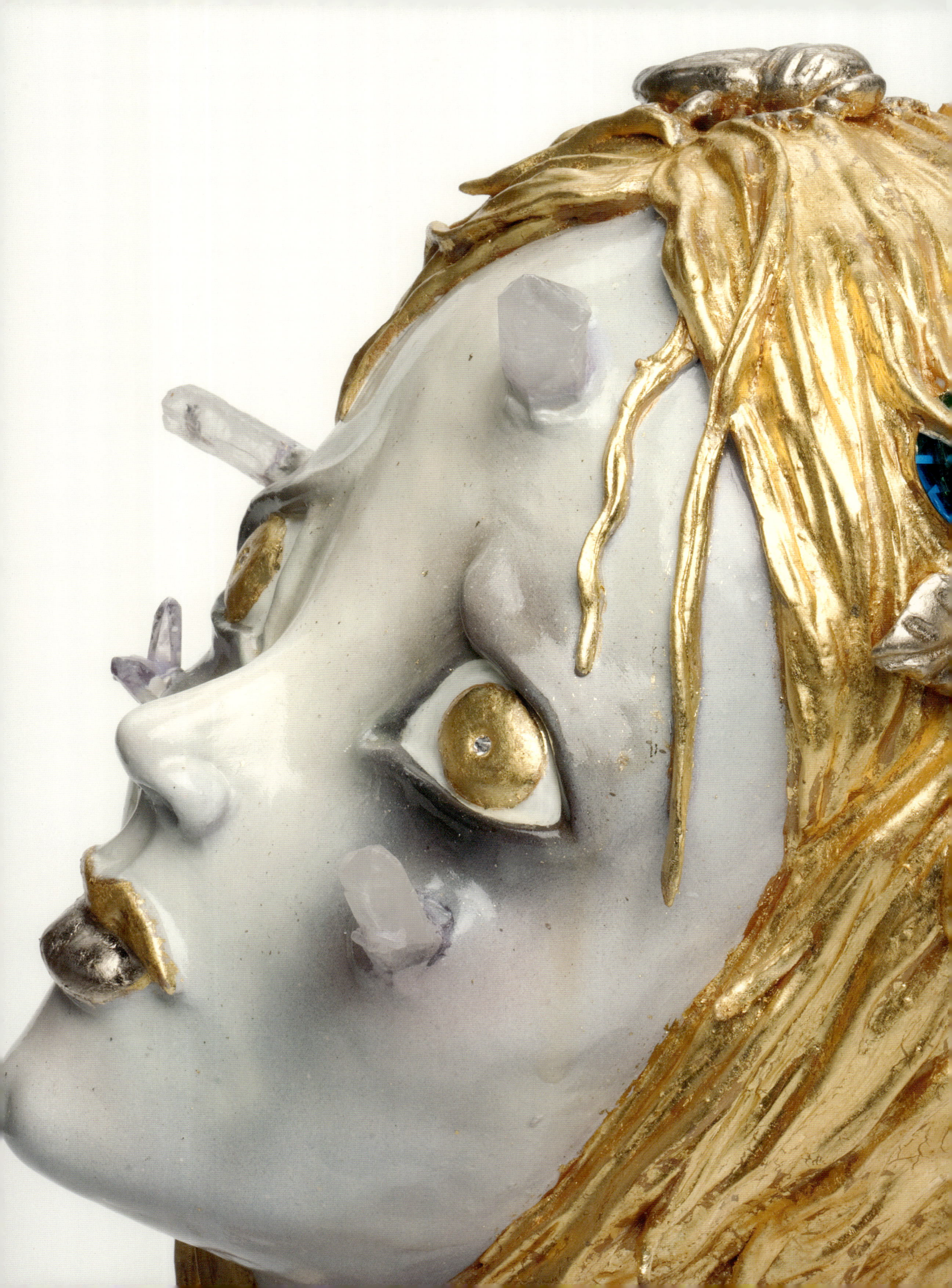

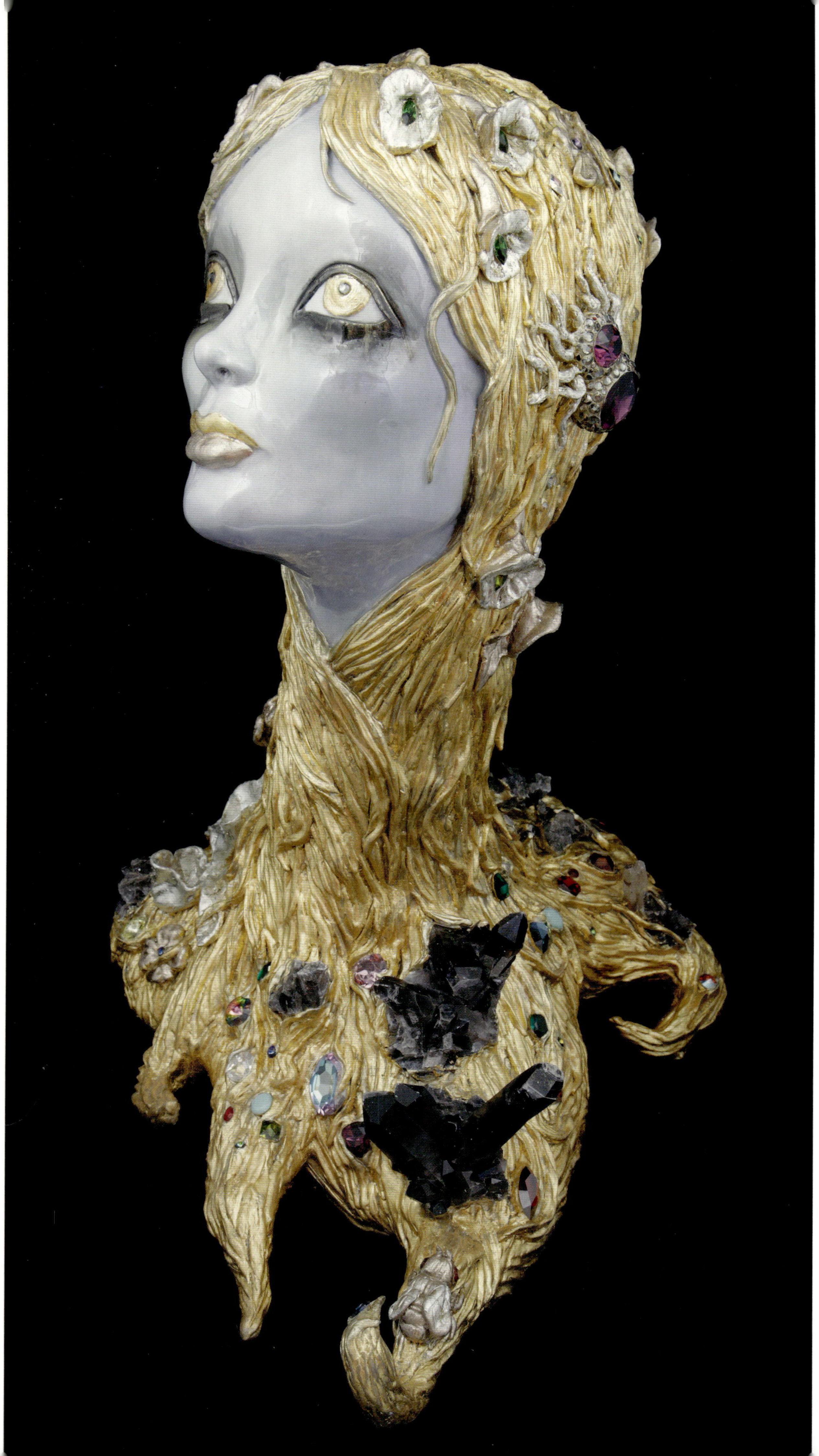

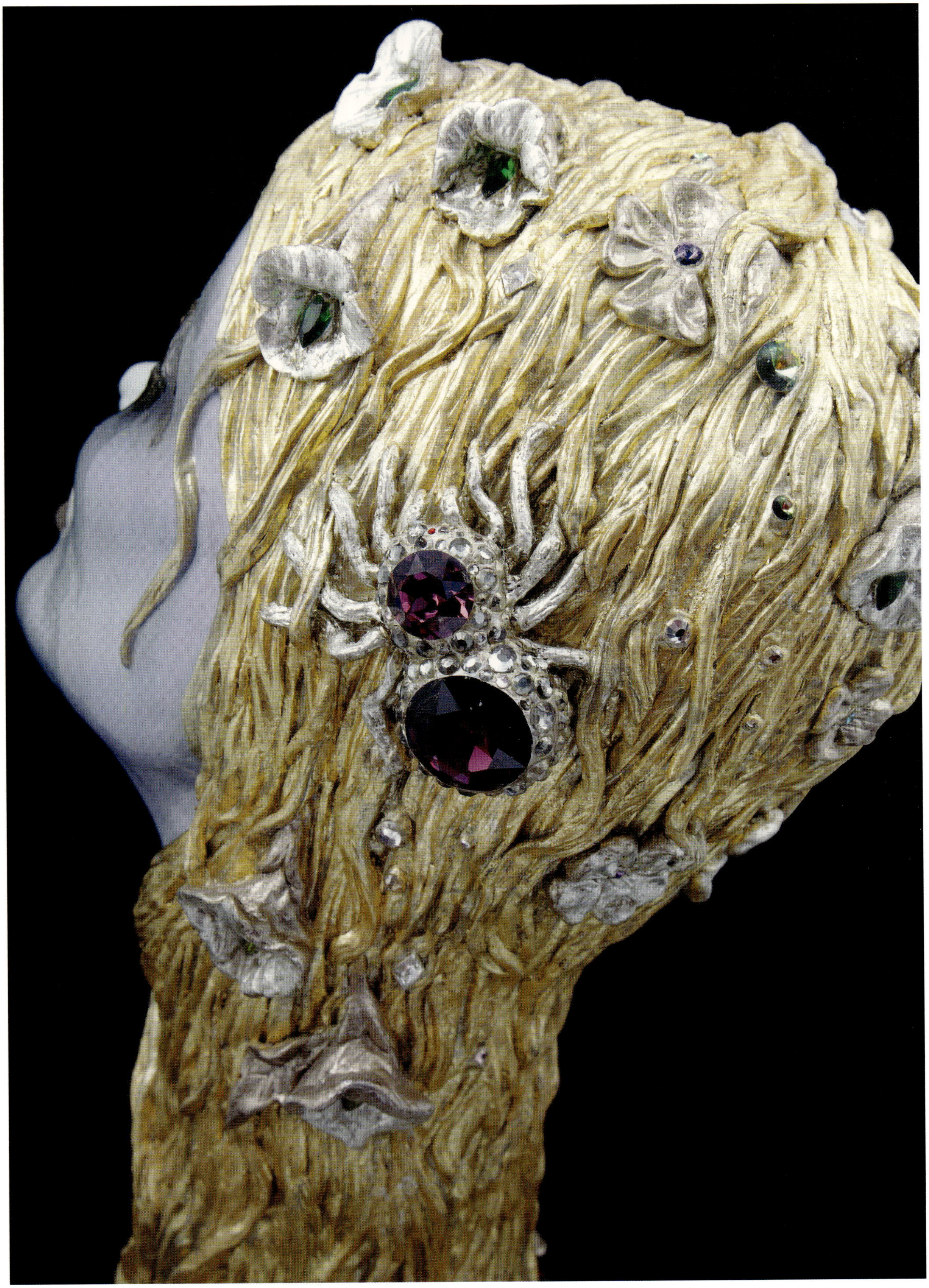

I could tell you quite a bit about Elizabeth McGrath's art career, but I'm not going to. I'd like to tell you the deep down dirty, the real life story, of what it's like to be her best friend.

My name is Winter and I met Liz about 66,666 beers ago. It was in some shitty dive bar in Pasadena, after I was told to go see this band with this chick in a Girl Scout uniform that screamed until her nose bled all over the stage. It was love at first sight for me. We exchanged numbers that night and several weeks later, she rode me on the handlebars of her bike while I balanced a twelve-pack of beer on my lap, straight into a dumpster, because we both had hair bleach dripping in our eyes. I woke up the next morning and I have never been blonder in my life. That one sealed the deal pretty much.

I was working as a professional dominatrix at the time and Liz was knocking out set design and doing claymation puppets for Sepultura. Liz lived in a warehouse that looked like H. R. Giger meets the stuffed animal section at the Salvation Army.

I wound up defaulting back to my fashion design career and Liz and I both started working for Trashy Lingerie in West Hollywood. Liz was doing window display and painting all the signs around the building, while I was getting yelled at for not making the crotchless crotch holes big enough for Elton John's lace panties. The job ruled on the days that Dolly Parton came in looking for custom underwear and when we were hanging out smoking cigs with Phyllis Diller in the alley. But the days that Dog the Bounty Hunter's wife showed up with those crazy tits, wanting a tiny little halter top… or Janice Dickinson showing up at the back door asking us to make custom shit on the side… we just ran down the alley screaming for our lives. We could not get fired if we doused that building with a can of gas.

The job enabled us to squirrel away a deposit on a 3500-sqare-foot loft in downtown Los Angeles, long before it was "hip" to live there. We moved in with nothing but a few blankets and Liz's stuffed animal collection. We had one pair of roller skates and a record player. Liz liked to skate around to the Stan Getz record with a bottle of Night Train… until we passed out with our blankets on the concrete floor. We had all this space and nothing in it. We scavenged alleys and found old junk that Liz turned into furniture and threw a benefit at Al's Bar, so we could get an industrial stove, because I liked to cook. Before long, there was a stripper pole installed in the kitchen so the customers we befriended from Trashy Lingerie could show us how to dance (though we never made it to the top of the pole).

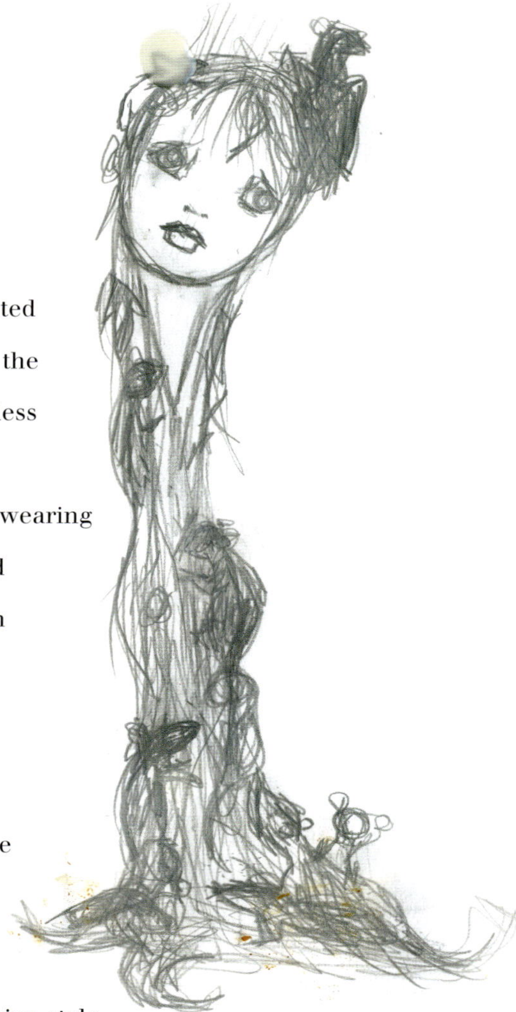

Within several months we had built ourselves a home in the middle of a dilapidated city, where the workers went home at five, everything shut down and after dark, the streets where filled with toothless crack whores hollering on corners, and homeless people shitting in front of our doorway. The filth was inspiring. We hung out in disgusting dives, drinking and dancing to the jukebox with fat homeless women wearing fanny packs, then came home and Liz would sculpt rabid and bloody two-headed animals until 6 a.m. We threw parties with strippers and donkeys and gay men in space suits. We ate raw meat and developed a fondness for all things bloody and wrong.

Before long, all of the ants from the *Hollywood* started migrating down, to the downtown, to get a little shit on their shoes. The parties got out of hand; everyone showed up including the fire department. On a regular basis. The gentrification of Downtown Los Angeles had begun.

Liz, never caring much for this Hollywood glamour, had started to develop a fashion style, where she felt most comfortable by looking broken. I would spend hours before parties and nights that her band played, wrapping her in casts, medical braces and applying the perfect trickle of blood coming from her ears, so she could stand on stage and harmoniously scream "motherfuckin' titty suckin' two-ball bitch. Your mother's in the kitchen cookin' red hot shit." But Liz's best look was at home when she wore the headless bear suit that she got from the Goodwill. Oh the stories she'd tell us at 3 a.m. in that bear suit. My apologies, but I cannot put these stories on record.

Liz's art style had begun to develop years before we met. She never attended any kind of art school or fancy college, she just mutated naturally. Her shattered childhood may have played some part in this after doing hard time in an abusive Christian girl's home. Liz was ejected out of a car, flew 40 feet onto the concrete and survived. There are so many tragic stories, many I have personally lived through with her during the last 66,666 beers and not only does this little girl shine every single day, she turns tragedy into beauty and this is her gift.

I hope the next time you take a look at one of Liz's art pieces that you look a bit longer and see her message of our bitter sweet existence. I hope that my story has helped you to understand her a bit better. I hope that you can meet her someday, because this will change your life forever. She sure did change mine.

Winter Rosebudd Mullender

Index

84–85 *Siamese Cat*, 2009, 16" x 12" x 6", tattoo line-work by Morgan Slade, photo by Larry Underhill, dedicated to Derek O'Brien

86 *Sickos Unite & FTW*, 2008, 8" x 10" x 9", photo & tattoo line-work by Morgan Slade, dedicated to Stacy Rodgers

87 *Death Before Dishonor*, 2006, 8" x 10" x 8", photo & tattoo line-work by Morgan Slade, dedicated to Jeremy Sims

88 *His*, 2009, 12" x 12" x 8", tattoo line-work by Morgan Slade, photo by Larry Underhill, dedicated to Cody Cox

89 *Hers*, 2009, 12" x 12" x 8", tattoo line-work by Morgan Slade, photo by Larry Underhill, dedicated to Ricci Cox

90 *Zombina*, 2009, 9" x 12" x 8", photo by Larry Underhill, dedicated to Natasha and Julie Garcia

91 *Lucky Gomez*, 2008, 9" x 12" x 8", photo by Morgan Slade

92 *Sad Sammy Saucier, the Dirty Little Piglet*, 2009, 10" x 15" x 10", tattoo line-work by Morgan Slade, photo by Larry Underhill, dedicated to Lightening Bill Woodcock

93 *The Butcher*, 2008, 6" x 9" x 4", photo by Larry Underhill

94 *Sailor Swift*, 2009, 25" x 10" x 10", photo by Larry Underhill, dedicated to Cristina Armisen

95 *Sammy the Sea Monkey*, 2009, 12" x 8" x 8", photo by Larry Underhill, dedicated to Morgan Night

96 *Black of Heart*, 2008, 9" x 16" x 7", photo by Larry Underhill

97 *Carlos*, 2009, 12" x 5" x 5", photo by Larry Underhill, dedicated to Jeff Nott

98 *Vampirates*, 2007, 9" x 10" x 9", photo by Larry Underhill

99 *White Teeth*, 2008, 17" x 10" x 10", tattoo line-work by Morgan Slade, photo by Larry Underhill

100 *We Are All Ships in the Night*, 2009, 20" x 7" x 7", photo by Larry Underhill, dedicated to Dan and Andrew Banales

102 *Black Gold*, 2009, 18" x 13" x 12", photo by Larry Underhill

103 *A Prayer On The Wind*, 2009, 20" x 7" x 7", photo by Larry Underhill, dedicated to Joeann Inco

104–105 *Honey Creeper*, 2006, 71" x 47" x 8", photo by Morgan Slade, dedicated to Yasha Young

106 *Scavenger Joe*, 2009, 22" x 10" x 5", photo by Larry Underhill

107 *Scavenger Judy*, 2009, 19" x 9" x 5", photo by Larry Underhill

108–109 *Drippy Muthus*, 2009, 29" x 34" x 9", photo by Larry Underhill, dedicated to Allen Scott

110–113 *Boxer*, 2009, 61" x 72" x 24", photo by Larry Underhill

114–115 *Ass to Ass*, 2006, 20" x 24" x 6", photo by Morgan Slade, dedicated to Anne Shackman

116–117 *Polar Wonder Where*, 2007, 20" x 28" x 16", photo by Larry Underhill

118–121 *Schwein Haben*, 2008, 48" x 36" x 18", photo by Larry Underhill, assisted by Peter Romberg

122–123 *Lioness*, 2008, 14" x 14" x 3", photo by Larry Underhill, dedicated to Karen Schaupeter

124–125 *Dandy Lion*, 2008, 15" x 15" x 4", photo by Larry Underhill, dedicated to WC Moriarty

126 *Bunnytooth*, 2008, 11" x 6" x 15", photo by Larry Underhill, dedicated to Jessicka and Christian Addams

127 *MerKitten*, 2012, 11" x 8" x 9", photo by Morgan Slade

128 *Savoy*, 2007, 44" x 22" x 22", photo by Larry Underhill, dedicated to Dave and Terry Perry

129 *Blue Deer Special*, 2007, 23" x 15" x 18", photo by Morgan Slade, dedicated to Heather Rae Brown

130 *Blue Bunny Special*, 17" x 9" x 9", photo by Morgan Slade

131 *White Castle*, 2008, 23" x 9" x 23" , photo by Morgan Slade, dedicated to John Tucker

132 *Gold Finger*, 2012, 4.5" x 7" x 3", photo by DanielBanales.com, dedicated to Robert and Alix Marbury

134–135 *The Hunger*, 1012, 17" x 9" x 9", photo by DanielBanales.com, dedicated to Ivan X

136–137 *Cerberus*, 2012, 16" x 15" x 15", photo by DanielBanales.com, assisted by Johannes Schleiwies

138–139 *The Dik Dik*, 2009, 24" x 33" x 9", photo by Morgan Slade, dedicated to Kirsten Anderson

140–141 *The Folly of St. Huberus*, 2012, 23" x 15" x 24", photo by DanielBanales.com

142–143 *The Royal Weasels*, 2008, 13" x 6" x 6", photo by Larry Underhill, dedicated to the Ramseys

144 *Lord Crane*, 2010, 23" x 11" x 9", photo by Morgan Slade

145 *Xing Xing*, 2012, 4" x 7" x 10", photo by DanielBanales.com, dedicated to SIA

146 *Pinktopus*, 2012, 10" x 8" x 8", photo by DanielBanales.com, dedicated to Mariah McMullen

147 *Little Urchin*, 2012, 13" x 8" x 8", photo by DanielBanales.com, dedicated to Amy Palmer

148–149 *Fevered*, 2012, 16" x 11" x 10", photo by DanielBanales.com

150–153 *The Entanglement*, 2009, 54" x 53" x 24", photo by Larry Underhill, dedicated to Tim Redman

154–155 *The Eyes of Ophelia*, 2012, 18" x 16" x 12", photo by Larry Underhill, dedicated to Dave Grey

156–157 *Heroine*, 2012, 26" x 18" x 14", photo by DanielBanales.com, dedicated to Janine Jarman

159 *Sketch for Ophelia*

162 *Vambunny*, 2009, 22" x 12" x 10", photo by Morgan Slade dedicated to Vareena and Mario, and Art Slave Wendy

Credits & Thanks

Special thanks to the people who helped make this book possible, my husband Morgan Slade who has been an unending source of inspiration, Colin Turner and the Last Gasp family for giving me the opportunity to put out another book, Debra Valencia for her amazing design skills, Alix Sloan for her invaluable guidance, Morgan Spurlock for his artistic insight, Winter Rosebudd for the memories she wrote about, Clint Catalyst for his special contribution, and to those who have shared their support and friendship, Billy Shire, Greg Escalante, Annie Adjchavanich, Doug Nason, Gary Pressman, Long Gone John, Gwynn and Juxtapoz magazine, Cecil B Feeder, WC, Clem Burke, Debbie Harry, Robert Williams, Michael Mortensen, Tracy Ferra, Helen Garber, Gino Joukar, my family, Mom and Dad, Ruth, Rachel and Sara McGrath, Madeline and Max, Lynn, Gary, Jenn and Andrew Slade, the Htains, the Ngos, the Westfalls, the Lims, Aunt PEM and Patrick RIP, and my good neighbors on Main St., The Canadians.

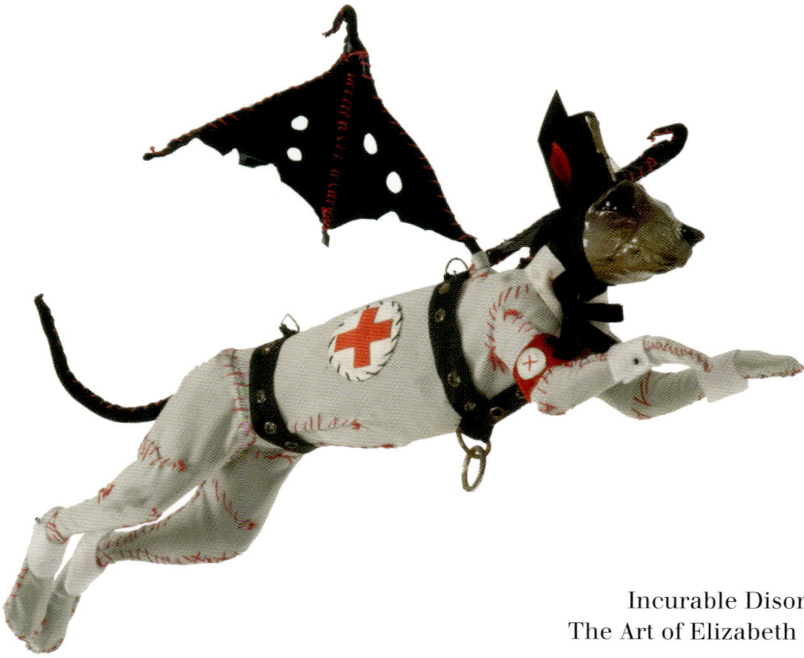

Incurable Disorder
The Art of Elizabeth McGrath

Published by Last Gasp of San Francisco

Ronald E. Turner, Publisher
Colin S. Turner, Editor

Last Gasp
777 Florida Street
San Francisco, CA 94110
www.lastgasp.com

Book Designed by Debra Valencia

ISBN-13:978-0-86719-776-1

First Printing

Printed in China

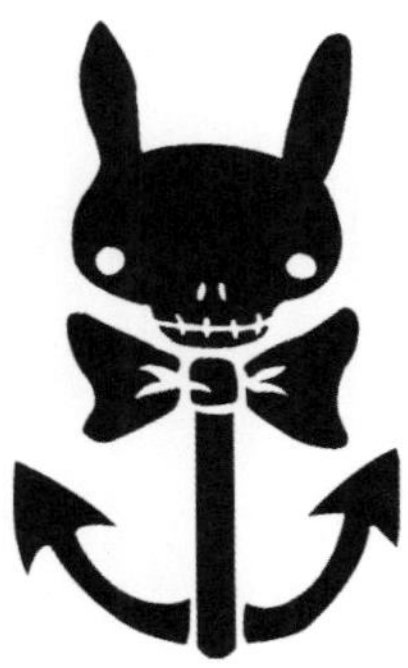

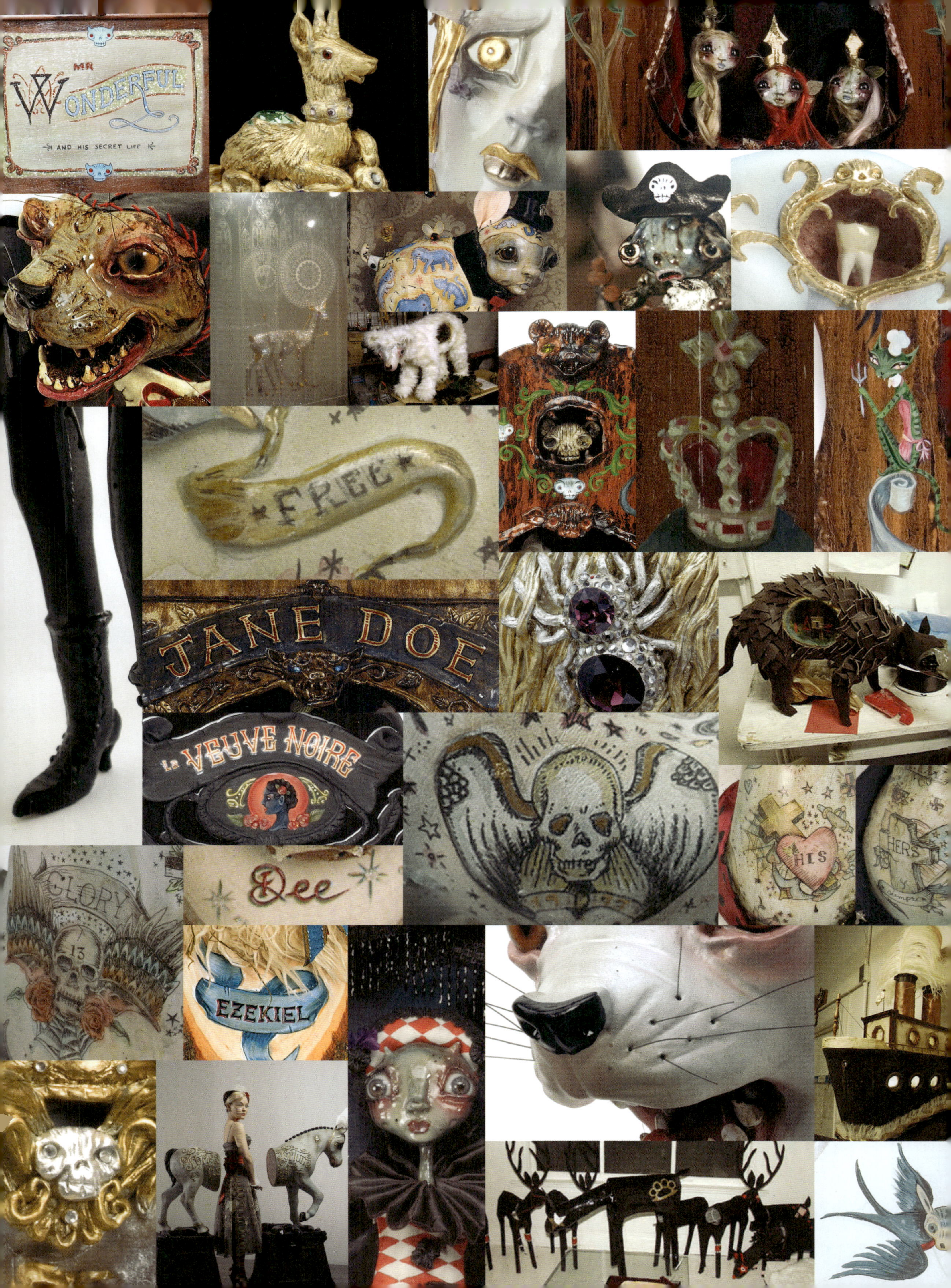
MR WONDERFUL
AND HIS SECRET LIFE
FREE
JANE DOE
La VEUVE NOIRE
GLORY
13
Dee
EZEKIEL
HIS
HERS